From a transcript of the conversation via cellular phone between Det. Tom Lange and O.J. Simpson during the June 17, 1994, Bronco chase

LANGE: Listen. No. We're not gonna say good-bye to your kids.

SIMPSON: I already have.

LANGE: You're gonna, you're gonna see them again.

SIMPSON: . . . aaah . . .

LANGE: You want to see them again. Please. You're scaring us. You're scaring them. Please, man.

SIMPSON: Hey, you've been a good guy to me.

LANGE: Thanks.

SIMPSON: And let me tell you. I know you're doing your job.

LANGE: I appreciate that.

SIMPSON: You were honest with me right from the beginning, just saying you're doing your job. I know you do a good job.

DET. TOM LANGE AND **DET. PHILIP VANNATTER**
AS TOLD TO DAN E. MOLDEA

EVIDENCE DISMISSED

THE INSIDE

STORY OF

THE POLICE

INVESTIGATION

OF O.J. SIMPSON

POCKET BOOKS
New York   London   Toronto   Sydney   Tokyo   Singapore

POCKET BOOKS, a division of Simon & Schuster Inc.
1230 Avenue of the Americas, New York, NY 10020

ISBN: 0-671-01938-4

First Pocket Books paperback printing September 1997

10 9 8 7 6 5 4 3 2 1

POCKET and colophon are registered trademarks of
Simon & Schuster Inc.

Cover photo by AP Photo/Los Angeles Police Department

Printed in the U.S.A.

This book is dedicated to our wives, Linda Lange and Rita Vannatter, who went through more than we could have ever imagined. Thank you for always being there for us.

Contents

CONTENTS

PART TWO: Evidence Presented

"A homicide detective carries a heavy responsibility when called upon to investigate a death, for he stands in the dead person's shoes to protect his interests against those of everyone else."

LAPD Homicide Manual
"The Investigation of a Death"
April 1981

Preface

For better or worse, we will be remembered for what has become our career-defining case, the O.J. Simpson murder investigation. We took over the probe of the Nicole Brown and Ronald Goldman homicides during the early morning of June 13, 1994, when it was just a few hours old, and then worked it for the next sixteen months. Fairly or unfairly, before a national television audience, we represented not just the Los Angeles Police Department but the 600,000 police officers across America. Our names became household words and our faces were almost as recognizable as those of Starsky and Hutch.

We built a case against Simpson that Los Angeles County District Attorney Gil Garcetti proudly called "a mountain of evidence." In fact, the documentation of Simpson's guilt was as solid as in any of the five hundred homicide cases we, together and individually, had investigated. But, in the end, it wasn't enough. A brilliantly pragmatic legal-defense team, led by Johnnie L. Cochran, used a handful of police errors and the racist views of one rogue detective, named Mark Fuhrman, to create a courtroom firestorm that, in the eyes of the jury, caused our "mountain of evidence" to melt down like a cup of Ben & Jerry's ice cream.

Simpson's legal team effectively placed the two of us and the controversial LAPD on trial, forcing the jury to choose between the police department that beat up Rodney King and one of the greatest sports heroes who ever lived. In the midst of overwhelming evidence of Simpson's guilt, a gray area peripheral to this complex case—namely, the recent history of the LAPD—became a decisive black-and-white issue at the trial. In the end, Simpson's acquittal led to a harsh verdict against America's law enforcement community. Many came to believe that "Cops do sloppy work. Cops plant evidence. Cops commit perjury. Cops are racists."

We flatly deny all of this and apologize, up front, for whatever contribution we made to these mistaken beliefs through our inability at the time to counter the false and misleading claims made against us and our investigation by Simpson's defense team. Now, through this book, we will finally respond to these charges while detailing our investigation.

We first heard about the murders at 3:00 A.M. on June 13; and we cleared our case to the district attorney's office at 7:20 A.M. on June 17. Soon after, we received the authority to arrest Simpson. Of course, that task took the rest of the day after Simpson fled, culminating with the slow-speed Bronco chase on southern California's 405 freeway.

After those five days, the prosecutors took center stage, forcing us into a defensive posture without providing us much support—even though we continued to work hard and to produce results. Subsequently, when Simpson's defense attorneys laid out their case, it primarily concentrated on allegations of our misconduct during that five-day period. In other words, after June 17, this story ceased to be a police story and became a tale of two legal teams who used us as their foil.

With the help of our friend and writing partner, veteran crime reporter Dan E. Moldea, who has been a critic of the LAPD, we have reconstructed in Part One of our book the five-day period between June 13 and June 17 with a blow-by-blow chronicle of our investigation. In Part Two, we tell our side of the events that followed during Simpson's criminal trial—including what we believe was crucial evidence that was never entered into that trial. We alert the reader that the endnotes following each chapter are very much a part of our story.

Although this book is consistent with the thousands of pages of our sworn testimony before the grand jury in 1994 and at the criminal trial in 1995, as well as during our depositions and appearances at the Simpson civil trial in 1996, we are fully aware that numerous bona fide O.J. experts and analysts will be critically reviewing this work—ranging from attorneys to Court TV addicts who have closely followed this case. We aim to be responsible to them by presenting an honest account while answering their questions about our tactics and behavior.

In those instances where we made mistakes, we admit them and explain why they happened. These were errors of omission rather than commission—which were later blown out of proportion by defense attorneys who had earned their reputations by distorting realities and turning them into reasonable doubts.

This work is *not* a vehicle of revenge or a means to fix blame on others. Rather, by re-creating events and conversations as they happened, we have attempted to provide a clear recitation of what we knew, when we knew it, and what we did when we found out about it.

This is our story.

Tom Lange and Philip Vannatter
Los Angeles
January 3, 1997

PART ONE

Trail of Blood

1

"We've got a double"

Monday, June 13, 1994

Their phones ring in the middle of the night.

Shortly before 3:00 A.M., Los Angeles Police Department homicide detectives Tom Lange and Phil Vannatter are awakened at their homes, one call right after the other, from their supervisor, Lieutenant John Rogers.

"The captain wants to buy you a cup of coffee," Rogers says. "We've got a double."

Without being told, the two detectives—partners since 1989 with over fifty years of police experience between them—know exactly what this means: It's time to go to work immediately. On call for the entire weekend but not summoned until now, both men are ordered to report to the scene of a double murder at 875 South Bundy. Lange recognizes the location as the high-rent area of West Los Angeles; Vannatter knows it as Brentwood's low-rent district between San Vicente and Wilshire Boulevards.

During these brief conversations, Rogers tells both detectives that one of the victims might be the wife of football legend O.J. Simpson. To Lange and Vannatter, it is just another murder investigation, just another job.

Rogers is Lange and Vannatter's boss in the Homicide Special Section of the LAPD's famed Robbery/Homicide Division, headed by Captain William O. Gartland, a thirty-nine-year veteran of the LAPD. The Homicide Special Section, which consists of only a dozen investigators, usually gets the call when a high-profile murder is committed or when the investigation crosses divisional boundaries within the LAPD. To many in the Los Angeles law enforcement community, Homicide Special detectives walk on water.

Six feet tall and built tough and wiry like a soccer player, the forty-nine-year-old soft-spoken Lange, mustachioed and balding, springs out of bed and jumps into the shower. Dressing quickly and finding his wire-rimmed glasses, he returns to his bedroom and kisses Linda, his wife of fifteen years, who still cannot get used to these middle-of-the-night assignments that potentially place her husband at risk. Hastening out of his home in Ventura County, Lange grabs an apple to eat during his forty-five-minute drive to Los Angeles.

Meantime, about twenty-five miles northeast in Valencia, a small valley community in northwestern Los Angeles County, the fifty-three-year-old Vannatter, a usually gregarious six-foot-one bear of a man with a full head of silver-and-gold hair, sits on the side of his bed. His wry sense of humor is well hidden this morning. He rubs his tanned face, weather-beaten from years in the sun. At the moment, he lacks any degree of enthusiasm for rushing out to another murder site.

Vannatter and his wife of twenty-nine years, Rita, hoped to retire a year ago. But they had to postpone their plans to move to Indiana near his wife's family because of the extensive damage to their home from the Northridge earthquake on January 17. Unable to afford the expensive repairs with his anticipated pension, Vannatter couldn't be more disappointed by this delay.

Just last night, during a quiet dinner with Rita at a local Italian restaurant, Vannatter had let out his feelings about his situation, expressing both anger and frustration at his inability to retire and to improve their quality of life. Recently a grandfather for the first time, the aging but rugged detective has seen enough slaughtered bodies and bloody crime scenes. He wants relief from his longtime mind-set of viewing murder victims as evidence instead of human tragedy. He just wants out.

But, shrugging off his personal concerns, Vannatter lumbers into the bathroom to clean up. A stylish but conservative dresser, Vannatter picks out a gray pin-striped suit from his closet.

Passing on breakfast this particular morning, he goes straight to his gray LAPD-issued 1994 Buick Regal and finds his way to the South Bundy address, an off-white stucco, three-level condominium with light beige trim. Vannatter parks his car on the east side of the road, just south of Dorothy Street, which already looks like a parking lot for black-and-whites and detectives' vehicles. Getting out of his car, Vannatter notices that the inner block around the location has already been cordoned off with the standard bright yellow police tape; uniformed patrol officers are posted around the perimeter. He walks up to Officer Miguel Terrazas, the patrol officer handling the crime scene log, and reports in at 4:05 A.M.

Almost immediately, West Los Angeles Division homicide detective supervisor Ronald Phillips, friendly and accommodating, greets Vannatter with a handshake and begins to brief him about the situation, knowing that the Robbery/Homicide Division has been assigned the case. Their handshake symbolizes the transfer of this murder investigation from the West L.A. Division to Homicide Special.

Phillips explains that Terrazas, along with his partner, Robert Riske, were the first cops to arrive at 12:17 A.M. While responding to a possible burglary across the street from the crime scene, the officers met a young married couple, Sukru Boztepe and Bettina Rasmussen. The couple had followed a white Akita with bloody paws back to its home where they found the body of a blood-covered woman lying on a walkway.[1] After this discovery, the couple ran across the street to the home of a neighbor and frantically knocked on her door, wanting to use her telephone to call the police. The neighbor believed that someone was trying to break into her house, so she called 911 to report a possible burglary.

When the police arrived at the neighbor's house, Boztepe and Rasmussen directed them to the dead woman—where the officers also found the body of a young man. Riske and Terrazas immediately called for paramedics and other backup police units.

While waiting for emergency personnel, Riske, who had stepped carefully around the bodies and the massive amounts of blood without disturbing any evidence, shined his flashlight in the male victim's eyes, which were wide open. Knowing that his first priority at any crime scene is to determine whether victims are alive or dead, Riske touched the man's eyeball, hoping for a reaction. There was none.

Riske did not bother to check the female victim. He could see that her head was nearly severed from her body.

Riske and Terrazas radioed for backup. A few minutes later, two other patrol officers, Edward McGowan and Richard Walley, as well as their sergeant, Martin Coon, arrived to help Riske and Terrazas secure the location and block traffic on South Bundy, which usually remained busy even late at night.

At 12:45 A.M., paramedics from a nearby fire station officially pronounced both victims dead at the scene. Seeing that the situation for the two victims was hopeless, the paramedics conducted no emergency lifesaving procedures and allowed the bodies to remain where they fell.

During the briefing, Phillips tells Vannatter that Riske and Terrazas had noticed a bloody left-hand glove near the body of the male victim. They did not see its matching right-hand glove in the area.

Riske and another patrol officer had gone to the front door of the residence, which was nearly wide open. Above the door a porch light, turned on, revealed a set of bloody shoe prints moving away from the two bodies, toward the back alley, and through a rear gate—which also had blood transfers, conveyed from one surface to another.

After going door-to-door and talking to neighbors, the officers tentatively identified the dead woman as Nicole Brown, who the neighbors said was the ex-wife of O.J. Simpson. Her "official" identification would not come until later, when Lange and Vannatter conduct their detailed crime-scene search.

Inside Brown's house—which contained neither bloody shoe prints nor paw prints—they noticed on a table near the front door an envelope that contained Simpson's return address at 360 North Rockingham Avenue in Brentwood. They saw a painting of Simpson and photographs of him as well, among other pictures of the dead woman's family. They concluded that the attractive blond woman in many of the photographs was most likely the slaughtered Nicole Brown now lying outside on the walkway.

The officers saw candles burning in Brown's sunken living room and heard soft New Age music playing on the stereo. A large knife was on the countertop of the stove in the kitchen. On a banister in the stairwell outside the kitchen, near the garage, a cup of Ben & Jerry's Chocolate Chip Cookie Dough ice cream was still melting; a spoon was on the steps.

Officer Riske had used the telephone in Brown's kitchen to call for additional backup. He feared that his radio would be monitored by reporters. Instinctively, he knew that this murder case would be big news, and he wanted the LAPD to have a jump on the media.

Upstairs, the patrol officers found two young children asleep in their rooms with their doors half opened. They had apparently slept through the brutal murder of their mother. Getting them up and dressed, the officers took them out the back door, avoiding the bloody scene in front, and arranged for them to be taken to the West Los Angeles Division until they could be positively identified and a member of their family located.

The children, nine-year-old Sydney and six-year-old Justin Simpson, were taken to the police station by Officers Joan Vasquez and Bill Heider. During the trip, Sydney was particularly upset, repeatedly asking, "Where's my mommy?"

Also, the officers arranged for an animal-control unit to impound the white Akita, which was sent to a pound in West Los Angeles, until it could be examined later.[2]

To preserve the existing evidence and to prevent contamination, the patrol officers at the scene created a "safe route" for those coming into the perimeter: south on South Bundy, west on Dorothy, then north into the alley behind the condominium. Everyone was to enter the residence through the garage in the rear.

Like every other cop, Riske and the other patrol officers knew well "the golden rule" of homicide investigation: "Never touch, change or alter anything until identified, measured and photographed. Remember that when a body or an article has been moved, it can never be restored to its original position."[3]

Phillips informs Vannatter that he arrived at 2:10 A.M., accompanied by Detective Mark Fuhrman—nearly two hours after the first officers arrived. The two of them had performed a "visual inventory" of the crime scene.

According to the official sign-in sheet, Phillips and Fuhrman were the sixteenth and seventeenth police personnel to log in. They were the first investigators at the scene, along with Brad Roberts,

Fuhrman's partner, who arrived at 2:30. During the prior two-hour period, a captain, three sergeants, and eleven patrol officers were listed on the sign-in sheet.

A few minutes after Roberts's arrival, Phillips received the notification from his superior, Lieutenant Frank Spangler, that detectives from Homicide Special would be handling the investigation. Phillips passed the word to his investigators, including Fuhrman, who had only begun to take some notes on his general observations. Other than the initial officers who had secured the crime scene, no one—not even Detectives Phillips, Fuhrman, or Roberts—had come near either the bodies or the evidence.

According to official LAPD procedure, *no one* may touch a dead body until a coroner's investigator is present—even to get to his or her identification in a wallet or purse. The only exception is to make a determination as to whether a person is alive or dead. In this case, that has already been done.

Also, standard operating procedure dictates that *no one* may touch any evidence at a crime scene until a criminalist from the police crime lab or the concerned investigator is present to document and collect it.

Phillips had called a photographer—Rolf Rokahr, a civilian employee with the LAPD's crime lab, who arrived at 3:25 A.M.—to document the crime scene. However, until Homicide Special arrived, Rokahr had to limit his photography to panoramic or establishing shots. He could not take close-up pictures of the bodies and evidence until the lead detective or SID criminalist was present to direct him.

Also, after being told that the West Los Angeles Division was no longer in charge of the case, Phillips decided not to call in either a criminalist from the LAPD's crime lab or a coroner's investigator. He had left those chores to the lead investigators, the boys from Homicide Special.

After this quick briefing of what had occurred since 12:17 A.M., Phillips takes Vannatter on a quick walk-through of the area, the usual means of orientation for detectives arriving at a crime scene. Lange is still en route; he'll get his own walk-through when he arrives. In the routine division of labor developed during their hundreds of homicide investigations, Lange generally handles the crime-scene search in the wake of a murder; Vannatter makes the calls and gets the witnesses. Vannatter hopes to pick up some leads during his tour with Phillips.

On the sidewalk in front of the condominium are the bloody paw prints from the white Akita, which has apparently stepped in the victims' blood and left a trail behind it as it walked south on the sidewalk along South Bundy and turned west on Dorothy, where the prints begin to fade.

Then, Phillips takes Vannatter under the yellow tape. Peering through the darkness, Phillips points to a location by the front gate of the residence. As they focus their flashlight beams, the two bodies are illuminated, lying crumpled on the ground and covered in blood.

Without touching the bodies, Vannatter and Phillips cannot be absolutely sure of the cause of death. Neither man gets within six feet of the two bodies or the physical evidence surrounding them. However, they can see from the wounds that the killer or killers had apparently stabbed and slashed them with a knife.

Nicole Brown is dressed in a short black cocktail dress and black-lace panties. The dead man—dressed in blue jeans, a light brown shirt, and cream-colored cloth boots—remains unidentified. Once again, without the presence of a coroner's investigator—the only law enforcement official in the state permitted to move a dead body—the detectives cannot touch him to look for his wallet for identification purposes. It is unclear whether one of the victims or both had been the chief target.

Vannatter and Phillips do see a number of items surrounding the dead man: a blue knit cap, a set of five keys, a beeper, and a white, blood-splattered envelope—as well as the bloody left-hand glove. Now, almost four hours after the first officers arrived, no one has seen its right-hand match. Vannatter, the twenty-sixth person on the log, knows that everything he is seeing are pieces of a jigsaw puzzle that they will begin to fit together after Lange arrives.

Entering the house through the safe route, Phillips and Vannatter begin their brief walk-through, touching nothing. After the tour through the residence, they stand at the front door and look out at the walkway, where Phillips shows Vannatter the trail of bloody shoe prints, apparently made by one killer as he exited away from the bodies. To the left of these shoe prints, they see five drops of blood—tailing west, away from the murder site and out to the back alley. Since the house appears undisturbed and the bloody shoe prints go past the front door, Vannatter and Phillips believe that the killer or killers never entered the residence.

After surveying the area around the murder site from the top of the stairs, carefully avoiding the bloody shoe prints and the five blood drops to their left, Vannatter tells Phillips, "Okay, that's good. I've seen enough. Let's go back out and wait for Lange. He should be here anytime now."

They return to the front of the house on South Bundy and are joined by Fuhrman—a tall, clean-cut detective in his early forties—whom Phillips introduces to Vannatter. Fuhrman, saying nothing, nods and shakes hands with the detective. Although he has never met him before, Vannatter has heard Fuhrman's name once in passing. Several months earlier, during a three-on-three basketball game between Homicide Special and the LAPD Officer-Involved Shooting Section, Lieutenant Bill Hall of OIS had mentioned to Vannatter that he was trying to hire a detective from the West Los Angeles Division who was also "a damn good basketball player." When Vannatter asked who, Hall replied, "Mark Fuhrman." Vannatter shrugged, saying he had never heard of him.[4]

At 4:25 A.M., Lange, parking his car near Vannatter's on Bundy, logs in. He sees his boss, Lieutenant Rogers, and the two of them walk over to Vannatter, Phillips, and Fuhrman. Like Vannatter, Lange has never met the other two detectives before.

While Phillips and Lange take their walk-through of the crime scene, Rogers tells Vannatter that Commander Keith Bushey, the chief of operations for the LAPD West Bureau, wants them to notify O.J. Simpson, who lives nearby, in person, of his ex-wife's death "as soon as humanly possible" before the media does. Bushey also wants the detectives to help Simpson get his children from the police station.

A few minutes later, Lange and Phillips return to Vannatter and Rogers, who, along with Fuhrman, are now standing near the northeastern corner of South Bundy and Dorothy under a street-light. Lange is still wincing a bit from his view of the two slaughtered bodies.

"This is a classic overkill," Lange reports to his partner. "This isn't just some robbery, then a cut and run. These people were mutilated and stabbed. They were beaten. Just look at their slashed throats. Phil, this is a rage killing." But, like Vannatter and Phillips before him, Lange doesn't know yet whether the killer was angry with one or both of the victims or a deranged maniac who had selected them at random. Actually, Lange doesn't even know for sure how many killers were involved.

Neither Lange nor Vannatter had originally given much thought to becoming police officers. Born in Milwaukee on April 14, 1945, and raised in Coral Gables, Florida, Frederick Douglas Lange—who had been nicknamed "Tom" by his two older sisters—moved to Los Angeles County with his mother after the death by heart attack of her estranged husband, Lange's father, in 1960. As a young teenager, Lange was a runaway in the San Fernando Valley and was detained twice by police for minor infractions. However, Lange straightened out, somewhat, while attending a strict Catholic school. A long-distance runner on his high school's cross-country and track-and-field teams, Lange remained rebellious and had no interest in college after graduation. Unlike many children of the 1960s, Lange expressed his rebellion by joining the U.S. Marines and going to Vietnam in June 1965. After a distinguished tour of duty with intensive combat experience, Sergeant Lange left the Marines in October 1966, refusing to re-enlist even after being offered Officers Candidate School.

After returning home from the war, Lange drifted for nearly a year, unable to land a decent job. He traveled around the country, visiting the families of war buddies who hadn't come home. Eventually, he wound up back in Los Angeles, putting up tents for large events and getting paid ten to twenty bucks a day. Then, he went to work for Clairol beauty supplies, putting little boxes into big boxes. He slept on his mother's sofa and spent most of his time hanging out with other vets.

Finally, while pumping gas in North Hollywood for Standard Oil, Lange became acquainted with a LAPD cop who gassed up at his service station. The officer encouraged Lange to take the tests for the LAPD. Lange did and passed with high marks.

He graduated from the LAPD Academy in January 1968. After a variety of assignments, he became an investigator at Central Juvenile and Central Detectives, earning his associate degree in Administration of Justice from Los Angeles Valley College in 1976. While working on the infamous Skid-Row Stabber Murders case, he became a member of the Robbery/Homicide Division in November 1978, working, at first, on loan from the Central Division.

He eventually solved the murders after identifying a mere palm print left by the killer at one of the crime scenes.[5] The following year, in October 1979—the same month as his marriage to his wife, Linda—Lange was permanently assigned to RHD, where he met Phil Vannatter.

Born on April 18, 1941, in Billy's Creek, West Virginia, near the birthplace of flying-ace Chuck Yeager, Vannatter grew up on a farm in the heart of Appalachia. The son of a coal miner who died of black lung disease in 1951 and the youngest of six children, Vannatter helped his mother run the farm until he was fourteen, when they moved to Culver City, California, to join one of his older brothers who had settled there. A three-letter man in high school— football, basketball, and baseball—Vannatter had been scouted by the Cleveland Indians for his pitching abilities. Although he didn't get a ticket to the major leagues, he did receive a nomination from his congressman to the U.S. Naval Academy. However, disappointment struck again when the academy rejected him because of his lifelong stuttering problem. Selected as his high school's top scholar-athlete by a local car dealership, Vannatter took his scholarship money and used it for speech therapy, eventually conquering his handicap.

After receiving his associate degree from Santa Monica College, where he played football, he received a football scholarship at Humboldt State University in Arcata, California. Because he had to support his mother, he dropped out in his junior year and took a job with an auto parts store. While working there, he met his wife—Rita, a nurse at UCLA—on a blind date and married her three months later. But two months after their marriage, Vannatter was drafted and spent thirteen months in Korea, serving as a Spec-5 and working in army communications. Honorably discharged, he returned to the United States in November 1968, at age twenty-seven. He went back to work at the auto parts store.

While watching television, he saw a public-service message about a LAPD recruitment drive. At the time, he was only making $600 a month; he and Rita had their first child on the way. Seeing that he could make nearly $750 a month as a police officer, he applied for the LAPD and was accepted. He graduated from the LAPD Academy in June 1969.

After making his bones as a patrol officer, Vannatter became an investigator, working in the Venice, Wilshire, and West Los Angeles

Divisions. In February 1979, Vannatter joined the Officer-Involved Shootings Section of the Robbery/Homicide Division and was later appointed to Homicide Special, where he became Lange's partner in 1989.

Since then, Lange and Vannatter have become close friends, as well as partners, complementing each other's strengths. Vannatter is known for his instincts and personal warmth; Lange is the bookworm who is highly regarded for his careful methodology.

In the complicated LAPD bureaucracy, Lange, Vannatter, and Ron Phillips all have the rank of Detective-III—although Lange and Vannatter share the responsibilities as the "lead detectives" on this case. Mark Fuhrman, who has spent nearly twenty years with the LAPD, is a Detective-II and the junior officer in this four-man group. Even though Fuhrman is the least senior man at this crime scene, Lange and Vannatter already pick up on his "been there, done that" attitude.

Phillips asks Fuhrman for his general observation notes taken during his earlier walk-through. When Fuhrman complies, Phillips hands them to Vannatter, who immediately gives them to Lange. This is their standard operating procedure, since Lange will conduct the crime-scene search and ultimately prepare the final murder follow-up report for the district attorney's office—should an arrest be made. Up to this point, neither Lange nor Vannatter has taken any notes of their own during their quick walk-throughs. The note-taking process will not start until they begin their detailed crime-scene examination.

As the detectives talk over their crime-scene strategy, Lieutenant Rogers joins the conversation and tells Lange and Phillips about Commander Bushey's order: They are supposed to contact O.J. Simpson, in person, to help him recover his children.

Vannatter asks, "Do we know where he lives?"

Phillips replies, "Well, Fuhrman says he was once up there on a four-fifteen radio call [a disturbance of the peace], some sort of domestic dispute. It's just a couple of miles away."

Vannatter hears Phillips say that Fuhrman had responded to a previous domestic dispute at Simpson's home, but he does not give it any thought; Lange only hears Phillips say that Fuhrman had once been there on some unspecific radio call.[6]

Phillips's comment about a previous "domestic dispute" between O.J. Simpson and Nicole Brown passes without further comment.

Lange says to Phillips and Fuhrman, "The four of us are going to go over to Simpson's place. We can meet the guy, make the notification, and get his cooperation for background information down the road. The two of you will stay with Simpson and help him make the arrangements for picking up his kids at your division. Then Phil and I will come back here and handle the bodies and the evidence."

Lieutenant Rogers, as Lange and Vannatter's supervisor, approves of this plan and takes charge of securing the South Bundy crime scene until Lange and Vannatter return. Considering that Simpson lives just two miles away, Lange and Vannatter assume that they will be back in twenty minutes or less.

At this moment, neither Lange nor Vannatter view O.J. Simpson—who, to most people, is a beloved American sports icon—as an *actual* suspect in the murders. However, as the ex-husband of the dead woman, they must consider him a *potential* suspect. This is consistent with routine police procedure: Anyone who has had any personal contact with a murder victim is a potential suspect until the case has been investigated. But, at this moment, the detectives have no physical evidence linking anyone, including O.J. Simpson, to this crime. And there is no discussion among the detectives of Simpson even being a potential suspect.[7]

Endnotes

1. Neighbor Steven Schwab, while walking his own dog, had found the Akita barking and seemingly walking aimlessly. He had left his home after watching *The Dick Van Dyke Show*, which ended at 10:30 P.M. The dog followed Schwab, who arrived back home before *The Mary Tyler Moore Show*, which began at 11:00. Schwab gave the Akita a bowl of water and noticed its bloody paws.

Forty minutes later, Schwab and his wife saw Boztepe and Rasmussen, with whom they were acquainted. The two couples talked, and Boztepe and Rasmussen offered to take the Akita home with them for the night. But when they arrived at their home, they noticed that the Akita kept pawing the door, apparently wanting to go out. Boztepe and Rasmussen obliged, leading to their discovery of Nicole Brown's body.

Also, another neighbor, Pablo Fenjves, reported to police that he had heard a dog's "plaintive wail" begin at about 10:15 to 10:20 P.M.

2. The LAPD later sent Sergeant Donn Yarnell of the animal-control unit to examine the Akita and to determine whether it was capable of being aggressive to the point of defending its owner. The final conclusion was that it was a docile dog that shied away even when threatened.

3. Lemoyne Snyder, *Homicide Investigation: Practical Information for Coroners, Police Officers, and Other Investigators*, 2nd ed. (Springfield, IL: Charles C. Thomas, 1972), p. 36. Snyder's book is strongly suggested reading among LAPD homicide detectives.

4. Just prior to the Brown-Goldman murders, the LAPD high command had rejected Fuhrman's transfer.

5. Charged with eleven counts of murder, the killer, Bobby Joe Maxwell, was later convicted and sentenced to life in prison without the possibility of parole.

6. In his book, *The Run of His Life*, author Jeffrey Toobin writes on pages 34–35: "In his report of the evening's activities, Lange summarized Fuhrman's information this way: 'Mr. Simpson and [Nicole Brown] had been embroiled in previous domestic-violence situations, one of these resulting in the arrest of Mr. Simpson.' (Phillips later testified he did not remember any such discussion that evening, although it is possible he simply did not hear what Fuhrman said to Lange.)"

Toobin raises a legitimate point, but it has a simple explanation. In short, Toobin is wrong about what Lange wrote "in his report about the evening's activities." Actually, Toobin is referring to Lange's "Murder Follow-Up Report"—which was filed with the district attorney's office on

Friday, June 17. The detective prepared this document in conjunction with the formal felony filing of the case. This June 17 report was a compilation of information the LAPD had received since the investigation began on Monday, June 13.

Lange *never* had any discussion with Fuhrman about a domestic-violence situation involving O.J. Simpson and Nicole Brown.

7. The Simpson defense team created a major ongoing controversy by arguing that Lange and Vannatter, in fact, had viewed Simpson as an *actual* suspect when they left South Bundy to make the notification at North Rockingham. If Simpson had been an actual suspect—with hard evidence linking him to the crime—when they later entered his property, the prosecution stood to lose all of the evidence that was recovered at Simpson's estate both before and after a search warrant had been obtained later that morning.

The defense team did not want to hear—and, certainly, did not want the jury to believe—the distinction between a *potential* suspect and an *actual* suspect.

2

Over the Wall

It is 5:00 A.M.

Phillips and Fuhrman, who needed to ask Officer Riske for directions to Simpson's home, are riding in the lead car. Lange and Vannatter follow close behind in Vannatter's Buick. The officers drive northbound on South Bundy to Sunset Boulevard, turn left, and drive westbound to North Rockingham Avenue, where they turn right and continue north.

As Lange and Vannatter turn the corner onto North Rockingham, Vannatter repeats their earlier discussion, saying that they will meet Simpson, give him the notification, solicit his future help for background data on his ex-wife, and leave Phillips and Fuhrman with him to arrange for the pickup of his children.

Neither Lange nor Vannatter are starstruck with this opportunity to meet yet another celebrity. In Los Angeles, they meet famous people all the time. In fact, they dread telling *anyone* of the death of a loved one, even though that's occasionally part of their job. But because they will be running this investigation, not Phillips and Fuhrman, they want Simpson to know them, personally, from the outset.

As the detectives drive up North Rockingham Avenue toward Ashford Street, Lange, sitting in the passenger seat, looks to his right as the lead car slows down and its brake lights click on. Through the darkness, he sees a large estate behind an iron gate and a stone wall. Parked near the gate—facing north and on the east side of the street—is a white 1994 Ford Bronco. The street is narrow and void of other parked cars. Lange notices that the Bronco is parked at an angle with its rear sticking out into the street.

Seconds later, Phillips and Fuhrman turn east on Ashford and park at the curb near a black Nissan 300ZX, which is up ahead on the south side of the street. Lange and Vannatter pull directly behind them. Nearly five minutes after leaving the South Bundy crime scene, they have arrived at O.J. Simpson's home.

After getting out of their cars, Lange and Vannatter look through a second iron-barred gate on Ashford and see a light on inside the house. They also observe two cars parked in the semicircular driveway, a Bentley and a Saab. It is too dark to see their tag numbers.

Fuhrman walks over to an intercom to the left of Simpson's gate and presses the button. No answer. Phillips steps in and presses it. Still no answer. For several minutes, the detectives take turns pressing the button on the intercom, still getting no response. Because of the cars in the driveway and the light in the house, they assume that Simpson is home and the intercom is broken.

While they are waiting for someone to talk to inside the house, Vannatter notices a sign for "Westec," a private security company, near the gate. He suggests that Phillips call and get a telephone number. Phillips complies, pulling out his cellular telephone and calling Sergeant David Rossi, the night-watch commander at the West Los Angeles Division. Phillips asks him to contact Westec and request someone to come to Simpson's residence.

By coincidence, while they are waiting for Westec to arrive, another Westec car cruises up North Rockingham on a routine patrol. Seeing the detectives, the Westec patrol officer pulls over and stops.

On his own initiative, Fuhrman walks over to the white Bronco near Simpson's gate on North Rockingham. Like Lange, he has noticed that the car appears to have been parked hastily—with its right front tire over the apron of the curb and the rear tires angling toward the street. Fuhrman shines his flashlight into the back window of the Bronco's cargo bay. Seconds later, he turns around and immediately calls out to Vannatter.

While Phillips and Lange talk to the Westec patrol officer,

Vannatter strides over to Fuhrman, who shines his flashlight again into the back of the Bronco. Inside, they see a long-handled shovel and a plastic sheet;[8] also, they can read the words on one of two packages—"Orenthal Productions." Like most football fans, Vannatter and Fuhrman know that "Orenthal" is Simpson's first name. Then, Vannatter shines his flashlight into the car and notices its lock knobs in the locked position.

Although he assumes that Simpson owns the Bronco, Vannatter, still wondering if the football star is home, asks Fuhrman to run a Department of Motor Vehicles inquiry on the Bronco, as well as the Nissan 300ZX parked on Ashford.

As Fuhrman runs the tag checks on his police radio, Vannatter returns to Phillips and Lange, who are now arguing with the Westec patrol officer. He is giving them a hard time about revealing Simpson's telephone number. "I can't give it out," the guard insists.

"Bullshit!" Vannatter exclaims to the security man. "Give us the goddamn phone number!"

Just before a second Westec patrol officer appears on the scene, the first one calls his supervisor, who orders him to provide the detectives with anything they want. After reluctantly giving up the number, the guard adds that as far as he knows, Simpson is inside the house. A live-in maid should be in there as well. He adds that if Simpson were away, he would have notified his home-security service.

A few minutes later, Fuhrman reports that the Bronco is registered to the Hertz Corporation—which, the detectives know, is represented on television commercials by Simpson running through airports; the Nissan 300ZX is registered to Brian Gerard Kaelin, who has an address not in this neighborhood.

After giving Vannatter that information, Fuhrman returns to the white Bronco, which has now become his focus of interest. Using his flashlight, Fuhrman conducts a brief inspection of the vehicle and calls Lange over to the car. "Hey," he says, "I think I've found blood."

Lange walks over to the Bronco, where Fuhrman is shining his flashlight on a red speck, smaller than a dime, above the outside door handle on the driver's side.[9] On his way, Lange notices a piece of wood, which is about a foot long, on the grass alongside the Bronco on the parkway. It looks freshly splintered and doesn't seem to fit anywhere in the area. It appears to have been broken off from a fence.[10]

Lange eyes the red speck and nods his head in agreement as Fuhrman shouts out to Vannatter, "Phil, come over here, I want you to see something."

When Vannatter returns to the Bronco, Fuhrman, shining his flashlight at the small speck, asks, "Is this blood?" Vannatter narrows his eyes, then puts on his reading glasses for a closer look. Surprised, he replies, "Jesus, it does look like blood."

Lange and Vannatter return to Phillips, telling him that there might be a small amount of blood on Simpson's car door. Now, the detectives don't know what to think.

As the Westec patrol officer leaves the area to respond to another call, Phillips calls Simpson's home on his cellular phone. It is now 5:36 A.M. All four of the detectives hear the phone ringing inside Simpson's house. Simpson's answering machine switches on, inviting the caller to leave a message. Phillips doesn't leave one.

Moments later, an LAPD black-and-white appears at Simpson's residence and parks. Two patrol officers, Richard Aston and Daniel Gonzalez of the West Los Angeles Division, climb out of their squad car. They have just come from the South Bundy crime scene where they have been since 12:30 A.M. Sergeant Rossi, the watch commander who contacted Westec, has ordered them to Simpson's estate to provide whatever assistance the detectives might need.

Immediately upon their arrival, Vannatter asks them to call for a criminalist. He wants an analysis of the red speck on the Bronco to determine whether or not it is, in fact, blood.

Vannatter then turns to the others and says, "Let's add this up: We have lights on in the house and cars parked in the driveway. Simpson and his live-in maid are supposed to be home, but no one is answering either the intercom or the phone. And, now, we have blood near the door handle on the driver's side of Simpson's Bronco, which is parked kind of funny in the street just a couple of miles from the scene of a double homicide. And one of the victims is Simpson's ex-wife. Do we have two connected crime scenes?"

Lange weighs in with his opinion, "Something's wrong. Lights on. Cars everywhere. No one's answering. What if Simpson and his maid are in trouble in there?"

The detectives look at each other momentarily. Then, they mutually agree that a potential emergency exists and that they must enter Simpson's estate. Under such exigent circumstances, real or perceived, police officers are permitted to enter a person's property without a search warrant.

At this moment, the question of whether Simpson is an *actual* or *potential* suspect is moot. The concern for the safety of Simpson and his maid overrides everything else.

But in order to enter Simpson's property, they will have to go over Simpson's thick, five-foot-high, vine-covered stone wall—which should be no great athletic feat. The younger and trimmer Fuhrman volunteers. "I'll go over if you want me to."

"Yeah," Vannatter readily agrees. "Go ahead."

At approximately 5:45 A.M., Fuhrman scales the wall, jumps over onto the other side, walks to the gate, and opens it, allowing the other three detectives to enter.

Vannatter orders Officers Aston and Gonzales to stand guard outside the Ashford Street gate—in case the detectives need additional backup support.

Walking south on Simpson's driveway, they encounter another dog. This one is a black Akita. Vannatter—who had been thrice bitten by dogs while on the job—approaches the dog carefully, allowing the Akita to sniff his hand, and then pets it. The dog is friendly, wagging its tail and making no noise.

With the Akita moving about nearby, the four detectives walk up to Simpson's front door and ring the doorbell. Hearing no response inside, they start knocking on the door.

Still hearing nothing, Phillips says, "Let's check out the back of the house."

The detectives, walking in single file—Phillips, Lange, Fuhrman, and Vannatter—go back up the driveway a few yards and turn right onto a walkway leading around the northern portion of the house. As they walk along the eastern side of the house, past a large swimming pool on their left, they see a row of three bungalows along the southeastern perimeter of the estate. Continuing to feel that something is very wrong, Vannatter has his flashlight on, scanning the area and looking for anything out of the ordinary. None of the detectives have drawn their guns.

At the first door, Fuhrman looks in a window and tells the others, "It looks like there's somebody inside." Phillips then pounds hard on the door.

Almost immediately, a disheveled man answers. He appears to

be in his thirties with long, blond surfer-boy hair and green bloodshot eyes. He looks like he has just been awakened from a sound sleep. Wearing a T-shirt and pajama bottoms, he asks, "What's going on?"

Phillips demands, "Who are you?"

"I'm Kato Kaelin, and I live here. What's going on?"

"Where's Mr. Simpson?" Phillips asks.

Kaelin, who is still half asleep, doesn't seem to know.

"Did anything unusual happen to you last night?" Phillips continues.

"I spent the night here at home," he responds.

Because Kaelin is acting oddly, Fuhrman pulls out his flashlight and gives him a nystagmus test to determine whether he is under the influence of something. The detective asks him to follow his finger to see whether his eyes jump. Kaelin passes the test.

Fuhrman also demands to see his shoes and the clothing he wore last night; Kaelin, again, offers no resistance. At this moment, Kaelin is under some suspicion because the officers have no idea why he's here. Westec didn't tell them anything about him living on the property. He shows the detectives a shirt and a pair of pants thrown over a chair, as well as a pair of work boots on the floor. Fuhrman looks for bloodstains but doesn't find any.

"Is anyone else here?" Lange asks.

"Well, yeah, Arnelle, O.J.'s daughter. She lives next door."

Saying nothing further, Lange and Phillips go to the door to the east of Kaelin's bungalow. Fuhrman remains behind with Kaelin while Vannatter hangs back in the courtyard in front of the bungalows.

At the next bungalow, Phillips again knocks on the door. Arnelle Simpson—an attractive young woman, who is Simpson's daughter by his first wife—answers in her nightgown. She is baffled by the sight of these strangers. "What's the matter?" she asks, very alarmed. "What's going on?"

"Is O.J. Simpson your father?" Phillips asks, showing his LAPD shield to her.

"Yes."

"Do you live here?"

"Yes, but what's going on?" she repeats.

Pointing toward Kaelin, who is standing with Fuhrman, Lange continues, "Do you know this fellow?"

"Yeah, that's Kato. He lives here."

Lange then asks, "And who drives the white Bronco parked out in the street?"

"Mostly my dad. It's his car," she replies.

"We're looking for your father," Vannatter says. "Can you tell us where he is?"

Arnelle steps out of her front door and points to the main house, asking, "Isn't he there?"

Lange immediately believes his worst fears have been realized. Simpson—and perhaps even his maid—are dead in the house in another double murder.

"Do you have a key?" Vannatter asks. "Can we go check?"

By this time, Arnelle has walked out near the pool area. Now, starting to wake up and realizing that four police detectives are at her home, she asks if everything is okay and whether something has happened to her father.

"We have an emergency," Lange says. "We need to talk to your father. Can we have that key?"

The detectives do not tell Arnelle about Nicole Brown's murder yet. They want her to remain composed in the event they need more help or information from her.

Cooperating fully, Arnelle replies that she does have a key and walks quickly to her bungalow to retrieve it.

When she returns, she leads Lange, Vannatter, and Phillips to the back door of her father's house while Fuhrman continues to talk with Kaelin back at his bungalow. After unlocking the door, she steps aside, allowing Lange, Vannatter, and Phillips to enter first. Once inside the house, Vannatter asks Arnelle, "Where's the maid's room?"

Arnelle takes him through the kitchen to a small hallway and opens a door on the left. She tells him, "This is where the maid lives."

As Arnelle then joins Lange and Phillips in the kitchen, Vannatter looks in and sees that the maid's bed is made and the room is in good order. Clearly, there has not been a struggle here or anywhere else that he can see.

Vannatter then walks toward the back door. Fuhrman steps into Simpson's house with Kaelin in tow, saying, "Phil, you gotta talk to this guy. You've gotta hear what he has to say."

"Okay," Vannatter says, "let's hear it." Vannatter and Kaelin sit at a semicircular bar in a large and comfortable television room. Following up on what he has just learned from Kaelin, Fuhrman leaves the room and goes back outside, allowing Vannatter and Kaelin to talk.

Kaelin explains that just last night, he and Simpson had gone out in Simpson's black 1988 Bentley to a local McDonald's, pulling up at the drive-thru. After getting their order and driving away, Simpson began eating his food in the car; Kaelin saved his to eat back home. When they returned to the estate, Simpson went into his house alone.

Kaelin recalls that at about 10:45 P.M., while talking on the telephone to his girlfriend, he heard a loud noise coming from outside the back of his bungalow, which he described as "three thumps." At first, Kaelin tells Vannatter, he thought that the sound had resulted from an earthquake. A picture frame on his wall had actually moved in response to the clamor. Kaelin, with a dim flashlight in his hand, had gone outside to check out the noise.

While outside—before he had a chance to walk behind his bungalow—he saw a limousine at the Ashford Street gate. Kaelin opened the gate, and the chauffeur parked in the driveway. The driver told Kaelin he was taking Simpson to the Los Angeles International Airport. But, the driver said, Simpson was late. A few moments later, Simpson walked out of his house. Kaelin and the driver helped Simpson put his luggage in the limousine.

Kaelin informed Simpson about hearing the "three thumps," adding that he was going to look around when he saw the limousine driver. Because Kaelin's flashlight didn't work very well, Simpson tried to find him one before leaving. Unable to find it quickly and telling Kaelin that he was still running late, Simpson left without giving him another flashlight.

Then Simpson and the driver left for LAX.

Soon after leaving, Simpson called Kaelin on the phone. Apparently concerned about the noises Kaelin heard, Simpson asked him to set the alarm at the main house. When Kaelin, who didn't even have a key to Simpson's residence, said he didn't know how to do it, Simpson gave him instructions and the code numbers.

Completing his note-taking, Vannatter asks Kaelin if he has the keys to Simpson's Bronco. Kaelin goes to a desk in the kitchen where Simpson usually kept a spare set. He cannot find them.

Meantime, Arnelle continues to talk with Lange and Phillips.

The two detectives haven't talked to Vannatter yet about what he has just learned from Kaelin. Arnelle—who had returned home in her Saab from a movie in nearby Westwood at about 1:00 A.M.—suggests that her father's personal assistant, Cathy Randa, might know where Simpson is, since she doesn't know.

Arnelle continues to ask the detectives, "What's the matter? What's going on?"

Phillips replies, "Let's call Cathy Randa to see where he is, and make sure he's okay."

Arnelle calls Randa. Lange can hear Arnelle saying, "Oh, okay. . . . My dad's in Chicago. . . . Oh, man. . . . Fine." He sees her jot something down on a piece of paper.

Hanging up the telephone, Arnelle breathes a sigh of relief and says, "Everything's cool." She gives Phillips the piece of paper with the telephone number for Simpson's hotel in Chicago, the O'Hare Plaza. He had flown there the night before.

Lange and Phillips are relieved, as well. Since he is obviously in Chicago, they do not go upstairs to his bedroom or conduct any search of the house.

Arnelle continues, "But what's going on?"

"Let's go and talk," Lange says as he takes her through a sunroom, adjacent to the kitchen, and out into the driveway. "This has to do with Nicole. I'm very sorry to tell you this, but she's been killed at her home."

At this moment, Arnelle falls apart, screaming and crying. As she tries to collect herself, she mutters over and over again, "I gotta call A.C. I gotta call A.C.," whom she identifies as Al Cowlings. Lange offers to call him for her, but she tearfully insists on making the call herself. Cowlings is O.J. Simpson's lifelong friend, as well as a former teammate from the days when the two men played football for the University of Southern California, then the Buffalo Bills, and later the San Francisco 49ers.

Despite Arnelle's distress, Lange manages to get from her the telephone number of Nicole Brown's father and mother, Louis and Juditha Brown. She tells Lange that they live in Dana Point, near Laguna Hills in Orange County.

As Lange returns to the kitchen, Phillips is just getting Simpson on the telephone. Phillips begins by saying, "Is this O.J. Simpson?"

"Yes, who's this?"

"This is Detective Phillips from the Los Angeles Police Department. First of all, I want you to know that your children are fine. But I do have some bad news for you: Your ex-wife has been killed."

"Oh, my God! Nicole is killed? Oh, my God, is she dead?"

Lange falls silent as Phillips listens solemnly to Simpson as he reacts with shock and disbelief.

"Mr. Simpson, please try to get hold of yourself. I have your children at the West Los Angeles police station. I need to talk to you about that."

Still extremely upset, Simpson replies, "What do you mean you have my children at the police station? Why are my kids at the police station?"

"We had no place else to take them," Phillips responds. "They're only there for safekeeping. I need to know what to do with your children."

"Well, I'm going to leave Chicago on the first available flight. I'll come back to Los Angeles."

At no time during this conversation did Simpson ask Phillips any details regarding the death of his ex-wife.

Endnotes

8. Lange and Vannatter later came to believe that Simpson might have been planning to place Brown's body in the plastic bag and then to bury her at a nearby location after the murder. They theorized that the surprise appearance of Ron Goldman at the crime scene caused Simpson to scuttle his plan to remove Brown.

Simpson's defense team mocked this theory during the criminal trial, claiming that Simpson used the large shovel as a pooper-scooper for his Akita—an explanation that was received with some skepticism by the prosecution. Also, Simpson's lawyers noted that the plastic bag, a standard accessory for the Ford Bronco, covered the spare tire and the jack. Conceding that, the detectives wondered why the tire and the jack had been removed from the large plastic bag, which was lying empty next to the shovel in Simpson's cargo bay on the night of the murders.

9. Fuhrman later testified that he also saw red stains on the bottom panel of the driver's door. Yet, at no time did he communicate this information to either Lange or Vannatter. The first time they heard about this was during his courtroom testimony.

10. Lange and Vannatter spent a considerable amount of time trying to match this splintered piece of wood to a broken fence or any other object on every conceivable route between South Bundy and North Rockingham. In the end, they could not determine where it came from or whether it had any connection to the murders.

3

The Second Crime Scene

After giving the news to Simpson, Phillips hands the telephone to Arnelle, who, upon completing her painful conversation with her father, tells the detectives that she will pick up the two children at the police station.

As Arnelle leaves the kitchen with Phillips, Lange reaches for the telephone number of the Brown family, who live at least ninety minutes away from Brentwood.

Lange must make a decision. He knows that he is overdue at South Bundy to conduct the crime-scene investigation. He also recognizes that the media will soon be all over this story—if they aren't already. If Lange sends someone to the Brown home for a personal notification, there's a better chance that the family will first hear the news on television.

Lange remembers that after the 1982 death of comedian John Belushi, the LAPD had failed to make a prompt personal notification to the members of his family. Consequently, the Belushi family received the news from a reporter, causing a wave of criticism against the police.

Rather than risk that, Lange decides to call the Browns on the telephone and deliver the horrible news himself before they hear it from a reporter.

At 6:21 A.M., again using the telephone in Simpson's kitchen, Lange calls the Brown home. It rings several times before Lou

Brown, Nicole's father, answers—almost simultaneously with daughter Denise, who is on another extension.

"This is Detective Tom Lange, LAPD. Have I reached the home of Nicole Brown's parents?"

"Yes, you have," Lou Brown replies quizzically.

"I'm terribly sorry to inform you about this, Mr. Brown, but your daughter has been killed at her home."

To Lange's complete surprise, Denise immediately starts screaming, "I knew he'd do it! I knew that motherfucker would kill her! I knew it! I knew it! O.J. did it! O.J. killed her! I knew that son of a bitch was going to do it!"

As Lange tries to continue talking to Lou Brown—who does not scream, cry, or accuse—he can hear a growing wave of wailing female voices in the background, screaming, "O.J. did it! O.J. did it! *O.J. did it!*"

Lou Brown remains composed as Lange assures him that his grandchildren are safe at the police station and that they will be picked up by Arnelle. After a few moments, Juditha Brown, Nicole's mother, takes the telephone and speaks to Lange. She tearfully tells the detective that the whole family had dinner together with several friends last night at a restaurant in Brentwood—after they had attended a dance recital to see their granddaughter, Sydney. Without making any accusations, she tells Lange that O.J. Simpson had also attended the recital but not the dinner.

Lange does not push the issue of Denise Brown's frenzied reaction against Simpson. But he knows he will talk to her and the rest of the family again in the very near future.

Almost immediately after Lange hangs up from his brief conversation with the Browns, the telephone rings again, and Lange answers it. Simpson is on the line, informing him, "I'm on my way back. I've got the next flight out of here."

With his mind still reeling from his conversation with Denise Brown and the accusatory cries in the background, Tom Lange simply replies, "Okay, fine."

While all of this high drama is happening on the telephone in the kitchen, Fuhrman, who has been gone for ten to fifteen minutes, returns to Vannatter, who is still talking with Kaelin in the television room, and says, "You gotta see what I just found."

Vannatter goes outside with Fuhrman—this time through the front door of Simpson's house. They turn left and go south along the front of the residence and past Simpson's garage. Just a few feet past the garage, Simpson's property ends, marked by a chain-link fence. They turn left, pass through an open gate, and go east along the fence, on a narrow cement pathway, partially covered in foliage. Another gate on the path is also wide open.

It is nearly dawn, but the walkway, for the most part, remains dark. Fuhrman stops just short of an air-conditioning unit that extends out of the rear of Kaelin's bungalow. This is the location where Kaelin said he had earlier heard the strange noises outside his back wall. Then Fuhrman switches on his flashlight and shines it on the ground at an object shrouded near the shrubbery.

Illuminated is a leather, bloodstained, right-hand glove, appearing moist and sticky and looking like the match to the left-hand glove found at the South Bundy crime scene.[11] Also on the ground—up against and on the other side of the cyclone fence and near the glove—is a blue plastic bag.[12]

Vannatter and Fuhrman say nothing to each other—although Vannatter does say out loud to himself, "I don't fucking believe this." The two detectives touch neither the glove nor the bag; they must wait for a criminalist.

Following Fuhrman's discovery, Vannatter and Fuhrman return to the front of Simpson's house. There, Vannatter says to Fuhrman, "I want you to go back to Bundy. I want you to look at the glove over there. Make sure that we have a match. And I want you to have the photographer photograph it. Then I want you to bring the photographer back here, so that we can photograph this one."

Fuhrman turns and starts looking for Phillips. Fuhrman had already pointed out the glove to him while Lange was on the phone with the Browns and Vannatter talked to Kaelin. Phillips is now in the kitchen, telling Lange about the discovery.

Before Fuhrman and Phillips leave for South Bundy, Fuhrman takes Lange to see the glove. This is the first time Lange, who has been busy doing other things, has seen Fuhrman in nearly twenty minutes. Like the others, Lange does not get closer than six feet from the glove, knowing that it will be collected by a SID criminalist.

By the time Lange and Fuhrman return to the front of the house at about 6:35 A.M., A.C. Cowlings has arrived to pick up Arnelle. He says nothing to the detectives—other than that he is going to drive Arnelle to pick up Simpson's children at the West Los Angeles Division.

As Phillips and Fuhrman head for the South Bundy crime scene, Lange and Vannatter meet in the driveway in front of Simpson's garage. Both men are deadly serious.

"We might have an extension of the Bundy crime scene here," Vannatter tells his partner.

"Yeah," Lange replies, "I agree with you."

Vannatter continues, "We're going to have to handle this as a possible second crime scene. There was no struggle here. His house is neat and clean. But look at what we've got: No one here at the house knew for sure where he was. And it turns out that he flew to Chicago late last night. . . . You know, Tom, I think Simpson's our suspect."

"The dead woman's sister thinks so," Lange says. "While I was on the phone with her and her father, giving them the bad news, she flat-out accused Simpson of killing her sister. And then I heard several voices in the background yelling that 'O.J. did it.' "

"You're kidding!" Vannatter exclaims. "Then, maybe, Simpson is our man."

Lange agrees and envisions, as he often does in his investigations, what might have happened. "We have the left-hand glove at Bundy," Lange says. "It probably got torn off while he was fighting the dead man. Before being killed, the guy injures the killer somewhere on his left side. We have a trail of blood to the left of the bloody shoe prints leading away from the bodies."

Vannatter adds it up: "So we do have two crime scenes: Bundy and Rockingham."

Pointing at the patrol car still outside the gate on Ashford Street, Lange continues, "I'm going to get one of the uniforms to take me back to Bundy. Let me get started on that crime scene. You handle whatever you find up here."

"Okay, no problem," Vannatter responds. "I'll keep the other uniform with me."

As the patrol officer drives off with Lange at about 6:40 A.M., dawn breaks in Los Angeles. With the early-morning light shining over the shadows cast by Simpson's house to the east, Vannatter walks west across the driveway, expecting the criminalist to arrive soon to check the red speck on the white Bronco and a photographer to take pictures of the right-hand glove.

At this point, none of the LAPD detectives have conducted any semblance of a search inside Simpson's house. They have opened no cupboards, drawers, or closets. They have not looked under his tables. They have not gone upstairs—and had no interest in doing so, especially after being told that Simpson had gone to Chicago.

Now, with the discovery of the right-hand glove, Vannatter is interested in Simpson's house. But he knows that he'll need a search warrant to find out if anything important is in there.

As the shadows continue to abate, Vannatter looks down on the pavement near the Bentley and the Saab parked in the driveway. There, Vannatter sees another red spot.

He puts on his glasses again and bends down to examine it; the spot appears to be a drop of blood. Looking ahead toward the west gate on North Rockingham, he sees another drop of blood—and another, and then several others.

Following this trail of blood, it leads out into the street to the rear of Simpson's Bronco.

With more light around him now, Vannatter peers inside the locked Bronco from the passenger side's window. Inside the car, he sees blood smears on the passenger side of the console and on the driver's side door.

Then, retracing the blood spots, he looks on the driveway to the east of the Bentley and sees more blood spots leading right to Simpson's front door.

Vannatter says out loud to himself, "My God! O.J. did do it!"

A few minutes later, Arnelle and Cowlings return to Simpson's home with his two children. As Vannatter walks around outside, they proceed inside with the kids. Although they now must know that something more is going on, Arnelle and Cowlings strangely ask no questions, and make no comments to either Vannatter or the patrol officer still guarding the Ashford Street gate.

Shortly after 7:00 A.M., Fuhrman returns to Simpson's home, accompanied by his partner, Detective Brad Roberts and LAPD photographer Rolf Rokahr, who has been at South Bundy taking pictures. Under Fuhrman's supervision, Rokahr has just taken a close-up photograph of Fuhrman pointing to the left-hand glove at the murder scene. Fuhrman tells Vannatter that the glove at South Bundy and the right-hand glove at Simpson's home appear to be a match. They seem to have the same dark brown color and style. Because Fuhrman could not touch either glove without a criminalist present, he did not know the brand name on the inside lining.

Loosening his tie and lighting a Marlboro, Vannatter then shakes his head and runs his hand through his thick hair. "O.J. Simpson," Vannatter says in astonishment to Fuhrman, Roberts, and Rokahr. "God, who would have thought it possible? . . . Let me show you guys something else."

Vannatter points out the blood spots in the driveway, as well as the blood smears inside the Bronco. He orders Rokahr to document any evidence in "plain view" outside Simpson's home. Vannatter and the others know that "plain view" evidence may be collected without a search warrant.

After being briefed by Vannatter, Roberts walks through the front door of the house and sees more drops of blood inside on the floor of the foyer. Roberts immediately tells Vannatter, who exclaims, "Jesus Christ, the blood goes right into the house!"[13]

Now seeing that the entire area, including the house, might contain additional evidence, Vannatter yells out, "That's it! Shut it down! I want this entire place sealed off! I don't want anyone coming or going!"

Vannatter walks up to Cowlings, who is now outside with Arnelle and Simpson's children, and introduces himself. Cowlings replies, "I'm A.C. Cowlings, a friend of the family."

"You're going to have to leave now," Vannatter tells him. "This is a crime scene. Do you have someplace to go with the children?"

Without any protest or questions, Cowlings simply replies, "Yeah. No problem."

At 7:10 A.M., Dennis Fung, a criminalist from the LAPD Scientific Investigation Division (SID), arrives at the North Rockingham location—along with his assistant, Andrea Mazzola, who is in her sixth month as a SID trainee.

The lead detective at a crime scene directs the police criminalist how to proceed with his documentation and collection of crime-scene evidence. Ultimately, the lead detective is responsible for everyone—and everything they do—at a crime scene once the investigation is under way.

Vannatter immediately gives Fung and Mazzola a tour of the new crime scene, insisting, "I want every blood drop, as well as the glove and anything else that's in 'plain view.' I also want the Bronco impounded and towed immediately."

Before Vannatter leaves the new crime scene, Fung conducts a presumptive test on the red speck on the Bronco. He quickly determines that it is, indeed, blood.

Then he writes the number "1" on a white evidence tag and places it by the blood near the outside door handle. The evidence tag denotes the item number as it will appear on the property report Fung will prepare. The tag is photographed from a distance and in a tight shot.

After that, Fung collects it by taking a cotton swab, wetting it with distilled water, placing it directly on the blood speck, and transferring it from the Bronco to a cloth swatch for analysis.

The speck of blood on the Bronco becomes the first piece of evidence collected in this case by Fung, who will be responsible for collecting and cataloging every piece of evidence in the case hereafter.

Then, turning to Fuhrman and Roberts, Vannatter says, "I want you to secure and control this crime scene, because I have to go write out the search warrant. I'll be back later when I've finished."

For all intents and purposes, Fuhrman's role in this investigation has ended. He will now simply become part of a general detail.

Endnotes

11. The Simpson defense team later created a major controversy, contending that Detective Fuhrman had planted the right-hand glove on Simpson's property in the midst of a police conspiracy to frame Simpson. The theory went that Fuhrman had actually found the right-hand glove at the South Bundy crime scene, picked it up, hid it, and then dropped it on Simpson's estate before Lange and Vannatter arrived at the crime scene.

For a variety of reasons that will later be addressed in this work, this scenario is impossible.

12. Scientific analysis indicated no blood or trace evidence in the plastic bag, which was deemed to have been trash.

13. At or about 7:30 A.M., Kato Kaelin was taken to the West Los Angeles Division by Detectives Brian Carr and Paul Tippin for routine questioning. While he was leaving with the detectives, Kaelin also saw the blood spots.

4

Collecting Evidence

Soon after arriving at the South Bundy crime scene at about 6:45 A.M., Lange grabs his briefcase, which contains his clipboard for taking notes, measuring devices, a variety of tools, and rubber gloves, among other items.

At 6:49, Lange asks Detective Phillips to arrange the "first call" to the coroner's office, placing its investigators on notice that he wants them to respond quickly when he makes his second call, which should be at about 8:00 A.M. Because he has to review and document all of the evidence at the crime scene before having the bodies moved, Lange is simply not ready for the coroner's people. Right now, they would just get in the way of everything else he has to do.

He assigns other detectives, who have also arrived at the scene, to search through garbage containers outside the yellow tape in back of the condominium and around the area, as well as to canvass the neighborhood for potential witnesses and to check the license tags of cars in the vicinity.

Also, Lange attempts to reach Simpson at the O'Hare Plaza Hotel in Chicago, but he has already checked out. Lange asks a couple of detectives under his command to find out when Simpson will arrive at LAX and on which airline.

At about 7:30, Vannatter returns to South Bundy to speak with his partner. Vannatter tells Lange, "After you left, we found more blood. We've got blood in the driveway. We've got blood in the entrance—along with the blood in and on the Bronco. The criminalist is there now."

"Are you getting a search warrant?" Lange asks.

"I'm on my way over to West L.A. now to write it up."

"Okay," Lange replies. "I'll be right here."

As Vannatter walks back to his car, Lange sees the growing number of reporters and film crews setting up on a hill across the street from Brown's condominium. Because the two bodies are still lying on the ground—with Brown's slaughtered corpse out in the open—Lange asks Officer Don Thompson to get him a clean sheet.

When Thompson returns, he says he can't find one, except for those already on Brown's and her children's beds. However, he has found a tightly knit hospital-style blanket in a bathroom cabinet upstairs. It is clean in appearance and neatly folded.

To block the media's view of the grotesque sight of Nicole Brown, lying in her own blood, Lange—without touching her body— spreads the blanket over her until the coroner's investigator arrives. Because the male victim cannot be seen from the street, Lange doesn't need to cover him.

Actually, Lange has two reasons for protecting Brown from view; the other, which is more important, is less for humanitarian reasons and more for investigative purposes.

Lange knows that Brown's body is evidence. The position it's in is evidence. Any of the dried blood drops on her body, any tailing of blood on the body, and any blood patterns on the body are evidence. The nature of her wounds is evidence. The jewelry she is wearing is evidence. Her scant clothing is evidence. The fact she is wearing no shoes is evidence.

Lange knows that the media is probably using long-lens cameras that can highlight a speck of blood at two hundred feet. He doesn't want such pictures made public because they could compromise all of the evidence Brown's body might give. Once the evidence becomes public, investigators will not be able to use it as effectively when they interview potential witnesses or suspects, as the detectives are trying to determine whether they are truthful.

As the investigator in charge of the crime scene, Lange wants to keep his edge in case someone steps forward and takes responsibility for committing these murders or claims to have knowledge about them. Other than police investigators, Lange wants only the killer and those he might tell about the murder to know all of the little details about such things as the position of wounds and the blood patterns. So Lange must ensure that the crime scene is protected from compromise, as well as contamination.[14]

After viewing and covering Brown's body, Lange has Phillips call the coroner's office for the second time at 8:08 A.M. Lange is now ready for the coroner's investigator to come to the South Bundy crime scene. Lange will soon need the coroner's office to move the two bodies so that he can continue his work.

With his clipboard in hand, Lange reenters the area through the "safe route" in the rear of the condominium. Everything is still in pristine condition; nothing has been disturbed. Nicole Brown's black Grand Cherokee Jeep is parked in her driveway with its passenger door slightly cracked open. Near her car, Lange sees two coins—a dime and a penny—on the pavement.[15] He sees a drop of blood near the coins. He also sees a plastic heart on the ground in front of the Jeep. Brown's other car, a white Ferrari, is in the garage. A maze of interlocking tire tracks are on the driveway and in the back alley.

From there, Lange moves into the garage leading to the back door of the house. At the bottom of the stairwell on a banister near the garage, he sees the cup of Ben & Jerry's ice cream, now almost completely melted. Still, no officer has touched it. Lange doesn't think there is much significance to the presence of ice cream, particularly in a house where children live.

Also, a long knife is on the edge of the stove's countertop in the kitchen, which, along with the ice cream, seems to be the only other item out of place. Lange wonders whether Brown had heard something and grabbed the knife for protection.

Walking through the brightly lit condominium toward the front door, Lange notices candles still lit in the sunken living room to his right—over seven hours after the first officers arrived at the scene. The soft New Age music continues to play. Seeing this romantic atmosphere, Lange wonders to himself, "Was she expecting the dead guy outside or someone else?" But Lange remembers how his own wife, Linda, enjoys lighting candles at their home—even when she's alone.

Lange goes upstairs to Brown's bedroom, continuing to take notes. He sees more candles burning—although the lights are on, as well as her television, which is tuned to the Prime Sports cable station.

Brown's bed appears to have been rested on but not slept in; the bedspread on top is rumpled. In her bathroom, even more candles are lit, three around the bathtub. When Officer Riske earlier went through the house, he observed that the bathtub was filled with water. Now it's empty. Lange notices that the tub has a faulty slip lever, which might have allowed the water to drain.

On the floor of the bathroom, Lange notices a pack of Marlboro Lights, alongside a rug that appears to have a slight red stain, which he will have the SID criminalist collect and analyze.[16] Lange knows from Vannatter that Dennis Fung is at North Rockingham, collecting the blood evidence. When he is done there, he will come to the South Bundy crime scene.

Next, Lange conducts a search of the children's rooms. Sydney's room has dolls throughout; Justin's room, which has bunk beds, is extremely neat. His clothing and toys are all put away.

Then, after surveying a sundeck on top of the house, Lange notes it and goes back downstairs. He carefully walks out the front door, making sure that he doesn't step on the bloody shoe prints or the drops of blood to their left, which pass by the door and continue west. He follows the trail of blood toward the back alley.

He sees that the gate at the west end of the walkway is open and has two drops of blood on its inside lower rung. Phillips had earlier pointed this out to him, and Fuhrman had mentioned this blood evidence in his notes.[17]

Although the bloody shoe prints fade as they approach the back alley, he sees a drop of blood just before the gate and another on the driveway, by the Jeep Cherokee and near the dime and penny he found earlier. Lange, who has now come full circle around the house, believes that the killer might have stopped to reach into his pocket for his car keys and dropped the two coins when he pulled out the keys. Lange can tell that the drop of blood near the coins is from a stationary source and not one in motion. This blood drop is concentric, while a blood drop from a source in motion would tail in the direction the source was moving.

Returning to the front of the house, Lange walks to the end of the walkway and to the top of the cement staircase, facing South Bundy. Nicole Brown's body is at the bottom of the stairs; the unidentified male is to Lange's left in a cramped fenced-in location. Lange can clearly see the blood-splattered white envelope between the two bodies, and the left-hand glove and a blue-knit cap partially hidden under bloodstained foliage near the feet of the dead man.

Carefully walking into the area around the bodies, Lange lifts the corner of the envelope with his pen. Inside, he sees a pair of eyeglasses.

Lange also spots other items, which do not appear to have any particular significance—but he makes a note for them to be collected and photographed anyway. These items include a faded label from a piece of Bonita Ecuador fruit and a carry-out menu from a local Thai restaurant that's found under Brown's right leg.

Lange is not required to pick up every piece of trash, every bloody leaf, and every rawhide dog bone at this or any other crime scene. These murders did not occur in a sterile laboratory; they have been committed outdoors in an area that is hardly contamination-free. He must use his best judgment, based upon his years of experience, to discriminate between possible evidence and trash—although everything is photographed just in case he's wrong.

Lange then checks the front gate, which locks when it's closed. A person must have a key to get in; or a visitor must call in on the intercom and then be buzzed in. However, Lange notices that the mechanism to buzz someone in is not working; the door release only makes a clicking sound and does not open.

Lange speculates that the dead man might have used the intercom, asking to come in. When Brown came out of her house to open the gate manually, the assailant attacked them both. Possibly, the assailant might have been visiting, and the dead man walked into the midst of an argument between them. Or the killer had a key and laid in wait for either Brown or her visitor to come to the gate.

Back at the detective bureau in the West Los Angeles Division, Vannatter finds an empty desk. He pulls out his notes from his brief interview with Kaelin and begins writing the search warrant.

On the basis of the notes, his recollection, and his experience as a homicide investigator, Vannatter chronicles the investigation.

While he's pulling information together for the warrant, a sergeant comes to his desk and tells Vannatter, "I've checked the computer on O.J. Simpson. He was involved in some domestic-abuse incident in 1989." After the sergeant hands him the computer printout, Vannatter sees that on January 1, 1989, at 3:30 A.M., Nicole Brown Simpson, then married to O.J., had made a 911 call, reporting that her husband had physically assaulted her. No other details are available.

After completing the draft of his search warrant at about 9:00 A.M., Vannatter calls Marcia Clark at her office in the Criminal Courts Building. She is a remarkably tough and aggressive forty-year-old deputy district attorney who has tried over twenty murder cases. Clark's most publicized case was her successful prosecution of an obsessed fan by the name of Robert Bardo, who stalked and subsequently shot and killed Rebecca Schaeffer, a twenty-one-year-old Hollywood actress who had starred in the popular television comedy series *My Sister Sam*.

Vannatter had worked with Clark twice before. He likes her and respects her work as a prosecutor. Vannatter first met Clark during a case with his first partner in Homicide Special, Kirk Mellecker. The investigation had centered on Jack Farnham, a young psychotic who had a passion for raping and killing elderly women.

As a result of the close working relationship among the detectives, the LAPD/SID crime lab, and Marcia Clark, Vannatter and Mellecker were successfully able to use fingerprint evidence to build their case against Farnham. Working with Vannatter and his partner, Clark prosecuted the case, convincing the jury of Farnham's guilt and persuading its members to recommend that the killer receive California's death penalty.[18] Through this experience, Vannatter and Clark became good professional friends and colleagues. Like a big brother to his kid sister, Vannatter has been very protective of Clark ever since.

In the other case, Vannatter, working solo on a murder case he had picked up from the LAPD Wilshire Division, again teamed up with Clark to gain a 1992 conviction against murderer Christopher Johnson on the basis of the DNA analysis of a single drop of the victim's blood found in the killer's car. This case was especially unusual because the victim's body was never found.

Considering the alarming amount of blood already discovered at South Bundy and North Rockingham—as well as Clark's experience with DNA—Vannatter decides to bring Clark into this case. Usually, the district attorney's office selects its own prosecutors for those matters the LAPD sends over. However, in this particular case, the detective has handpicked the prosecutor he wants to handle it. Although this is rare, to say the least, Vannatter's decision demonstrates the seriousness of this investigation. He trusts Clark and doesn't want another prosecutor, assigned by the DA, to jeopardize it.

When Vannatter gets Clark on the telephone to discuss the Simpson case, he says, "Marcia, I have a double murder—the ex-wife of O.J. Simpson and an unidentified male, white. O.J. Simpson is a suspect."

"So who's O.J. Simpson?" she replies rather sarcastically. "He's just a has-been football player."

"Well, Marcia, regardless, this is going to be a really high-profile case, and the media's already all over it. I'm writing out the search warrant, and I want to read it to you to make sure it's okay."

"Sure, Phil," she says with considerable interest. "Go ahead."

Vannatter reads Clark the search warrant, word for word.

When he finishes reading, she asks, "What's your physical evidence?"

Vannatter then repeats the litany of evidence they have already identified.

After she hears all of this, Clark replies, "Sounds great to me."

"Should I do anything different?" Vannatter asks.

"No," she replies. "Once you get it signed, call me back."

Vannatter then adds, "I want you to be there when we do the search."

"Well, I want to be there, so call me back."

Placing the finishing touches on his search warrant at a little after 10:00 A.M., Vannatter walks over to the West Los Angeles municipal courthouse on Purdue Street. He goes to the courtroom of Judge Linda Lefkowitz and asks her bailiff for an audience with the judge, who is in chambers. The bailiff takes him to her.

After looking at the warrant, Judge Lefkowitz remarks, "Oh, my gosh, you have a lot of blood evidence."

"Yeah," Vannatter responds. "We've got all kinds of blood evidence."

"Well, hold on, I'll be right back."

The judge takes the search warrant and leaves her chambers to confer with another judge. When she returns twenty minutes later, Vannatter and Judge Lefkowitz sign the warrant at 10:45 A.M.; the judge also initials each page.

The final search warrant reads:

SW No. 94-0093

STATE OF CALIFORNIA - COUNTY OF LOS ANGELES

SEARCH WARRANT AND AFFIDAVIT
(AFFIDAVIT)

Philip L. Vannatter , being sworn, says that on the basis of the information contained within
(Name of Affiant)

this Search Warrant and Affidavit and the attached and incorporated **Statement of Probable Cause**, he/she has probable
cause to believe and does believe that the property described below is lawfully seizable pursuant to Penal Code Section 1524
as indicated below, and is now located at the locations set forth below. Wherefore, affiant requests that this Search Warrant be
issued.

_____ , NIGHT SEARCH REQUESTED: YES [ ] NO [X]
(Signature of Affiant)

(SEARCH WARRANT)

THE PEOPLE OF THE STATE OF CALIFORNIA TO ANY SHERIFF, POLICEMAN OR PEACE OFFICER IN THE COUNTY

OF LOS ANGELES: proof by affidavit having been made before me by _____Philip L. Vannatter_____
(Name of Affiant)

that there is probable cause to believe that the property described herein may be found at the locations set forth herein and that
is lawfully seizable pursuant to Penal Code Section 1524 as indicated below by "x" (s) in that it:

___X___ was stolen or embezzled

_____ was used as the means of committing a felony

_____ is possessed by a person with the intent to use it as means of committing a public offense or is possessed by another to whom he or she may have
delivered it for the purpose of concealing it or preventing its discovery.

___X___ tends to show that a felony has been committed or that a particular person has committed a felony,

_____ tends to show that sexual exploitation of a child, in violation of P.C. Section 311.3, has occurred or is occurring;

YOU ARE THEREFORE COMMANDED TO SEARCH:

360 Rockingham, Avenue, West Los Angeles, California. A single family
residence located on the southeast corner of Rockingham Avenue and
Ashford Street. The residence is two stories constructed of light
brown wood trim and beige stucco. The property is fence by a solid
plant hedge with green wrought iron gates facing Rockingham Avenue and
Ashford Street. The number 360 is clearly painted on the curb adjacent
to the Rockingham Gate.

FOR THE FOLLOWING PROPERTY:

Presence of traces of human blood, clothing, surfaces, or any material
that may contain blood, any object that may have been used to inflict
the fatal injuries to the victims, including but not limited to objects
capable of inflicting blunt force trauma, firearms or knives.
Paperwork indicating the identity of the occupants of the residence to
show dominion and control of the residence. Any and all garages or
outbuildings associated to the residence to which the occupants have
access, and the 1994 Ford Bronco, California license 3CWZ788.

AND TO SEIZE IT IF FOUND and bring it forthwith before me, or this court, at the courthouse of this court. This Search Warrant
and incorporated Affidavit was sworn to and subscribed before me this _13th_ day of _June_ , 19_94_
at _10:35_ A.M./P.M. Wherefore, I find probable cause for the issuance of this Search Warrant and do issue it.

_____ , NIGHT SEARCH APPROVED: YES [ ] NO [ ]
(Signature of Magistrate)

Judge of the Superior/Municipal Court, ___Los Angeles___ Judicial District

OA-1506-A-76S346W3—8 86

SW & A1

EVIDENCE DISMISSED

1   Your affiant Philip L. Vannatter #14877 is a Police Detective
2   for the Los Angeles Police Department, assigned to Robbery-Homicide
3   Division, Homicide Special Section. Your affiant has been a police
4   officer for the City of Los Angeles for over 25 years. Your
5   affiant has been assigned to Robbery-Homicide Division for the past
6   15 years working the Officer-Involved Shooting Section and Homicide
7   Special Section.

8   Your affiant worked homicide at West Los Angeles and Wilshire
9   Division prior to being assigned to Robbery-Homicide Division, and
10 has investigated in excess of 200 homicides. Your affiant has
11 attended numerous training sessions and seminars, and has qualified
12 in Los Angeles County Municipal and Superior Court as a homicide
13 expert.

14 On Monday June 13, 1994 at 0430 hours you affiant and his
15 partner F.D. Lange #13552 were assigned the investigation of the
16 double murder of Nicole Brown AKA Nicole Simpson and an
17 unidentified male, White at 875 South Bundy Drive, West Los Angeles
18 the residence of Nicole Brown. The facts contained herein are
19 summarized as follows:

20 During the course of the investigation it was determined that
21 Nicole Brown was the ex-wife of O.J. Simpson and had two children
22 by Simpson. The children were located and were removed from the
23 residence on Bundy Drive.

24 During the course of the investigation detectives followed up
25 to 360 Rockingham Avenue, West Los Angeles, the residence of O.J.
26 Simpson in an attempt to make a notification. Upon arriving at the
27 location detectives were unable to arouse anyone at the residence.

ehl

1   Detectives observed a 1994 White Ford Bronco, California license

2   3CWZ788 registered to Hertz Corporation parked at the west side of

3   the residence headed north on Rockingham Avenue. Detectives

4   observed what appeared to be human blood, later confirmed by

5   Scientific Investigation personnel to be human blood on the drivers

6   door handle of the vehicle.

7   Detectives subsequently aroused O.J. Simpson's daughter,

8   Arnell Simpson at the residence and determined Simpson was not at

9   home. During the interview of Simpson's daughter, she identified

10   the Ford Bronco as belonging to her father who was the primary

11   driver. Blood droplets were subsequently observed leading from the

12   vehicle on the street to the front door of the residence.

13   During the securing of the residence a man's leather glove

14   containing human blood was also observed on the south side of the

15   residence. This glove closely resembled a brown leather glove

16   located at the crime scene at the feet of the unidentified male,.

17   White victim. *the by interviews of Simpson's daughter and a friend*

18   *Brian Kaelin*

    It was determined Simpson had left on an unexpected flight to

19   Chicago during the early morning hours of June 13, 1994, and was

20   last seen at the residence at approximately 2300 hours, June 12,

21   1994.

22   It is prayed that a search warrant be issued to search 360

23   Rockingham Avenue for the presence of traces of human blood,

24   clothing, surfaces, or any material that may contain blood, any

25   object that may have been used to inflict the fatal injuries to the

26   victims, including but not limited to objects capable of inflicting

27   blunt force trauma, firearms or knives. Paperwork indicating the

EVIDENCE DISMISSED

1   identity of the occupants of the residence to show dominion and
2   control of the residence. Any and all garages or outbuildings
3   associated to the residence to which the occupants have access, and
4   the 1994 Ford Bronco, California license 3CWZ788.

ebl

Returning to the West Los Angeles Division to make several copies in the detective bureau, Vannatter calls Clark again. "Marcia, I have the signed warrant. I'm going to leave here, and go by Bundy and let Tom know what's going on. Then I'm heading up to Rockingham in order to organize this search."

"Okay," Clark replies, "I'll get there."

While Vannatter has selected his own prosecutor for this case, he realizes that he must now break the news about this decision to his partner.

Back at the South Bundy crime scene, coroner investigator Claudine Ratcliffe arrives at about 9:10 A.M., followed by her driver/assistant John Jacobo. Lange meets them in the street in front of Brown's condominium and takes them around back to the "safe route" through the crime scene. As is standard operating procedure, Lange gives the coroner's investigator her walk-through of Brown's residence.

After opening Nicole Brown's purse, which is found in her bedroom, Lange and Ratcliffe "officially" identify her through a driver's license and her German citizenship papers; Brown had been born in Frankfurt, Germany. Then, Lange and Ratcliffe go outside to her body and that of the still-unidentified male.

According to California law, the number one law enforcement officer in each county is not the county sheriff, the chief of police, or the homicide detectives. It is the county coroner. Once again, only authorized personnel from the county coroner's office may touch or move a body at a crime scene.

So, with Ratcliffe present, Lange has his first close-up look at the bodies: Nicole Brown is lying on her left side in a semifetal position; her head points in a northeasterly direction. A portion of her legs are beneath a side stationary gate, pointing, more or less, in a southerly direction. Her right ankle rests against an outside power outlet. Lange sees blood smears on her outer right calf and thigh and on her inner left knee and thigh.

Her right arm is beneath her body; her left arm and hand, which are both smeared with blood, are extended in what Lange calls "a death grip," or a cadaveric spasm. Her fingernails are intact, but Lange notices blood underneath them.[19]

He sees a silver ring on her left thumb and a ring with a clear stone on her left ring finger; she has another ring on her right ring finger. Also, she is wearing a Swiss Army wristwatch on her left wrist and a pair of gold earrings, one of which is loose and tangled in a portion of her blood-matted, long blond hair.

She is wearing no shoes. However, the bottoms of her feet are clean. From this, Lange deduces that she had been struck down before the probable fight between the killer and the unidentified male and died where she fell, never stepping into anyone's blood—not even her own.

A runoff of blood from the deep slash in her neck—from the center of her neck to her right ear, which nearly took off her head—flows east down the sidewalk. The bloody paw prints from the Akita lead through the blood and out onto the sidewalk.

Lange can see an odd pattern of blood droplets on her back. They tail off in all directions. He believes that, possibly, the blood could have come from the killer or perhaps even from the killer's weapon.

The problem is that neither Ratcliffe nor Jacobo are criminalists. Only a coroner's criminalist may collect such evidence as blood patterns on a dead body.[20] Unfortunately, the only coroner's criminalist on call is back at the office, suffering with a broken leg in a large cast. He is not going to roll out to South Bundy or anywhere else for a while.

However, while Lange is talking to Ratcliffe, he tells her about the blood pattern on Brown's back and says he wants it collected. Because a coroner's criminalist is not present, this will have to be done back at the coroner's lab prior to Brown's autopsy.

To document the dried blood pattern on Brown's back—which has not been disturbed by the blanket that earlier had been placed over her body—Lange asks the LAPD/SID photographer to take pictures. Ratcliffe, who is holding a Polaroid camera, takes pictures of the body from numerous angles. Regardless of how the body is moved now, its original position has been documented.

However, Lange knows that SID criminalist Dennis Fung should be there to collect the evidence around the body as it is being moved. The LAPD has no hard-and-fast rule about when one of its criminalists must arrive at a crime scene. The key is to safeguard the evidence for his examination when he does arrive.

To Lange, even though Fung is still busy at North Rockingham, nothing is being compromised by his absence at South Bundy. It is simply a frustrating inconvenience. Lange and Ratcliffe will have to begin removing the bodies.

Endnotes

14. Lange clearly understands the controversy that resulted from his decision to cover Brown's body with a blanket taken from her home. He certainly does not recommend this procedure as a matter of policy. Nevertheless, he insists that all crime scenes are different; no two are the same. Consequently, all crime-scene investigators are occasionally faced with making decisions that might later be challenged in court. Lange stands by this decision.

15. Simpson's defense team later tried to create a controversy when they revealed that Lange—in his thirteen pages of handwritten notes taken at the crime scene—had noted that *two* dimes and *two* pennies were present. Lange has admitted making this minor error, pointing to the photographs taken at the scene. Regardless of what he jotted down in his notes, the photographs depict that only two coins were actually discovered, *one* dime and *one* penny.

16. Scientific analysis later determined that neither the rug nor the knife found in the kitchen contained any blood evidence.

17. Fuhrman claimed in his notes that he had also observed a bloody fingerprint on the locking mechanism of the rear gate at the South Bundy crime scene. However, no such fingerprint was seen by anyone else. Also in his notes, Fuhrman speculated that the victims died from gunshot wounds, and that the killer had possibly been bitten by Brown's dog.

18. As of this writing, Farnham is still on death row, awaiting execution.

19. Scientific analysis later revealed that the blood under Brown's fingernails was her own blood and not her killer's. She had been found lying in her own blood.

20. SID criminalists, such as Dennis Fung, may collect any and all evidence at a crime scene but *not* if it's on a body. All evidence found on a body, including blood patterns and even a weapon, must be collected by the coroner's own criminalist. The coroner's office has full legal jurisdiction over bodies, and everything on them, at a crime scene.

5

The Faces of Murder

At 10:15 A.M., Dennis Fung, already overloaded with blood and evidence work, finally arrives at South Bundy, along with his assistant, Andrea Mazzola, after completing their "plain-view" blood and evidence collection for Vannatter at Simpson's residence. Lange stops his work, as well as Ratcliffe's, and gives Fung and Mazzola their walk-through of the crime scene.

Returning to the bodies, all of the investigators snap on new pairs of latex gloves and begin their examination of Brown's body, noting the location and type of wounds. As Ratcliffe begins her work by prying apart the limbs of the rigor-laden Brown, Lange is taking measurements on and around the body. Consistent with the orientation photographs—which show the exact location of existing evidence—they measure the distance from the body to other objects around it, including, among other things, the nearby fence, the gate, and the still-unidentified male. As all of this is being done, more photographs are being taken of the bodies and everything around them.

Under the direction of Ratcliffe, Lange and Jacobo spread out a light gray plastic body wrap on the walkway. They place Brown's lifeless body on the plastic, wrap her up in it, and carry her out to the coroner's van. The blanket that has been used to cover her body is left on the walkway.

At about 10:40 A.M., in the coroner's brown van and with Lange present, Ratcliffe unwraps Brown, draws a small circle on her abdomen, and rams a thermometer with a spiked tip into the center of the circle and into her liver. Ratcliffe removes it a few moments later; Nicole's liver temperature is eighty-two degrees. This information will later be used by the medical examiner to help estimate the time of death.

After rewrapping Brown, Lange and Ratcliffe walk to the body of the blood-covered unidentified male, who lies four feet, ten inches to the north of where Brown died. He is lying on his right side with his torso bent at the waist. His head, which is resting at the foot of a tree trunk, is pointed in a westerly direction. His eyes are still open. His face has scrape marks and dried blood that has run downward from his nose and left ear.

His right leg is bent at the knee at a ninety-degree angle; his left leg, which is straight, appears to have been badly cut. His blood and mud-stained brown and light brown shirt has been pulled up around his upper back—indicating that the killer might have grabbed him and jerked him around in the midst of a fight.[21]

His throat has been cut on both its left and right sides—although neither cut is anywhere nearly as dramatic as the wide slash across Brown's neck. He has another stab wound on his lower left side and on his upper left outer thigh.

Ratcliffe is a rather large woman who has to get into a tight area to remove the body. In the process of trying to lift the dead man, she nudges the white envelope and the blue knit cap, slightly moving them from their original position.

Although Lange is miffed that these two pieces of evidence have moved, he knows that both have already been well photographed.[22]

As the dead man is removed from the spot where he died, Lange notices a pager by his body, which is near the north metal-rung fence.

Like Brown before him, the unidentified male is taken out on the walkway and placed on a gray plastic sheet. Ratcliffe immediately reaches into the victim's back pocket and pulls out his wallet. This is the first opportunity to identify him.

Looking at his driver's license and Union Bank card, she identifies the young man as twenty-five-year-old, six-foot-one-inch, 170-pound Ronald Lyle Goldman, who has brown hair and eyes. Because a coroner's investigator has identified him, a member of the coroner's staff will make the death notification to Goldman's family.

As with Brown, Goldman is examined and photographed while lying on the walkway. At 10:47 A.M., during the examination, Goldman's pager starts to beep quite audibly. Without touching it, Lange takes note of the telephone number that registers on the device and orders one of his detectives to investigate. The detective finds out that the call was made by a bartender at Mezzaluna Trattoria, a nearby restaurant.[23]

Instead of waiting to get Goldman into the coroner's van, Ratcliffe opens his shirt and takes his liver temperature right there on the walkway. It is the same as Brown's: eighty-two degrees. Ratcliffe confirms what Lange already suspects: Brown and Goldman were killed at basically the same time.

Lange examines Goldman's hands, which show defense wounds such as fresh abrasions, cuts, and scrapes. However, these minor injuries do not appear over the knuckles as they would have if Goldman had doubled his fist and struck someone. Instead, they are over the fingers and on the back of his hand, indicating that he might have been flailing around and accidentally hit his hands on something. Objects around him included a large tree with very coarse bark, a smaller tree, a metal-rung fence, and a metal pole, as well as the tree stump that had been under his body. There is no blood under his fingernails.

The sole of Goldman's left boot contains a blood drop that appears to have a pattern similar to that on Nicole Brown's back, indicating that this might have been "castoff" blood from either the killer or the killer's knife.[24]

Considering the five blood spots to the left of the bloody shoe prints, which Fung has approximated were made by a size-twelve shoe, Lange believes that it is likely that the killer might have been wounded during his fight with Goldman. However, he also knows that the drops could have come from blood dripping from a knife that the killer held in his left hand. The SID crime lab's blood analysis will solve this mystery.

As Goldman's body is rolled away on a gurney, Lange and Fung examine the left-hand glove—the only glove found at the scene. The item is an Aris-Isotoner, extra large, dark brown glove made in the Philippines. Cashmere lined, it looks expensive.

* * *

Soon after Goldman's body is removed at about 11:00 A.M., Vannatter returns to the South Bundy crime scene to update Lange. Vannatter gives his partner a copy of the search warrant and tells him that he has contacted Marcia Clark.

"Marcia Clark?" Lange asks in disbelief.

"Yeah, is that a problem?"

Nodding his head, Lange reminds Vannatter about an earlier dispute Lange had with Clark. In mid-1983, Lange began a murder-for-hire investigation that would go on for over ten years. Finally, in late 1993, Lange received a call from a source who offered him information about the killer. As Lange developed his relationship with the source, he became concerned that the murderer might kill the source if he discovered that he was an informant.

By early 1994, Marcia Clark had been selected by the district attorney to handle the case. Lange briefed her on the new developments. She appeared completely supportive, promising to get protection for the source, who had agreed to testify in open court. Based upon the representations he had received from Clark, Lange told the victim's family that the case would be prosecuted; and he told the source that he would be protected in the wake of his testimony.

But in the midst of Lange's continuing investigation, Clark went behind his back and talked to Vannatter. Clark told Vannatter, "Phil, I'm not going to file Lange's case. I can't. I don't like it." Vannatter, always loyal to his partner, advised Clark to tell Lange directly. When she didn't, Vannatter told Lange what Clark had said and done.

Lange believed that Clark had not only forced him to break his promises to the victim's family and to his source—but that she had placed the life of his source in jeopardy.[25] Lange viewed Clark's action as a blatant breach of trust. From then on, he had stayed away from her and, for the most part, refused to talk to her. But he had had no confrontation with her in the wake of this falling-out.

After being reminded about this, Vannatter, who still respected Clark, explains to Lange, "Tom, listen, we need somebody, and I know Marcia. She's smart and tough. She can deal with all this blood evidence. And she knows DNA."

Lange has more to do at the crime scene and does not want to argue with his partner. "Fine," he responds, disgruntled. "Just do it! Get it done!"

After a few uncomfortable moments of silence, Vannatter asks, "How are you doing here?"

"Well, I'm trying to wrap it up," Lange says, still upset. "I have more to do; plus I have the final walk-through."

"Okay," Vannatter says, "I'm going over to Rockingham and run the search. Come over as soon as you finish up here."

Then, just before leaving at about 11:45 A.M., Vannatter asks, "By the way, do you know what the status of Simpson is?"

"I bet he's en route to Rockingham right now," Lange predicts.

Endnotes

21. Scientific analysis later determined that a head hair consistent with Simpson's hair was on Goldman's shirt.

22. The original positions of the envelope and knit cap were documented by the crime-scene orientation pictures—which is the point of photographing a crime scene before anyone touches or moves anything. If the exact positions of these items ever becomes an issue, the photographs speak for themselves.

23. Stewart Tanner, the bartender, left this message. He was trying to reach Goldman, who had failed to appear at a local bar where the two men had arranged to have drinks the previous night.

24. Scientific analysis later revealed that this blood drop on the bottom of Goldman's left boot contained a mixture of blood from both Brown and Goldman. In other words, the blood probably came from the killer's knife.

Also, further examination later revealed that Goldman's cloth boots had cut marks on each. Lange believed that Goldman, attempting to ward off his assailant, might have kicked into the killer's knife at least twice, which could account for the slices in his boots.

25. As of this writing, the source is alive, but the murder suspect is still free.

6

Simpson Unhooked

When Vannatter arrives back at Simpson's estate a little before noon, television cameras and reporters are surrounding the North Rockingham location. Vannatter thinks to himself, "Well, the circus has begun!"

When he sees Simpson's white Bronco, which he had ordered impounded five hours earlier, still parked on the street and not being guarded, he becomes furious. Reporters are using it as a table for their coffee cups. Vannatter sternly tells an officer on perimeter security, "Damn it! Let's get the Bronco out of here! Impound it! Now! Until then, get someone to guard it!"[26]

With the exception of Fung and the LAPD's photographers, no one else has done anything or has been authorized to do anything, other than to secure and protect this second crime scene. Everyone has been waiting for Vannatter's return with the search warrant.

At the North Rockingham gate, Vannatter walks over to patrol officer Don Thompson, who is standing guard. The officer had been at the South Bundy crime scene between 6:55 and 8:05 A.M. He had helped Lange place the blanket over Nicole Brown's body. Since then, he has been reassigned by his watch commander to Simpson's home.

Vannatter says to Thompson, "I have the search warrant, and I'm going to get to work. I want you to keep this area tightly secured. Don't let anybody in. O.J. Simpson might be on his way from the airport. If he tries to get in, detain him, and let me know he's here."[27]

As Vannatter and Thompson finish their conversation, Los Angeles attorney Howard Weitzman, whom Vannatter knows by reputation as a prominent criminal attorney, comes up to them at the gate. Weitzman, who had represented auto executive John DeLorean and Michael Jackson, introduces himself, explaining that Simpson had called and asked him to meet him at his home.

Surprised that Simpson has already called a lawyer, Vannatter walks across the driveway toward the house. As Vannatter steps in, he is met by Detective Bert Luper, who also works in the Homicide Special Section of the LAPD's Robbery/Homicide Division. Vannatter says to Luper, "Bert, I've got the search warrant. I want us to go room to room in a pattern."

The time is just after 12:00 noon. As Vannatter and Luper discuss the logistics of the search, they hear a commotion outside. Looking out a window, Vannatter is somewhat startled when he sees a handcuffed O.J. Simpson walking on his front lawn with Thompson and Detective Brad Roberts, who is holding Simpson's travel bag.

"Jesus!" Vannatter says to Luper. "Simpson's here!"

Vannatter hands Luper a copy of the search warrant, telling him, "You're in charge.[28] I want you to run the search. . . . I'm going out to talk to O.J."

Vannatter walks out the front door and catches up with Thompson and Simpson, who is wearing a white golf shirt, dark slacks, and slip-on sandals. Thompson tells Vannatter that Weitzman and Skip Taft, one of Simpson's personal attorneys, want to come onto the property.

"Let them in!" Vannatter says in an accommodating tone.

Weitzman and Taft walk up to Vannatter, Roberts, Thompson, and Simpson. Weitzman asks, "Do we need these handcuffs?"

"No, we don't," Vannatter replies. "In fact, let me take them off." Vannatter pulls his universal handcuff key from his pocket and unhooks Simpson.[29] While uncuffing him, Vannatter notices that the middle finger of Simpson's left hand is bandaged, but Vannatter doesn't want to make an issue of it at this particular moment.

Vannatter has no intention of arresting Simpson right now. The detective recognizes that he has a mandatory forty-eight-hour filing deadline with the district attorney's office after an arrest is made. If he takes Simpson into custody and doesn't file his paperwork within that period of time, he must, under law, release him. With the whole world already watching this case, Vannatter knows that Deputy District Attorney Marcia Clark, as well as the LAPD, will want the blood-analysis work completed before the case is formally cleared and filed with the DA's office. Vannatter knows that they are several days away from receiving the critical blood reports from the LAPD/SID crime lab.

In lieu of arresting Simpson, Vannatter asks, "O.J., will you come downtown, so we can sit and talk?"

"Yes," Simpson politely replies, with no hesitation.

Turning to Weitzman, Vannatter tells him, "I've asked your client to go with me down to Parker Center."

"Okay," Weitzman responds, looking at his client. "Can I come?"

"Yeah, sure," Vannatter says to the veteran attorney. "Meet us downtown at Robbery/Homicide. You know where it is."

Vannatter sees Cliff LeFall, a detective in the Robbery/Homicide Division and Bert Luper's partner, and asks him to accompany Simpson and himself. Before they leave, Roberts hands Vannatter the travel bag he took from Simpson; Vannatter puts it on the front-passenger floorboard of his car.[30]

At about 12:10 P.M., with Simpson and LeFall in the back seat and Vannatter driving, the three men head for Parker Center, a thirty-minute drive in midday traffic. While turning east onto Sunset Boulevard from North Rockingham, Vannatter reaches for his car radio and tells a dispatcher at detective headquarters, "Get in touch with Lange. And tell him that I'm en route to Robbery/Homicide Division with the number one 'witness' in the case."

Vannatter deliberately does not use the word "suspect," because he realizes that the media is monitoring the broadcast.

Hearing that, Simpson replies sarcastically, "Yeah, the number one suspect." Vannatter is struck by Simpson's remark. He thinks to himself: If Simpson really believes that he's the "number one suspect" and is innocent, shouldn't he be outraged instead of sarcastic about all of this? This is the only thing Simpson says during the trip downtown, other than his quick replies to Vannatter's only two questions: "How are you doing?" and "Are you all right?" Simpson responds "Okay" and "Yes," in that order.

He *never* asks what happened to his ex-wife. He *never* asks if there are any other suspects. He doesn't ask any of the questions the detectives usually hear from victims' families.

Back at South Bundy, Lange is interviewing John DeBello, the general manager of the Mezzaluna Trattoria restaurant on San Vicente Boulevard, a trendy and upscale Italian restaurant in Brentwood near Brown's home. DeBello has come to the crime scene after hearing that Goldman might be the then unidentified man found with Nicole Brown. Goldman had worked as a waiter for DeBello at Mezzaluna for nearly four months, and DeBello is grief-stricken after receiving confirmation of his employee's murder.

Lange takes notes as he interviews DeBello, reporting:

> The witness states that he has observed O.J. Simpson and victim Brown at the restaurant in the past on at least one occasion. The witness went on to state that both victims frequented the Mark Stevens Gym on San Vicente near the restaurant.
>
> On 6-12-94 at approximately 1900 hours, the victim (Brown) came to the restaurant with a party of ten. They had reservations.
>
> In conversation, victim Goldman states to the witness that he had been seeing victim Brown socially. . . . The Brown party left the restaurant at approximately 2100 hours. Victim Goldman left the restaurant at approximately 2145/2150 hours. Prior to Goldman's departure, the witness admonished Goldman to use caution in his relationship with Nicole Brown. The witness feels that although Goldman listened to this advice, he seemed 'non-affected' by it.

After interviewing DeBello, Lange gets the message that Vannatter will be waiting for him at Parker Center so that they can interview a "witness." He knows exactly who the "witness" is.

By now, Lange has completed his work at the crime scene— while Fung continues to work with the photographer and the print specialists from the SID crime lab who are lifting fingerprints from a variety of areas. Among other locations, Lange has had the fingerprint specialists dusting the front and rear doors of Brown's condominium, the moldings around the doors, her mailbox, the intercom device, all telephones in the residence, the knife on the kitchen counter, the front and back gates, the fence around the victims, the railings along the staircases and walkways around and near the condominium, Brown's Jeep Cherokee and white Ferrari, the banister on the stairwell inside her home, the bedposts, her television sets, the bathtub and the counters in her bathroom, and the pack of Marlboro Lights found in the bathroom.[31]

Normally, Lange prefers to wait at the crime scene until everyone has completed their work. Then, routinely, he will do a final walk-through with the criminalist, the photographer, the print experts, and other detectives, making sure that all of the investigators have done what he has instructed them to do.

However, Lange has to get downtown to interview Simpson. He decides there will be no final walk-through—at least, not now. Lange places Senior Lead Officer Carson Pierce in charge of the crime scene—ordering the patrol officers to keep the area secure, especially with the growing legion of press people in the area, who are standing behind the bright yellow police tape. There is no need to leave a specific person in charge other than for perimeter security. The various crime-scene technicians are going about their work and left to their own areas of expertise.

At 12:15 P.M., Lange logs out and drives to Parker Center, a massive eight-story structure, nicknamed "The Glass House" and built in 1955. Located on North Los Angeles Street in downtown L.A., Parker Center is named after William H. Parker, the former police chief who was credited with cleaning up corruption in the LAPD during the 1940s.

As Vannatter, LeFall, and Simpson pull into the underground parking lot at Parker Center at about 12:45 P.M., Vannatter explains to Simpson, "What's going to happen, O.J., is we're going to go to the Robbery/Homicide Division, which is on the third floor. My partner, Detective Lange, is going to meet us there. We're going to interview you regarding the death of your ex-wife, and see if you can help us out with that. Your attorney, Mr. Weitzman, is going to meet us upstairs."

Simpson nods his head, saying nothing more.

When they walk through the large Robbery/Homicide office, past the two parallel rows of connecting desks, the other detectives and staff stare at Simpson momentarily but quickly return to their own work.

Vannatter takes Simpson through a door in the back of the room into the small area occupied by the division's three secretaries. Vannatter places Simpson in one of two small interrogation rooms.

Seeing that neither Lange nor Weitzman has arrived, Vannatter says to Simpson, "Listen, we're going to wait for your attorney here. Would you like a soft drink, a cup of coffee or something?"

Simpson asks for a Pepsi-Cola, which Vannatter buys for him from a nearby machine.

A few minutes later, Weitzman arrives, along with Skip Taft, followed almost immediately by Lange. Everyone is introduced and shakes hands.

Weitzman says to Lange and Vannatter, "You know, I don't know what you've got here. I'm more of a celebrity lawyer and I probably won't be handling this."

"Okay," Lange replies, asking, "what do you want?"

"Could we have a little time to talk to Mr. Simpson alone?"

"Absolutely," Vannatter says. "You can have all the time you want."

Lange and Vannatter leave the room and close the door.

As Simpson speaks to his attorneys, Lange looks at Vannatter and says, "The middle finger of his left hand is bandaged. When did he injure that?"

Vannatter shrugs, replying, "I don't know. Let's ask him—if the lawyers let us talk to him."

Lange adds, "If they do, maybe they'll let us examine that finger, and draw some blood from him, too."

"Hell," Vannatter laughs, "I'll be happy if they just let us talk to this guy!"

As Lange and Vannatter discuss what they have learned at the two crime scenes since they last spoke at South Bundy, they predict that Weitzman will advise his client not to speak to them.

After talking for about twenty minutes, Weitzman and Taft step out of the room.

Vannatter asks, "Can we interview your client?"

To Lange and Vannatter's complete surprise, Weitzman replies, "Yeah! Sure, you can!"

Trying to hide how thoroughly shocked they are for this unexpected access, the two detectives listen as Weitzman continues, "I only want you to do two things. I want you to tape-record the interview. And I want you to advise my client of his constitutional rights."

"Not a problem," Vannatter says, still stunned that Weitzman is allowing this to happen. He adds, "Do you want to be present during the interview?"

Weitzman replies, "No, Skip and I are going to go to lunch. He's all yours."[32]

Lange and Vannatter cannot believe what they've just heard.

Seconds later, Weitzman and Taft walk out of the Robbery/Homicide Division, leaving their celebrity client, the chief suspect in an already highly publicized double murder, with two experienced LAPD homicide detectives.

Endnotes

26. Because of budgetary problems, the LAPD does not have a central garage to perform all possible tests on impounded cars. On June 15, Simpson's Bronco was towed from the Print Shed, the LAPD's location for impounded vehicles, to Viertel's Tow, a private operation under contract with the police department. Later, the LAPD moved it to Keystone Tow, another private company under contract with the LAPD, where the final tests were conducted.

Simpson's defense team created a major controversy by arguing that the Bronco had been poorly secured while impounded. Between June 15 and August 26, 1994, the Bronco had been parked in a tow yard in downtown Los Angeles—with no sign-in log for those who entered the area.

In fact—*before* the SID had completed its analysis of the blood evidence in the Bronco—a tow-truck driver did enter Simpson's vehicle and remove a dry-cleaning receipt, five credit card receipts, and a Hertz rental agreement. All of these papers contained Simpson's signature. Boasting of his discoveries, the driver went to co-employees and showed them his O.J. souvenirs. One of them turned him in to their employer, who confronted the driver and fired him. The employer waited about a week before contacting the LAPD.

However, the SID's failure to collect all of the blood evidence in the Bronco before it was illegally entered was the source of a legitimate controversy.

27. Simpson's defense team later created a controversy over this conversation. Thompson testified that Vannatter told him to "hook him up," which means handcuff him; Vannatter insisted that he simply told Thompson to "detain" Simpson and nothing more. The act of handcuffing someone is a prelude to making an arrest. However, Vannatter had no intention, at that time, of arresting Simpson.

28. Luper authorized the creation of another crime-scene log at Simpson's home, which was maintained by Officer John Flowers. According to this sign-in sheet, Detective Ron Phillips was at this crime scene from 12:00 noon to 1:28 P.M., from 4:30 to 4:35 P.M., and 5:30 to 6:50 P.M.

Detective Mark Fuhrman was present from 11:45 A.M. to 4:15 P.M. and then, with Phillips, from 5:30 to 6:50 P.M.

Fuhrman's partner, Detective Brad Roberts, signed in from 8:30 A.M. to 1:28 P.M. and with Phillips and Fuhrman from 5:30 to 6:50 P.M.

29. After television cameras recorded Vannatter uncuffing Simpson, complaints began that the LAPD treated celebrities differently from other citizens.

Essentially, the LAPD finds itself in a catch-22 situation in such high-profile cases. When a case involving a celebrity receives no special handling, the media reports that the police are being indifferent. When special handling is given to a celebrity case—mostly because of the intense media interest—the police are accused of pandering.

In the Simpson case, many of those who believed Simpson to be guilty accused the LAPD of favoritism toward him because of his celebrity status. On the other hand, many of those who believed Simpson to be innocent accused the LAPD of framing him.

30. Unknown to the police at the time, Simpson's Louis Vuitton garment bag was taken by another friend and attorney, Robert Kardashian, who was also among those in the crowd outside the gate when Simpson arrived at his home from the airport at about noon on June 13. Although Kardashian resisted prosecution efforts to question him, neither Lange nor Vannatter believed that this garment bag, which was later produced at Simpson's criminal trial, was significant to the murder investigation.

However, they did believe that another piece of luggage Simpson had taken with him, a half-moon-shaped bag—which has not been seen since the night of the murders—might have carried the bloody clothing Simpson wore at the crime scene, as well as, possibly, the murder weapon.

This matter will be discussed further in Part Two.

31. Simpson's fingerprints were *not* among the seventeen sets of prints found at the South Bundy crime scene. A person wearing gloves, of course, would not leave any.

32. In *American Tragedy*, Lawrence Schiller wrote on page 10: "Simpson had arrived at Parker Center and was about to be interviewed by Vannatter and his partner, Detective Tom Lange, when Weitzman and Taft walked in.

"Vannatter didn't want Weitzman in the interview room. [']The only way we'll interview him is with you not here,['] [Vannatter] said. [']His lawyer doesn't have to be present. He isn't under arrest.['] As blunt as that.

"Weitzman knew Vannatter was bluffing. But O.J. insisted he could handle this himself, no problem, nothing to hide."

This entire statement is incorrect. First of all, Weitzman and Taft were in the office *before* Lange arrived. And both Lange and Vannatter invited Weitzman to be present during the interview.

Weitzman made the decision not to participate.

In fact, after Weitzman left for lunch with Taft, he did not complain to the media. Instead he said to waiting reporters, "O.J. is upstairs trying to get his wits about him and is answering whatever questions he can to help law enforcement investigate this case."

7

Walking a Tightrope

It is 1:32 P.M. and O.J. Simpson is sitting patiently, even confidently, on one of four metal chairs in the spartan interrogation room. He only glances at the detectives when they walk in, continuing to look at the bare, dirty beige walls, with their corklike tiles, and the metal table in front of him. There is no window in the room.

Vannatter sets up a tape recorder, as per Weitzman's request. He tells the suspect, "Now this is what your attorney has told me: He wants me to tape-record the interview that we have with you. And he wants me to advise you of your constitutional rights. Do you understand that? I mean, did you talk to him about that?"

"Yes," Simpson replies, "I understand that. We talked about it."

Immediately, both Lange and Vannatter believe that Simpson has probably rejected Weitzman's advice not to talk without an attorney. If Simpson had taken Weitzman's advice, either Simpson would not be here now or Weitzman would be sitting beside him for the interview. The detectives now assume that Simpson wants to talk.[33]

Still shocked that they'll have this free shot at Simpson, Lange and Vannatter have not really taken the opportunity to discuss their method of interviewing him—such as working out the details for applying their tried-and-true "good cop–bad cop" routine. Lange usually plays the sensitive good cop who only wants to help the suspect while Vannatter generally acts the part of the aggressive and impatient bad cop who is ready to strap the suspect in the gas chamber.

Lange and Vannatter will not use that tack this time. While Simpson is the primary suspect, they have no solid evidence against him yet; they have nothing with which to pin him down. Yes, they have plenty of blood, but no test has been completed to connect the blood to Simpson. Because he has not been arrested, Simpson must realize that they do not have enough evidence to hold him.

In other words, Lange and Vannatter, like most other police investigators, conduct either interrogations or interviews. And there is a clear distinction between these two devices. In order to *interrogate* a suspect, the detectives must have hard evidence—such as a completed blood analysis, fingerprints, or even an eyewitness—linking the suspect directly to the crime. In these cases, the detectives will become confrontational and accusatory, because they recognize that they have the evidence they need to nail the suspect.

In those circumstantial cases lacking hard evidence, the detectives will *interview* the suspect for investigative purposes. They attempt to draw out inconsistencies and other conflicting statements that can move their case forward. In short, Lange and Vannatter do not conduct contentious and accusatory interviews. Instead, they try to gain the cooperation of the witness, allowing him to talk and to disclose information.

The detectives also recognize that Simpson is savvy enough to see through a con. They view this entire interview, for however long it will last, as a gift. If they overplay their hand with Simpson or get in his face, he might easily end the interview and walk out of the building. It's his choice. He doesn't have to be here, and he knows it.

In effect, Lange and Vannatter will be flying blindly through the interview. Assuming that a jury might someday hear this tape, the detectives know they must be careful in how they question him.

The key is getting Simpson talking about himself. The longer he feels in control, the longer he'll talk. The detectives' goal is to get his statement on the record, particularly about his whereabouts on the night before, hoping that he will view himself as invulnerable and, thus, back himself into a corner.

But, as much as they want Simpson's story, they also want to have enough goodwill with him by the end of the interview that he will agree to be fingerprinted, permit the freshly injured middle finger of his left hand to be photographed before it heals, and allow the LAPD to take a blood sample. This is the tightrope Lange and Vannatter must walk. Regardless of what comes out of the interview, that blood sample, if Simpson's really guilty, will be the smoking gun the detectives need to clear this case.

They realize that his voluntary consent to these procedures could help solve this case—without the need for a court order or sweating a confession out of him. Consequently, they will run this interview until Simpson—who already appears tired from his trip to and from Chicago—becomes agitated enough to ask for his attorney or until he simply runs out of "juice."

With these thoughts in mind, Lange and Vannatter turn on the tape recorder at 1:35 P.M. and begin:

VANNATTER: We're in an interview room in Parker Center. The date is June 13th, 1994, and the time is 1335 hours. And we're here with O.J. Simpson. Is that Orenthal James Simpson?

SIMPSON: Orenthal James Simpson.

VANNATTER: And what is your birth date, Mr. Simpson?

SIMPSON: July 9th, 1947.

VANNATTER: Okay. Prior to us talking to you, as we agreed with your attorney, I'm going to give you your constitutional rights. And I would like you to listen carefully. If you don't understand anything, tell me, okay?

SIMPSON: Yes.

VANNATTER: Okay. Mr. Simpson, you have the right to remain silent. If you give up the right to remain silent, anything you say can and will be used against you in a court of law. You have the right to speak with an attorney and to have an attorney present during questioning. If you so desire and cannot afford one, an attorney will be appointed for you without charge before questioning. Do you understand your rights?

SIMPSON: Yes, I do.

VANNATTER: Are there any questions about that? . . .

SIMPSON: No.

VANNATTER: Okay, do you wish to give up your right to remain silent and talk to us?

SIMPSON: Ah, yes.

VANNATTER: Okay. . . . We're investigating, obviously, the death of your ex-wife and another man.

SIMPSON: Someone told us that.

VANNATTER: Yeah, and we're going to need to talk to you about that. Are you divorced from her now?

SIMPSON: Yes.

VANNATTER: How long have you been divorced?

SIMPSON: Officially? Probably close to two years, but we've been apart for a little over two years. . . .

VANNATTER: Have you? What was your relationship with her? What was the . . .

SIMPSON: Well, we tried to get back together, and it just didn't work. It wasn't working, and so we were both going our separate ways.

VANNATTER: Recently you tried to get back together?

SIMPSON: We tried to get back together for about a year, you know, where we started dating each other and seeing each other. She came back and wanted us to get back together, and—

VANNATTER: Within the last year, you're talking about?

SIMPSON: She came back about a year and four months ago about us trying to get back together, and we gave it a shot. We gave it a shot the better part of a year. And I think we both knew it wasn't working, and probably three weeks ago or so, we said it just wasn't working, and we went our separate ways.

VANNATTER: Okay, the two children are yours?

SIMPSON: Yes.

LANGE: Does she have custody?

SIMPSON: Yeah—. We both have joint custody. But she has—

LANGE: It's already been through the courts?

SIMPSON: We went through the courts and everything. Everything is done. We have no problems with the kids, we do things together, you know, with the kids.

VANNATTER: How was your separation?

SIMPSON: The first separation?

VANNATTER: Yeah, were there problems with that?

SIMPSON: For me, it was—big problems. I loved her. I didn't want us to separate.

VANNATTER: Uh huh. I understand that she had made a couple of crime reports . . . some warning crime reports or something?

[Vannatter had learned about this earlier that morning while drafting his search warrant at the West Los Angeles Division.]

SIMPSON: Ah, we had a big fight about six years ago on New Year's, you know, she made a report. I didn't make a report. And then we had an altercation about a year ago maybe. It wasn't a physical argument. I kicked her door or something.

VANNATTER: And she made a police report on those two occasions?

SIMPSON: Mmm hmm. And I stayed right there until the police came, talked to them.

LANGE: Were you arrested at one time for something?

SIMPSON: No. I mean, five years ago we had a big fight, six years ago, I don't know. I know I ended up doing community service.

LANGE: So you were arrested?

SIMPSON: No, I was never really arrested.

LANGE: They never booked you in or anything like that?

SIMPSON: No. No.

LANGE: Can I ask, when's the last time you slept?

SIMPSON: I got a couple of hours sleep last night. I mean, you know, I slept a little on the plane, not much, and when I got to the hotel I was asleep a few hours when the, when the phone call came.

LANGE: Did Nicole have a housemaid that lived there?

SIMPSON: I believe so, yes.

LANGE: Do you know her name at all?

SIMPSON: Avia, Alvia, Avia something like that.

LANGE: We didn't see her there. Did she have the day off perhaps?

SIMPSON: I don't know. I don't know what schedule she had her on.

LANGE: Okay. Phil, what do you think? We can just maybe recount last night . . .

VANNATTER: Yeah. When was the last time you saw Nicole, O.J.?

SIMPSON: We were leaving the dance recital. She took off, and I was talking to her parents.

VANNATTER: Where was the dance recital?

SIMPSON: Paul Revere [Middle] School.

VANNATTER: And was that for one of your children?

SIMPSON: Yeah, for my daughter, Sydney.

VANNATTER: And what time was that yesterday?

SIMPSON: It ended about 6:30, quarter to seven, you know,

something like that, I, you know, in the ballpark, right in that area. And they took off.

VANNATTER: They?

SIMPSON: Her and her family—her mother and father, her sisters, my kids.

VANNATTER: Your children. And then you went your own separate ways?

SIMPSON: Yeah, actually she left, and then they came back and her mother got in a car with her, and the kids all piled into her sister's car, and they . . .

VANNATTER: Was Nicole driving?

SIMPSON: Yeah.

VANNATTER: What kind of car was she driving?

SIMPSON: Her black car, a Cherokee.

VANNATTER: Cherokee?

SIMPSON: Jeep Cherokee.

VANNATTER: What were you driving?

SIMPSON: My Rolls-Royce, my Bentley rather.

VANNATTER: Do you own that Ford Bronco that sits outside?

SIMPSON: Hertz owns it, and I, you know, Hertz lets me use it.

VANNATTER: So that's your vehicle, the one that was parked there on the street?

SIMPSON: Mmm hmm. Yeah.

VANNATTER: And it's actually owned by Hertz?

SIMPSON: Hertz, yeah.

VANNATTER: Who's the primary driver on that? You?

SIMPSON: I drive it, the housekeeper drives it, you know, it's kind of a . . .

VANNATTER: All-purpose-type vehicle?

SIMPSON: All-purpose-type, yeah. Yeah. It's the only one that my insurance would allow me to let anybody else drive.

VANNATTER: Okay.

LANGE: When you drive it, where do you park it at home?

SIMPSON: It depends. All kinds of [places].

LANGE: Where it is now, it was in the street or something?

SIMPSON: Always park it on the street.

LANGE: You never take it in behind the . . .

SIMPSON: Oh, rarely. I mean, I'll bring it in after I come from golf and switch the stuff, you know, and stuff like that. You know, I did that yesterday.

LANGE: When did you last drive it?

SIMPSON: Yesterday.

VANNATTER: What time yesterday?
SIMPSON: In the morning, in the afternoon.

[Simpson will later say that he parked the Bronco at seven, eight, or nine o'clock on the night of the murders.]

VANNATTER: Okay, you left her, you're saying, about 6:30 or 7, you or she left the recital?
SIMPSON: Yeah.
VANNATTER: And you spoke with her parents?
SIMPSON: Yeah, we're just sitting there talking.
VANNATTER: Okay, what time did you leave the recital?
SIMPSON: Right about that time. We were all leaving. We were all leaving then. And they, her mother said something about me joining them for dinner, and I said "no thanks."

[The Brown family will later deny that they invited Simpson to dinner.]

VANNATTER: Where did you go from there, O.J.?
SIMPSON: Ah, home, ah, home for a while, got in my car for a while, tried to find my girlfriend for a while, came back to the house.
VANNATTER: Who was home when you got home?
SIMPSON: Kato.
VANNATTER: Kato? Anybody else? Was your daughter there, Arnelle?
SIMPSON: No.
VANNATTER: Isn't that her name, Arnelle?
SIMPSON: Arnelle, yeah.
VANNATTER: So what time do you think you got back home, actually physically got home?
SIMPSON: Seven-something.
VANNATTER: Seven-something?
SIMPSON: Yeah.
VANNATTER: And then you left, and . . .
SIMPSON: Yeah, I'm trying to think, did I leave? You know, I'm always . . . you know I had to run and get my daughter some flowers. That was actually during the recital, so I rushed and got her some flowers, and then I came home, and then I called Paula as I was going to her house, and Paula wasn't home.
VANNATTER: Paula is your girlfriend?
SIMPSON: Girlfriend, yeah.
VANNATTER: Paula who?
SIMPSON: Barbieri.[34]

VANNATTER: Could you spell that for me?

SIMPSON: B-A-R-B-I-E-R-I.

VANNATTER: Do you know an address on her?

SIMPSON: No, she lives on Wilshire, but I think she's out of town.

LANGE: You got a phone number?

[Simpson gives the detectives Barbieri's telephone number.]

VANNATTER: So you didn't see her last night?

SIMPSON: No, we'd been to a big affair the night before, and then I came back home. I was basically at home. I mean, any time I was . . . whatever time it took me to get to the recital and back, to get to the flower shop and back, I mean, that's the time I was out of the house.

VANNATTER: Were you scheduled to play golf this morning, some place?

SIMPSON: In Chicago.

VANNATTER: In Chicago. What kind of a tournament was this?

SIMPSON: Ah, it's a Hertz, with clients, special clients.

LANGE: Oh, okay. Well that's the whole thing with Hertz?

SIMPSON: Yeah.

VANNATTER: What time did you leave last night, leave the house?

SIMPSON: To go to the airport?

VANNATTER: Mmm hmm.

SIMPSON: About . . . the limo was supposed to be there at 10:45. Normally, they get there a little earlier. I was rushing around—and somewhere between there and 11 o'clock.

VANNATTER: So approximately 10:45 to eleven.

SIMPSON: Eleven o'clock, yeah, somewhere in that area.

VANNATTER: And you went by limo?

SIMPSON: Yeah.

VANNATTER: Who's the limo service?

SIMPSON: I don't know, you have to ask my office.

LANGE: Did you converse with the driver at all? Did you talk to him?

SIMPSON: Yeah, he's a new driver probably. Normally, I have a regular driver I drive with that converses.

LANGE: Remember his name?

SIMPSON: No, just about rushing to the airport, about how I live my life on airplanes, and hotel food and so on, that type of thing.

LANGE: What time did your plane leave?

SIMPSON: Ah, 11:45 the plane took off.

VANNATTER: What airline was it?

SIMPSON: American.

VANNATTER: American? And it was 11:45 to Chicago?

SIMPSON: Chicago.

LANGE: So yesterday you did drive the white Bronco?

SIMPSON: Mmm hmm.

LANGE: And where did you park it when you brought it home?

SIMPSON: Ummm, the first time probably by the mailbox. I'm trying to think, or did I bring it in the driveway? Normally, I will park it by the mailbox, sometimes I will . . .

LANGE: On Ashford, or Ashland?

SIMPSON: On Ashford, yeah.

LANGE: Where did you park it yesterday for the last time, do you remember?

SIMPSON: Right where it is.

LANGE: Where it is now?

SIMPSON: Yeah.

LANGE: Where, on . . . ?

SIMPSON: Right on the street there.

LANGE: On Ashford?

SIMPSON: No, on Rockingham.

LANGE: You parked it there?

SIMPSON: Yes.

LANGE: About what time was that?

SIMPSON: Eight-something, seven . . . eight, nine o'clock, I don't know, right in that area.

[Just a few minutes earlier, Simpson had said that he had last driven the Bronco "in the morning, in the afternoon."]

LANGE: Did you take it to the recital?

SIMPSON: No.

LANGE: What time was the recital?

SIMPSON: Over at about 6:30. Like I said, I came home, I got my car, I was going to see my girlfriend. I was calling her and she wasn't around.

VANNATTER: So you drove the . . . you come home in the [Bentley], and then you got in the Bronco. . . .

SIMPSON: In the Bronco, because my phone was in the Bronco. And because it's a Bronco. It's a Bronco, it's what I drive, you know. I'd rather drive it than any other car. And, I you know, and as I was going over there, I called her a couple of times and she wasn't there, and I left a message, and then I checked my

73

messages, and she had left a message that she wasn't there, and that she may have to leave town. And then I came back and ended up sitting with Kato.

[Later, during a sworn deposition, Simpson would state that he wasn't aware that Barbieri had left a message earlier that morning, ending their relationship.]

LANGE: Okay, and about what time was this again that you parked the Bronco?

SIMPSON: Eight-something, maybe.

LANGE: [INAUDIBLE]

SIMPSON: Relatively, he hadn't taken a, he hadn't done a Jacuzzi, we hadn't gone, we had went and got a burger, and I'd come home and kind of leisurely got ready to go. You know, I mean, we had done a few things after this.

[Later, Simpson will state that, as opposed to "leisurely" getting ready to go, he was "rushing to get out of my house."]

LANGE: You weren't in a hurry when you came back with the white Bronco.

SIMPSON: No.

LANGE: The reason I asked you, the cars were parked kind of at a funny angle, that stuck out in the street.

SIMPSON: Well, it's parked because . . . I don't know if it's a funny angle or what. It's parked because when I was hustling at the end of the day to get all my stuff, and I was getting my phone and everything off it, I was just, when I pulled, you bring it out of the gate there, it's like it's a tight turn.

LANGE: So you had it inside the compound, then?

SIMPSON: Yeah, yeah, yeah, yeah.

LANGE: Oh, okay.

VANNATTER: O.J. what's—

SIMPSON: I brought it inside the compound to get my stuff out of it, you know, and then I put it out, and I'd run back in the gate before the gate closes.

VANNATTER: O.J. What's your office phone number?

[Simpson gives Vannatter the telephone number.]

VANNATTER: How did you get the injury on your hand?

[The detectives note that this is where Simpson begins to give varying versions about how he cut the middle finger of his left hand.]

SIMPSON: I don't know. At the first time, I know I had it when I was in Chicago and all, but at the house I was just running around. . . .

VANNATTER: How did you do it in Chicago?

SIMPSON: I broke a glass. I just was—. You had—. One of you guys had just called me, and I was in the bathroom, and I just kind of went bonkers for a little bit.

LANGE: Is that how you cut it?

SIMPSON: Mmm, it was cut before, but I think I just opened it again. I don't know. I'm not sure. Because going there—

LANGE: Do you recall—

SIMPSON: Pardon me?

LANGE: Do you recall bleeding at all in your truck, in the Bronco?

SIMPSON: I recall bleeding at my house, and then I went to the Bronco. The last thing I did before I left, when I was rushing, was went and got my phone out of the Bronco.

[Later, Simpson will recant this, saying he wasn't retrieving his phone but rather his phone equipment.]

LANGE: Mmm hmm.

SIMPSON: [Or] whatever that is.

LANGE: Where's the phone now?

SIMPSON: In my bag.

LANGE: Oh, you have it . . . ?

SIMPSON: Right in that black bag.

LANGE: You brought a bag with you here?

VANNATTER: Well, yeah, it's in my car. I left it in my car.

LANGE: So do you recall bleeding at all?

SIMPSON: Yeah, I mean, I knew I was bleeding, but it was no big deal. I bleed all the time. I mean, it's—. I play golf and stuff, so there's always something, nicks and stuff here and there.

LANGE: So did you do anything? When did you put the Band-Aid on it?

SIMPSON: Actually, I asked the girl this morning for it.

LANGE: In Chicago?

SIMPSON: Yeah, because last night I just put a—. When Kato, when I was leaving, he was saying something to me, and I was rushing to get my phone, and I put a little thing on it, and it stopped.

[The detectives do not receive a clearer answer as to how Simpson cut his finger.]

75

LANGE: Do you have the keys to that Bronco?

SIMPSON: Yeah.

LANGE: Okay. We've impounded the Bronco. I don't know if you know that or not.

SIMPSON: No. That's fine.

LANGE: . . . Take a look at it. Other than you, who's the last person to drive it.

SIMPSON: Probably Gigi. When I'm out of town, I don't know who drives the car, maybe my daughter, maybe Kato.

LANGE: The keys are available?

SIMPSON: I leave the keys there, you know, when Gigi's there because sometimes she needs it, or Gigi was off and wasn't coming back until today, and I was coming back tonight.

LANGE: So you don't mind if Gigi uses it, or . . .

SIMPSON: This is the only one I can let her use. When she doesn't have her car, or sometimes her husband takes her car, I let her use the Bronco.

LANGE: When was the last time you were at Nicole's house?

SIMPSON: Mmm, I mean—I don't go in, I won't, I don't go in her house. I haven't been in her house in, well, a week, maybe five days. I go to her house a lot. I'm always there. I'm dropping the kids off, picking the kids up, fooling around with the dog, you know.

LANGE: How does that usually work? Do you drop them at the porch, or do you go in with them?

SIMPSON: No, I don't go in the house. I go—

LANGE: That electronic gate out front?

SIMPSON: Yeah.

LANGE: But you never go inside the house?

SIMPSON: Up until about five days, six days ago, I haven't been in the house. Once we, once I started seeing Paula again, I kind of avoid Nicole.

LANGE: Is Nicole seeing anybody else that you know?

SIMPSON: I have no idea. I really have absolutely no idea. I don't ask her. I don't know. Her and her girlfriends, they go out, you know, they've got some things going on right now with her girlfriends, and so I'm assuming something's happening, because one of the girlfriends is having a big problem with her husband because she's always saying she's with Nicole until three or four in the morning. She's not. You know, Nicole tells me she leaves her at 1:30 or 2 or 2:30, and the girl doesn't get home until 5, and she only lives a few blocks away.

VANNATTER: Something's going on, huh?

SIMPSON: Yeah, yeah.

LANGE: Do you know where they went, the family, for dinner last night?

SIMPSON: No. Well, no. I didn't ask!

LANGE: I just thought maybe there's a regular place that they go.

SIMPSON: No. If I was with them, we'd go to Toscano. I mean, not Toscano, Poponi's.

VANNATTER: You haven't had any problems with her lately, have you, O.J.?

SIMPSON: I always have problems with her, you know? Our relationship has been a problem relationship. It's probably lately for me, and I say this only because I said it to Ron yesterday at the—Ron Fischman, whose wife is Cora—at the dance recital, when he came up to me and went, "Oooh, boy, what's going on?" and everybody was beefing with everybody. And I said, "Well, hey, man, I'm just glad I'm out of the mix." You know, because I was like dealing with him and his problems with his wife and Nicole and with evidently some new problems that a guy named Christian was having with his girl, and he was staying at Nicole's house, and something was going on, but I don't think it's pertinent to this.

VANNATTER: Did she have words with you last night?

SIMPSON: Pardon me?

VANNATTER: Did Nicole have words with you last night?

SIMPSON: No, not at all.

VANNATTER: Did you talk to her last night?

SIMPSON: To ask to speak to my daughter, to congratulate my daughter, and everything. Because they're out of there so—

VANNATTER: But you didn't have a conversation with her?

SIMPSON: No, no.

VANNATTER: What were you wearing last night, O.J.?

SIMPSON: What did I wear on the golf course yesterday? Some of these kind of pants. I mean, I changed different for the whatever it was. I just had on some what do they call these?

VANNATTER: Just these black pants.

SIMPSON: Yeah. They're called Bugle Boy.

VANNATTER: Bugle Boy? Is that what you wore to the recital?

SIMPSON: No. No. To the recital I wore, what did I wear to the recital? I wore a white T-shirt. And some slacks and stuff.

LANGE: These aren't the pants?

SIMPSON: No.

LANGE: Okay, where are the pants that you . . . ?

SIMPSON: They're hanging in my closet. You know?

LANGE: These are washable, right? You just throw them in the laundry?

SIMPSON: Yeah, I got 100 pair. They give them to me free, Bugle Boys, so I've got a bunch of them.

LANGE: Do you recall coming home and hanging them up, or . . . ?

SIMPSON: I always hang up my clothes. I mean, it's rare that I don't hang up my clothes unless I'm gonna lay them in my bathroom for her to do something with them, you know those are the only [two] that I don't hang up. But something, when you play golf, you don't necessarily dirty pants. You know, they get holes—

VANNATTER: What kind of shoes were you wearing?

SIMPSON: Tennis shoes.

[A blow-up photograph of Simpson with his daughter taken at the recital shows that he was not wearing tennis shoes.]

VANNATTER: Tennis shoes? Do you know what kind?

SIMPSON: Probably Reeboks, that's all I wear.

LANGE: Are they at home, too?

SIMPSON: Yeah.

LANGE: Was this just to be a short trip to Chicago, so you didn't take a whole lot?

SIMPSON: Yeah, I was coming back today.

LANGE: Just overnight?

SIMPSON: Yeah. Gonna play golf today.

VANNATTER: That's a hectic schedule, drive back here to play golf, and then come back.

SIMPSON: Yeah, but I do it all the time.

VANNATTER: Do you?

SIMPSON: Yeah. That's what I was complaining with the driver about, you know, about how my whole life is on and off airplanes.

[Long pause]

VANNATTER: O.J., we've got sort of a problem.

SIMPSON: Mmm hmm.

VANNATTER: We've got some blood on and in your car, we've got some blood at your house, and sort of a problem.

SIMPSON: Well, we'll take my blood test, and you'll see.

LANGE: Well, we'd like to do that. We've got, of course, the cut on your finger that you don't, aren't real clear on.

SIMPSON: Can't be any clearer than I am.
LANGE: Okay. Do you recall having that cut on your finger the last time you were at Nicole's house?
SIMPSON: A week ago?
LANGE: Yeah.
SIMPSON: No. I'm pretty sure. Yeah. Yeah. It was last night.
LANGE: Okay, so it's last night that you cut it.
SIMPSON: Yeah. Yeah.

[The detectives note that Simpson has again said that he cut his finger on the night of the murders while he was still in Los Angeles and before leaving for Chicago.]

VANNATTER: Somewhere after the recital?
SIMPSON: Somewhere when I was rushing to get out of my house.

[Just a few minutes earlier, Simpson had said that he was "leisurely" getting ready to go.]

VANNATTER: Okay, after the recital.
SIMPSON: Yeah.
LANGE: What do you think happened? Do you have any idea?
SIMPSON: I have no idea, man.
LANGE: Had she been getting threatening phone calls?
SIMPSON: You guys haven't told me anything. I have no idea what happened. When you said to my daughter, who said something to me today, that somebody else might have been involved, I have absolutely no idea what happened. I don't know how, why, or what. But you guys haven't told me anything. Every time I ask you guys, you say you're going to tell me in a bit.

[Neither Lange nor Vannatter have given Simpson's daughter, Arnelle, any information about the case. And, up to this point, Simpson has not asked either detective any questions about the case. Even if he had asked, the detectives' intention was to be evasive, concentrating instead on what Simpson, now the top suspect, knew.]

VANNATTER: Well, we don't know a lot of the answers to these questions yet ourselves, O.J., okay?
SIMPSON: I've got a bunch of guns, I got guns all over the place. You know? You can take them, they're all there. I mean, you

can see them. I keep them in my car for an incident that happened a month ago that my in-laws, my wife, and everybody knows about. You know?

LANGE: What was that?

SIMPSON: Going down to . . . and cops down there know about it, because I've told two marshals about it at a mall. I was going down for a christening, and I had just left our set and it was like 3:30 in the morning, and I'm in a lane, and also the car in front of me is going real slow, and I'm slowing down, I figure he sees a cop, because we were all going pretty fast. And I'm going to change lanes, but there's a car next to me, and I can't change lanes. Then that goes for a while, and now I'm going to slow down and go around him but the car butts up to me, and I'm like caught between three cars. They were Oriental guys, and they were not letting me go anywhere. And finally I went on the shoulder, and I sped up, and then I held my phone up so they could see the light part of it, you know, because I have tinted windows, and they kind of scattered, and I chased one of them for a while to make him think I was chasing him before I took off.

LANGE: Were you in the Bronco?

SIMPSON: No.

LANGE: What were you driving?

SIMPSON: My Bentley. It has tinted windows and all, so I figured they thought they had a nice little touch . . .

LANGE: Did you think they were trying to rip you off maybe, was that it?

SIMPSON: I thought definitely, they were. And then the next thing, you know, I was, Nicole and I, you know, I went home. I got real, I got, at four in the morning I got down there to Laguna, and when we woke up, I told her about it, and told her parents about it, told everybody about it, you know? And when I saw two marshals at a mall, I walked up and told them about it.

LANGE: What did they do, make a report and all?

SIMPSON: They didn't do nothing. I mean, they'll remember me and remember I told them.

LANGE: Did Nicole mention that she'd been getting any threats lately to you? Anything she was concerned about or the kids' safety?

SIMPSON: To her?

LANGE and VANNATTER (in unison): Yes.

SIMPSON: From?

LANGE and VANNATTER (in unison): From anybody.

SIMPSON: No, not at all.

LANGE: Was she very security conscious? Did she keep that house locked up?

SIMPSON: Very.

LANGE: I know the intercom didn't work apparently, right?

SIMPSON: I thought it worked.

LANGE: Oh, okay. Does the electronic buzzer work on the gate?

SIMPSON: The electronic buzzer worked to let people in.

LANGE: Do you ever park in the rear when you go over there?

SIMPSON: Most of the time.

[The detectives note that the killer parked in the rear of Brown's condominium.]

LANGE: You do park in the rear.

SIMPSON: Most times when I'm taking the kids there, I come right into the driveway, blow the horn, and she, a lot of times or the housekeeper, either the housekeeper opens or they'll keep a garage door opener up on the top of the thing, you know, and make that, but, yes, when I'm dropping the kids off and stuff, when I'm going in. And then sometimes I go to the front because the kids have to hit the buzzer and stuff.

VANNATTER: Did you say before that up until about three weeks ago you guys were going out again and trying the, trying to reconcile?

SIMPSON: No, we'd been going out for about a year, and then the last six months we've had . . . it ain't been working, so we tried various things to see if we can make it work. We started trying to date, and it wasn't working, and so, you know, then we just said the hell with it, you know?

VANNATTER: And that was about three weeks ago?

SIMPSON: Yeah, about three weeks ago. It was like we just we stopped—

VANNATTER: So you were seeing her up to that point?

SIMPSON: To say I was seeing her, yeah, I mean, yeah. Yeah. We were trying—. It was like it was—. It was—. It was a—. It was a done deal. It just wasn't happening. You know, I was gone. I mean, I was in San Juan doing a film, and I don't think we had sex since I've been back from San Juan, and that was like two months ago. So it's been like, for the kids we tried to do things together, we didn't go out together, you know, we didn't really date each other. Then we decided let's try to date each other. We went out one night, and it just didn't work. You know?

VANNATTER: When you say it didn't work, what do you mean?

SIMPSON: Ah, the night we went out it was fun. Then the next night we went out it was actually when I was down in Laguna, and she didn't want to go out. And I said, "Well, let's go out because I came all the way down here to go out," and we kind of had a beef. And it just didn't work after that, you know? We were only trying to date to see if we could bring some romance back into our relationship. We just said, let's treat each other like boyfriend and girlfriend instead of, you know, like seventeen-year-old married people. I mean, seventeen years together, whatever that is.

LANGE: How long were you together?

SIMPSON: Seventeen years.

LANGE: Seventeen years.

VANNATTER: Did you ever hit her, O.J.?

SIMPSON: Ah, one night we had a fight. That night we had a fight. Hey, she hit me! You know? And as I said, they never took my statement, they never wanted to hear my side, and they never wanted to hear the housekeeper's side. Nicole was drunk. She did her thing, she started tearing up my house, you know? And I, I didn't punch her or anything, but I you know—

VANNATTER: . . . slapped her a couple of times.

SIMPSON: No, no, I rassled her, is what I did. I didn't slap her at all. I mean, I rassled her. Nicole's a strong girl. She's a . . . one of the most conditioned women. Since that period of time, she's hit *me* a few times, but I've never touched her after that, and I'm telling you, it's five, six years ago.

[The detectives later will receive the police report of the 1989 incident in which Nicole claimed that he had beaten her, as well as photographs of his battered wife.]

LANGE: What is her birth date?

SIMPSON: May 19th.

LANGE: Did you get together with her on her birthday?

SIMPSON: Yeah, her and I and the kids, I believe.

LANGE: Did you give her a gift?

SIMPSON: I gave her a gift.

LANGE: What did you give her?

SIMPSON: I gave her either the bracelet or the earrings.

LANGE: Did she keep them or did she return them?

SIMPSON: Oh, no, when we split she gave me both the earrings and the bracelet back. I bought her a very nice bracelet—I don't know if it was Mother's Day or her birthday—and I bought her the earrings for the other thing, and when we split—and it take credit to her—she felt that it wasn't right that she had it, and I said good because I want them back.

LANGE: Was that the very day of her birthday, May 19, or was it a few days later?

SIMPSON: What do you mean?

LANGE: You gave it to her on the 19th of May, her birthday, right, this bracelet or earrings?

SIMPSON: I may have given her the earrings. No, the bracelet, May 19th. When was Mother's Day?

LANGE: Well, Mother's Day was around that time.

SIMPSON: No, it was probably her birthday, yes.

LANGE: And did she return it the same day?

SIMPSON: Oh, no, she ret—. I mean this is, I get into a funny place here on this, all right? She returned it—both of them—I mean, I took—three weeks ago or so, because when I say I'm in a funny place on this it was because I gave it to my girlfriend and told her it was for her, and that was three weeks ago. Told her I bought it for her. You know? What am I going to do with it?

LANGE: Did Mr. Weitzman, your lawyer, your attorney, talk to you anything about this polygraph we brought up before? What were your thoughts on that?

SIMPSON: Should I talk about my thoughts on that?

LANGE: I mean, it's up to you.

SIMPSON: I'm sure eventually I'll do it, but it's like hey, I've got some weird thoughts now. And I've had weird thoughts, you know when you've been with a person for seventeen years, you think everything.[35] And I don't, I've got to understand what this thing is. I don't, you know, if it's true blue, I don't mind doing it.

LANGE: Well, you're not compelled at all to take this thing, number one, and number two—I don't know if Mr. Weitzman explained it to you—this goes to the exclusion of someone as much as the inclusion.

SIMPSON: Now you do that, too. Yeah. Yeah.

LANGE: Now [and] then we do that to eliminate people. And just to get things straight.

SIMPSON: But does it work for elimination?

LANGE: Oh, yes. We use it for elimination more than anything.

SIMPSON: Well, I'll talk to him about it.

LANGE: Understand, the reason we're talking to you is because you're the ex-husband.

SIMPSON: I know I'm the number one target, and now you're telling me I've got blood all over the place.

LANGE: Well, there's blood at your house in the driveway, and that footstep, we've got a search warrant, and we're going to go and get the blood. We found some in your house.

VANNATTER: Is that your blood that's dripped there?

SIMPSON: If it's dripped, it's what I dripped running around trying to leave.

[Once again, the detectives note, Simpson has indicated that he cut himself before leaving for Chicago.]

VANNATTER: Last night?

SIMPSON: Yeah, and I wasn't aware that it was . . . I was aware that I . . . And I was trying to get out of the house. I didn't even pay any attention to it, I saw it when I was in the kitchen, and I grabbed a napkin or something, and that was it. I didn't think about it after that.

[The LAPD did not find a bloodstained napkin during its search of Simpson's house.]

VANNATTER: That was last night after you got home from the recital, when you were rushing?

SIMPSON: That was last night when I was . . . I don't know what I was . . . I was in the car getting my junk out of the car. I was in the house. I was throwing hangers and stuff in my suitcase. I was doing my little crazy what I do . . . I mean, I do it everywhere. Anybody who has ever picked me up says that O.J.'s a whirlwind at the end. He's running, he's grabbing things, and that's what I was doing.

[Again, Simpson had earlier said that he was "leisurely" getting ready to go.]

VANNATTER: Well, I'm going to step out and I'm going to get a photographer to come down and photograph your hand there. And then pretty soon we're going to take you downstairs and get some blood from you.

SIMPSON: Okay.

VANNATTER: Okay? I'll be right back.

[Vannatter leaves the room.]

LANGE: So it was about five days ago you last saw Nicole? Was it at the house?

SIMPSON: Okay, the last time I saw Nicole, Jesus, physically saw Nicole . . . I saw her obviously last night. The time before, I'm trying to even think . . . I went to Washington, D.C., so I didn't see her, so I'm trying to think . . . I haven't seen her since I went to Washington. I went to Washington—what's the date today? I mean today is Monday, right?

LANGE: Today's Monday, the 13th of June.

SIMPSON: Okay, I went to Washington on maybe Wednesday. Thursday I think I was in . . . Thursday I was in Connecticut, then Long Island Thursday afternoon and all of Friday. I got home Friday night, Friday afternoon. I played, you know . . . Paula picked me up I believe at the airport. I played golf Saturday, and when I came home I think my son was there. So I did something with my son. I don't think I saw Nicole at all then. And then I went to a big affair with Paula Saturday night, and I got up and played golf Sunday, which pissed Paula off, and I saw Nicole at . . . so it was about a week before, I saw her at the, you know.

[At this point, Lange realizes that Simpson is giving him nothing but evasive patter. Knowing that he has no hard evidence with which to confront him, the detective senses that Simpson will offer nothing more. If Lange gets in Simpson's face on the basis on the inconsistencies he has already made, then the detective chances agitating Simpson and stands to lose the opportunity to fingerprint Simpson, photograph his injured middle finger while the wound is still fresh, and take his blood sample.]

LANGE: Okay, and the last time you saw Nicole, was that at her house?

SIMPSON: I don't remember. I wasn't in her house, so it couldn't have been at her house, so it was, you know, I don't physically remember the last time I saw her. I may have seen her even jogging one day.

LANGE: Let me get this straight. You've never physically been inside the house?

SIMPSON: Not in the last week.

LANGE: Ever. I mean, how long has she lived there? About six months?

SIMPSON: Oh! Christ, I've slept at the house for many, many, many times, you know? I've done everything at the house, you know? I'm just saying in the last— . . . You're talking in the last week or so.

LANGE: Well, whatever. Six months she's lived there?

SIMPSON: I don't know. Roughly. Last week—. I was at her house maybe two weeks ago, or ten days ago. One night her and I had a long talk, you know, about, you know, how can we make it better for the kids, and how can we do things better, you know? And, okay, I can almost say when that was. That was when I . . . I don't know, it was about ten days ago. And then we, I had her . . . The next day I had her dog do a flea bath or something with me. Oh, I'll tell you, I did see her one day. One day I went . . . I don't know if this was the early part of last week, I went because my son had to go and get something, and he ran in, and she came to the gate, and the dog ran out, and her friend, Faye [Resnick], and I went looking for the dog. That may have been a week ago, I don't know.

LANGE: [To Vannatter who has returned] Got a photographer coming?

VANNATTER: No, we're going to take him up there.

LANGE: We're ready to terminate this at 1407.

Endnotes

33. Lange and Vannatter have been widely criticized for the manner in which they conducted the Simpson interview.

For instance: On page 102 of his book *Outrage*, former prosecutor Vincent Bugliosi wrote: "The detectives were rather inexpert questioners who failed to pin Simpson down as much as they could have on his precise activities throughout the entire previous evening. They also did not ask good follow-up questions, and most unfortunately, it was they who terminated the interview. Since, at the time of the interview, they already strongly suspected he was guilty, why didn't they try to elicit from him as much as they could, continuing until either he said he didn't want to talk anymore or his celebrity lawyer finally deigned to enter the room and instruct Simpson or insist that he not answer any more questions? Isn't this just common sense?"

However, Bugliosi then stated on page 107: "So the statement Simpson gave the police—which by itself was enough to convict him—not only wasn't used by the prosecutors to help their case, but it actually hurt them."

And, then, Bugliosi added on page 109: "[W]hat's *in* the statement crucified Simpson, out of his own lips, with virtually nothing in the statement helping him."

In *The Run of His Life* Jeffrey Toobin revealed on page 67: "When the prosecutors heard the tape, they knew immediately how dreadfully the detectives had botched this opportunity. They seethed with frustration—in private. To berate Vannatter and Lange would have been futile, and might also have damaged a partnership that faced a long and difficult investigation. But among themselves the prosecutors had a nickname for the police interview of the defendant on June 13: 'the fiasco.'"

On page 193–194 of *The Prosecution Responds* Hank Goldberg, a member of the Simpson prosecution team, wrote: "It was about as hardball an interrogation as a celebrity interview with Larry King. They allowed Simpson to be so vague that virtually nothing he could testify to on the stand would have been inconsistent with what he told the detectives. . . . Vannatter and Lange, who the defense claimed were evil co-conspirators, had treated Simpson with a level of deference I would hope would be denied the president of the United States. . . . Phil and Tom may have sensed that a sympathetic public might view an effort to press Simpson as police coercion."

However, Lange and Vannatter defend their strategy during the Simpson interview in the text that follows this endnote number.

34. Paula Barbieri, a tall and willowy woman, had worked as a model for *Vogue*.

35. These "weird thoughts" Simpson admitted having later came up in a different context. Ron Shipp, a longtime acquaintance of Simpson and a former LAPD officer at the West Los Angeles Division, would testify that during a private moment with Simpson on the night of June 13 while he was at Simpson's house, "He [Simpson] kind of jokingly just said, you know, 'To be honest, Shipp, . . . I've had some dreams of killing her.'" Shipp also insisted that Simpson had asked him how much time a crime lab needed to analyze DNA blood evidence. Shipp speculated that such testing would take two or three months.

However, members of Simpson's family—who were also present at Simpson's house that night—argued that Shipp had been drinking, and that he never had the private moment with Simpson he described.

Lange and Vannatter believe that Shipp told the truth.

8

The Vial of Blood

Tom Lange takes Simpson downstairs to the LAPD's Latent Print Unit on the second floor. Simpson continues to be very cooperative. The detective arranges for Simpson to give a full set of fingerprints to a print technician, who smiles at Simpson but says nothing directly to him. The prints will be needed for crime-scene comparison or elimination.

After Simpson wipes the ink off his hands, Lange escorts him to the fourth floor, where Simpson and the injuries on the middle finger of his left hand will be photographed. Like the fingerprint technician, the photographer smiles at Simpson but says nothing to him—other than routine instructions about the position of his left hand.

Before the pictures are taken, Lange examines both of Simpson's hands, especially the now unbandaged and exposed finger. He has two wounds. One is a jagged, horizontal cut, about a half-inch long, on the middle knuckle, which is quite swollen and has been bleeding. There is a smaller nick, about half the size of the other wound, that's on the first knuckle.

These two cuts alone are the only fresh wounds on Simpson's hands that Lange observes.

While all of this is taking place, there is virtually no conversation going on between Lange and Simpson, not even any inconsequential small talk. Lange is in the process of collecting evidence from a murder suspect, and Simpson knows he's under suspicion. Under these circumstances, there really isn't much to say.

After the photographs are taken, Lange and Simpson return to the Robbery/Homicide Division, where they pick up Vannatter. Weitzman and Taft still have not returned from their lunch.

The two detectives and Simpson then walk to the medical dispensary at the city jail in Parker Center. On duty is Thano Peratis, an elderly male nurse whom the detectives have known for over twenty years. With Lange and Simpson standing outside the door, Vannatter walks in to Peratis's office to make the request for a blood sample.

"I'm real busy," Peratis replies. "I don't have time for all of this. Make an appointment, Phil."

Saying nothing, Vannatter points to the doorway. Peratis sees Simpson with Lange. "Yeah," Peratis says, "bring him on in."

Although Peratis is used to drawing blood from suspected drunk drivers, he is not accustomed to taking it from celebrities, like Simpson. Like the other technicians, Peratis is polite but only talks to Simpson when he needs information or to give him instructions. For instance, Peratis must fill out an official form in order to conduct the blood test, and Simpson must sign the form, indicating that he is taking it voluntarily.

With Simpson facing him on a chair at the side of his desk, Peratis takes Simpson's blood pressure. Then he wraps a thin rubber tourniquet around the upper portion of Simpson's left arm and asks Vannatter to hand him a glass vial from a nearby box.

The vial contains EDTA, a preservative that protects blood and other substances from quick deterioration—or, in the case of blood, until it can be refrigerated.

Peratis inserts the needle and draws Simpson's blood into the syringe. As Peratis is taking Simpson's blood, Lange is puzzled. "Why is Simpson doing all of this?" he wonders. "I sure wouldn't be."

Consistent with standard operating procedure, Vannatter is doing the paperwork, indicating that he has requested and will take custody of Simpson's blood sample, which is now in a vial.

Showing Lange the sample but not specifying any particular measurement, Peratis simply asks Lange, "Is this enough?"

"Yeah, fine," Lange replies. "We just wanted some blood."

Understandably, Lange and Vannatter would have been happy with a thimbleful. They have not asked for any particular amount. And Peratis has neither recorded nor noted how much blood he has just drawn from the suspect.[36]

Since Lange has Simpson with a trained medical professional, he asks Peratis to examine Simpson's injured finger and possibly treat it. Also, Lange wants Peratis to document the injuries in his report. For the first time—even after discussing the injury during the interview and allowing it to be photographed—Simpson balks, saying, "No, it's no big deal. Don't worry about it."

Lange replies, "Just let the nurse take a look at it. He can probably put something on it for you. He can bandage it up for you."

"No, no," Simpson tells them, seemingly not wanting to make a fuss. "That's all right. No big deal. Don't worry about it. I don't need that."

Finally, Simpson relents, allowing Peratis to examine his cuts, which require no medical treatment other than a general cleaning.

Just before the two detectives leave with Simpson at about 3:20 P.M., Peratis gives Vannatter a receipt, puts a label on the vial of blood, and then hands it over to him. Vannatter takes a loose LAPD analyzed-evidence envelope from Peratis's desk and places the vial inside.

Because Lange and Vannatter have been in constant motion since receiving their calls to report to South Bundy over twelve hours ago, they have not obtained a Division of Records or DR number for this case from the LAPD West Los Angeles Division. Actually, because this is a double murder, two DR numbers will be assigned, one for each victim.[37]

Receiving a DR number—which is designed for record-keeping purposes—is not a top priority during the initial stages of any investigation. However, any property report or analyzed evidence report must be accompanied by the case's DR number before being circulated. And *nothing* may be booked as evidence at the LAPD Property Division—unless it is accompanied by an appropriate DR number. In other words, property must be booked in sequence; and, without a DR number, it may not be booked at all.

Further, in this particular case, the sequence of evidence is being arranged by SID criminalist Dennis Fung, who has been collecting and identifying evidence at both the South Bundy and North Rockingham crime scenes. Even though the case does not have its DR number, the criminalist is still assigning item numbers to evidence that has been collected. Fung is preparing the property report, cataloging all of the items he books as evidence. Hours earlier, Fung had documented and collected the first item in his sequence: the blood stain on Simpson's Bronco.

Just before leaving Peratis's office, Vannatter filled out the form on the front of the analyzed evidence envelope, leaving blank the DR number, which has not yet been assigned.

When the detectives arrive back at their office with Simpson at about 3:30 P.M., his attorneys, Weitzman and Taft, now back from their lunch, are waiting.

Because he and Vannatter still appear to have Simpson's cooperation, Lange pushes Simpson for even more, saying, "Our people are still at your home conducting the search. But you're welcome to go back whenever you want. You might be able to help us there."

Simpson smiles and nods. Then, with little else said, Weitzman and Taft leave with their client. Simpson has left behind his taped statement, his fingerprints, photographs of his injured finger, and a vial of his blood.

With Simpson and his lawyers now gone, Lange and Vannatter go into the office of Captain Gartland, the commanding officer of the Robbery/Homicide Division, to give him an interim report.

"Let's go over what this guy said to you," Gartland says.

"First of all," Lange replies, "he said that he had parked his Bronco between seven and nine o'clock in front of the house. Just before that he said that he had last driven the car either in the morning or the afternoon."

"What about the cut on his finger?" Gartland asks.

Vannatter responds, "First he says that it was cut before and that he must have reopened it—although he didn't feel it."

Lange then says, "And he said he was dripping blood while running around, trying to leave his house. This was after he said that he had been 'leisurely' getting ready to go."

"Then, he changes all that by saying that he might have cut himself in Chicago."

"He's not clear on his alibi, which is obvious from his inconsistent statements," Lange continues. "And he's playing games with the polygraph. The key is just waiting for the blood results to come in."

After hearing his detectives' summary, Gartland asks Lange what he thinks.

Lange replies, "I'm ninety percent convinced he did it."

"And you, Phil?" Gartland asks.

"He did it. There's no doubt in my mind."

When the detectives return to their desks, Lange receives word that a car Ron Goldman had borrowed the night before has been found on Dorothy Street, just east of the alley in back of Brown's condominium. The owner of the car, a red Toyota, is Andrea Scott, a close friend of Goldman, who is in Canada on a modeling assignment.

While talking to another detective, Vannatter learns that Chicago Police Detective Ken Berris, at the earlier request of Detective Bert Luper, had gone to the O'Hare Plaza Hotel and seized room 915, the suite which had been occupied by Simpson. Berris has already found a broken drinking glass in the sink, which contains no apparent bloodstains. But red stains are visible on a washcloth and on his bedding.

There is no blood anywhere on his telephone, from which Simpson had made several calls after hearing of his ex-wife's death, including one to his home which Lange had answered. Also, after receiving the initial notification call from Phillips, Simpson made forty-eight calls from his cellular phone, alone, between 6:41 A.M. and 11:25 A.M. No fewer than eighteen went to his personal attorney, Skip Taft.[38]

Because the blood evidence is so crucial to their case, Vannatter, who is pumped up after the events of the past few hours, wants to get Simpson's vial of blood to Dennis Fung as quickly as possible. He recognizes that the media is all over this story. While in his office that afternoon, he has even seen himself, unlocking Simpson's handcuffs at North Rockingham, on a television set in the Robbery/Homicide Division. That scene has become the lead news story of the day across the country.

The political pressure will soon begin either to arrest or to vindicate Simpson after such a public spectacle. This case has now gone Hollywood. Gone CNN. Gone worldwide. Not many people care that some cases take years to solve. Lange and Vannatter realize that this one must be wrapped up in the time it takes to air a five-part mini-series on television.

Vannatter receives word from another RHD detective returning from Simpson's estate that Dennis Fung is now at Simpson's estate. Fung came from the South Bundy crime scene, which shut down at 3:45 P.M.[39]

At about 4:20 P.M., because he has no DR number for booking purposes, Vannatter decides to take the vial of Simpson's blood with him back out to North Rockingham and deliver it, personally, to the criminalist. They need Simpson's blood booked and analyzed as quickly as possible and to have it compared to the blood evidence found at the two crime scenes. With all the attention this case is already receiving, the obvious question becomes: What if the blood tests come back, and they don't match Simpson? One way or the other, Lange and Vannatter need to know—and fast.

Already, this is no ordinary situation. This is clearly a high-profile case, and—unlike most such cases, especially so soon after the crime—they have evidence in their possession that could provide them with a "smoking gun" and prove the guilt or innocence of their top suspect. In other words, if, for example, the blood analysis shows the victims' blood in Simpson's Bronco or Simpson's blood at the South Bundy crime scene, this immediately becomes a dead-bang case. But Simpson's blood needs to be cataloged before the analysis can begin. And the man doing the cataloging is Dennis Fung, who is still at Simpson's estate.

At about 4:30 P.M., Lange and Vannatter walk to their separate cars in the subterranean garage at Parker Center and drive back to North Rockingham.

Just before leaving, Vannatter—who has kept custody of Simpson's travel bag since just after noon when it was seized—is sitting in his car alone. He opens Simpson's bag and begins to go through it, searching for any trace of blood evidence. He finds none.[40] When he returns to the North Rockingham crime scene, he will return the travel bag and all of its contents to Simpson.

Vannatter arrives first at North Rockingham at 5:17 P.M. in the midst of throngs of reporters and cameras. LAPD patrol officers have kept the area secure since Vannatter left earlier that afternoon, while Detective Luper, whom Vannatter had placed in charge, directed the search of the Simpson estate.

As the media looks on and memorializes nearly every movement on the grounds, Vannatter approaches the front door of Simpson's home and immediately sees Dennis Fung, who is getting ready to leave. Prior to 10:15 that morning, Fung had collected all of the known blood evidence at the scene, including, among other things, the blood drops in Simpson's driveway and foyer and the bloody right-hand glove on the south side of the house.

Now, as a television camera records the scene, Vannatter hands Fung the analyzed evidence envelope containing the vial of blood, telling him, "Here's a blood sample from Simpson. It's part of the evidence package."[41]

Fung takes custody of Simpson's blood at exactly 5:20 P.M., three minutes after Vannatter's arrival. Thus, the chain of custody of the vial of blood from Vannatter to Fung has just taken place—in accordance with standard operating procedure, LAPD regulations, and state law.

After handing over the vial of blood, Vannatter regains control of the search from Detective Luper, asking Luper and the other detectives for reports about seized evidence. Among those items collected during the day have been a pair of socks, which were recovered on a rug in Simpson's bedroom.[42]

During the search, no weapons or knives have been taken.

A brief flurry of activity did erupt after red stains were found on the clothing in Simpson's washing machine. But Fung quickly determined that the red stains had merely been caused by some rust along the rim of the washer.

The LAPD, for routine administrative purposes after the service of a search warrant, uses video cameras to show that locations they looked through have not been trashed by police investigators. During the search of Simpson's home an LAPD videographer walks around the house, filming rooms that have just been scrutinized.[43]

As the search winds down, LAPD Commander John White, the chief of detectives, and his adjutant, Lieutenant Bob Salkeld, arrive at Simpson's estate. Vannatter and Luper brief both of them about the search.

Officially, the following items have been booked by Fung and are listed in his formal property report:

- Item #1: "Cloth swatch used to transfer red stain—recovered from 360 N. Rockingham . . . from a white Ford Bronco, Ca license #3CWZ788 on the driver door exterior . . . adjacent to the handle."
- Item #2: "Stick, wood—recovered from the grass . . ."
- Item #3: "Butt, cigarette, 'Marlboro'—recovered from the street . . ."
- Item #4: "Cloth swatch used to transfer red stain—recovered from . . . the south curb . . ."[44]
- Item #5: "Cloth swatch used to transfer red stain—recovered from the driveway . . ."
- Item #6: "Cloth swatch used to transfer red stain—recovered from the . . . north driveway edge."[45]
- Item #7: "Cloth swatch used to transfer red stain—recovered from the driveway . . ."[46]
- Item #8: "Cloth swatch used to transfer red stain—recovered from the driveway . . ."
- Item #9: "Glove, right hand, leather, brown, with red stains—recovered from the walkway . . . east of the west wall, . . . south of the south wall of the house."[47]
- Item #10: "Bag, plastic, blue—recovered from the ground . . . east of the west wall, . . . south of the south wall of the house, on the south side of the chain link fence."
- Item #11: "Cloth swatch used to transfer red stain—recovered from the wire, . . . east of the west wall, . . . south of the south wall . . ."
- Item #12: "Cloth swatch used to transfer red stain—recovered in the foyer . . ."[48]
- Item #13: "Socks, navy blue—recovered from the master bedroom . . ."[49]
- Item #14: "Cloth swatch used to transfer red stain—recovered from the master bathroom floor . . ."[50]
- Item #15: "Receipt, airline ticket—recovered from the bathroom south of foyer, from the trash can in the southwest corner."
- Item #16: "Tag, baggage—recovered from the bench, outside the front door."
- Item #17: "Blood, within vial labelled 'O.J. Simpson 6-13-94'—received from Det. Vannatter #14877 at 1720 hrs."

Lange has not been to the North Rockingham crime scene since early in the morning. This is the first time he has seen Simpson's estate in broad daylight.

After his survey of the grounds, Lange goes inside the house and up to Simpson's bedroom, off of which is an outside patio overlooking his pool. The bedroom walls are beige in color with dark wood trim and light beige carpeting. Along the north wall are built-in cabinets with a television on one of its shelves. The room contains a large bed, stone fireplace, and light beige sectional sofa. Between the foot of the bed and the stone fireplace is a two-tone beige throw rug—upon which Simpson's socks had been found earlier.

As Lange looks around the bedroom, Simpson is present and asks the detective whether the police have found and collected a cache of money and checks hidden in his closet. Lange knows nothing about this and simply replies, "We'll give you an inventory of anything we seize."[51]

Lange then asks Simpson, "What did you wear last night?"

"Like I told you at the interview," Simpson replies, acting both cooperative but impatient, "I don't remember. I probably had on a pair of Bugle Boy slacks. I wear them all the time. I don't know which pair I wore."

Lange looks into Simpson's walk-in closet, an immaculate display of clothing and clothing care. Everything is neatly hung and well organized.

Lange asks, "Which shoes did you wear?"

Pointing to a pair in his closet, Simpson says, "I think I was wearing those Reeboks. I have a lot of those, too."

"Which ones?" Lange asks, looking at a wide variety of shoes and Reeboks sneakers.

"That pair right there."

Lange picks up the pair of Reeboks Simpson is pointing to and asks, "These?"

"Yeah, those."

As Lange looks at the pair of Reeboks in his hand, he sees what appears to be red spots on them. He doesn't know whether the spots are blood or not. He will have to have them analyzed.

Lange says firmly, "I'm going to take these, O.J."

Shrugging, Simpson simply replies, "Okay, fine. Hell, take them all if you want."

Lange also notices that they are about the same size as the shoes that made the bloody shoe prints at the South Bundy crime scene. But he recognizes immediately that the soles are different. He looks at the soles of the other shoes in the closet but can't find a pair that matches the bloody-shoe pattern at South Bundy.

Nevertheless, because Simpson claims that he wore the Reeboks the night before, Lange seizes them and none others. Although Lange will ask the crime lab to check the red spots on these Reeboks, he primarily takes them to establish Simpson's shoe size.

Other investigators continue their search. Two detectives rummage through Simpson's laundry bin, searching for clothing possibly worn the night before; others are in the shower stall, searching for trace evidence. An LAPD photographer roams from room to room through the house, receiving instructions from Homicide Special detectives about what to shoot.

At 7:10 P.M., Lange logs out, carrying Simpson's Reeboks. Lange cannot give them to Dennis Fung, because he has already left the scene for the day. And the LAPD Evidence Control Unit at Piper Tech has closed. Even if it was open, he would face the same problem Vannatter had earlier with his handling of Simpson's vial of blood: The case doesn't have a DR number yet and won't have one until the following day.

Lange decides to go straight home and take the Reeboks with him.

Seeing Vannatter, Lange holds up the Reeboks and says to his partner, "This is what Simpson told me he was wearing last night. And I'm going to take them home with me."

"Okay, fine," Vannatter replies. "I'm going home pretty soon myself."

As Lange heads for his police-issued four-door 1988 Chevrolet outside the gate, he is mobbed by reporters who want him to comment about the case. Refusing, Lange quickly gets into his car, placing the Reeboks on the front seat next to him, and drives away.

When he arrives at his home in Simi Valley fifty minutes later, he places the shoes in a cardboard box in the trunk of his car. He plans to give them to the SID Serology Unit the following morning for an analysis of the red spots and shoe sizing.

When Lange walks into his house, Linda and his two young daughters are sitting in front of the television set, watching the coverage of the case. When Linda sees him come in, she smiles and says to her husband, "Hard day at the office, honey?"

Lange has a quick bite to eat—chicken soup and a tuna

sandwich—and then joins his family in front of the television. He sees the film of Vannatter taking the handcuffs off Simpson at North Rockingham, just before they interviewed him; he already sees coverage of himself walking away from Simpson's house with the Reeboks. He also watches videotape of Claudine Ratcliffe and John Jacobo from the coroner's office wheeling away the bodies of the two victims, close-ups of the blood all over the walkway in front of Brown's home, as well as aerial views of both the South Bundy and North Rockingham crime scenes.

Watching the media frenzy already developing, Lange knows he has another hard day ahead tomorrow. He also realizes that every move he makes will be memorialized—and, ultimately, second-guessed. Lange has been here before. He remembers his 1981 investigation of the brutal Laurel Canyon murders involving porno-movie star John Holmes and the 1982 contract killing case of Hollywood actor Frank Christi.

Exhausted, Lange goes to bed at 9:30.

Over in Valencia, Vannatter is still keyed up over the day's events, knowing that he and Lange have a case they can probably send over to the district attorney's office by the end of the week. Wanting to discuss it, he calls Marcia Clark at her home at about 8:00 P.M., saying, "Hey, I think we've got this thing nailed down pretty good. We're going to have to do some more blood work."

"So I've heard," she replies. "It looks like a great case."

"I've got a blood sample from Simpson and gave it to the criminalist. I'll get back to you with the preliminary testing as soon as possible."

"As *soon* as possible," she emphasizes.

Endnotes

36. The Simpson defense team later created a controversy after Peratis testified both during the grand jury and preliminary hearings that he had drawn about eight cc's of Simpson's blood—which was nothing more than a wild guess. Since the LAPD/SID could document its possession of only 6.5 cc's—about a quarter of a teaspoon's difference—Simpson's attorneys tried to make the case that the police had planted Simpson's unaccounted-for blood at key locations and on specific objects at the South Bundy and North Rockingham crime scenes.

During the prosecution's rebuttal case, the elderly Peratis—who had a serious heart condition and had recently undergone triple-bypass surgery —appeared on videotape, saying that he had overstated the amount of blood drawn from Simpson in his initial statement. In fact, he had never even recorded how much blood he had drawn from Simpson. Lange and Vannatter asked for a vial of Simpson's blood on June 13, 1994, and Peratis conducted the procedure—without ever knowing for sure how much blood he had drawn.

37. In order to receive a DR number for any crime under investigation in Los Angeles, the detective-in-charge reports to the division of occurrence —one of eighteen LAPD divisions. (In this case, the DR number comes from the West Los Angeles Division.)

The lead detective of the case gives the division general information, including the victim's name, date of birth, description, date and time of the crime, the location, and a list of any known witnesses, among other data. After providing this information, the detective receives a DR number for his case.

However, in the event of a multiple murder, each victim receives a DR number. The first number in the set becomes the master number, under which all record-keeping is cataloged.

38. Simpson didn't use his cellular phone again until Friday, June 17 at 12:45 P.M.—the day of the Bronco chase.

39. Officers Delaney Jones and Yvette Perridine shut down the South Bundy crime scene at 3:45 P.M. on June 13. Also present at that time, according to the log, were Officers Dorian Henry and Carson Pierce, whom Lange had placed in charge of perimeter security.

40. Interestingly, during a forty-seven-minute period—between 4:30 and 5:17 P.M. on June 13—Vannatter was alone and in possession of Simpson's travel bag from Chicago and all of its contents, as well as Simpson's blood. If Vannatter had been predisposed to plant blood evidence on

Simpson's property—as he was later accused by Simpson's defense team—this was his big chance. In fact, Vannatter found no blood on any of the contents of the travel bag.

41. Jeffrey Toobin, author of *The Run of His Life*, claimed that Vannatter's decision stemmed more from his own "laziness than malevolence." Toobin wrote on pages 328–329: "Rather than reflecting conspiratorial behavior, Vannatter's delivery of the blood merely illustrated his own laziness; by giving the blood to Dennis Fung at O.J.'s house, Vannatter spared himself the headache of stopping at another location and doing the paperwork on the evidence."

In short, unaware of police procedure—the need for a DR number and the process in which evidence is and is not booked—Toobin simply did not know what he was talking about in this instance.

42. Scientific analysis later confirmed that blood consistent with Nicole Brown's blood was found on Simpson's socks. Simpson's defense team, via defense expert witness Frederic Rieders, created a controversy claiming that the blood on these socks, as well as on Brown's rear gate, contained EDTA, a preservative. Rieders's testimony would bolster the claim that a portion of the vial of blood taken from Simpson on June 13—which contained EDTA—was planted.

Actually, EDTA is also found in numerous other substances, such as laundry detergents and paints—which easily explains why it had appeared on laundered socks and a painted gate. Rieders admitted that he had not done any independent testing of the blood evidence.

Also, during Simpson's criminal trial, forensic scientist Herbert MacDonell, a defense expert witness, testified that the blood pattern on Simpson's socks appears to have been more likely caused by smearing on the socks than by accidental splattering.

However, MacDonell conceded on cross-examination that the smearing pattern did not necessarily indicate that it had been done intentionally or unintentionally by the police. The smearing could have been caused by one of the victims, Simpson himself, or an object Simpson had rubbed up against.

43. The Simpson defense team later created a controversy after LAPD videographer Willie Ford testified at the criminal trial that he did not see Simpson's socks on the rug when he videotaped Simpson's bedroom. The problem was that Dennis Fung's records showed that he had collected the socks *after* the time registered on Ford's film. Consequently, the defense team insisted the police must have planted the socks.

However, the clock on the video camera Ford had used that day had not been reset after a long period of inactivity. In other words, Fung had actually collected the socks *before* Ford arrived to videotape Simpson's bedroom.

Supervisor David Atkins of the LAPD/SID Photo Unit accompanied

Willie Ford during his videotaping of Simpson's bedroom at or about 3:00 P.M. on June 13. According to an LAPD interview report, "[Atkins] was supervising various photography functions relative to the warrant service. At approximately 12:00 noon, the witness was in the upstairs master bedroom when he observed a pair of dark-colored socks on the bedroom floor in plain view. . . . At approximately 1500 hrs. on 6-13-94, the witness returned to the bedroom with video cameraman Willie Ford who videotaped the master bedroom."

Fung had collected the socks between noon and 3:00 P.M. on June 13.

44. Scientific analysis later determined that this blood spot was consistent with Simpson's blood.

45. Scientific analysis later determined that this blood spot was consistent with Simpson's blood.

46. Scientific analysis later determined that this blood spot was consistent with Simpson's blood.

47. Scientific analysis later determined that this glove contained hairs consistent with both Nicole Brown and Ron Goldman, as well as fibers consistent with Goldman's shirt and fibers consistent with the carpet in Simpson's Bronco.

Further, the blood found on the glove was consistent with a mixture of Brown's, Goldman's, and Simpson's blood.

48. Scientific analysis later determined that this blood spot was consistent with Simpson's blood.

49. Scientific analysis later determined that a blood stain on the ankle of one of these socks was consistent with Brown's blood. In fact, DNA/RFLP testing showed that the frequency that this bloodstain would be that of anyone *but* Brown's blood was 1 in 7.7 billion.

Another blood stain on the toe of one of these socks was consistent with Simpson's blood. In fact, DNA/RFLP testing showed that the frequency that this bloodstain would be that of anyone *but* Simpson's blood was 1 in 5.7 billion.

50. Scientific analysis later determined that this blood spot was consistent with Simpson's blood.

51. Author Lawrence Schiller wrote on page 55 of his book, *American Tragedy*, that Simpson believed that the LAPD had stolen "$8,000 in cash and checks" from his closet during the June 13 search of his property. However, in the end, Simpson realized that he had simply misplaced it, as the money "turned out to be under a sweater in the closet after all."

9

Bodies as Evidence

Tuesday, June 14, 1994

After waking up at 5:00 A.M., Lange arrives at the SID crime lab at 7:00. He meets with Greg Matheson, the supervisor of the serology unit, and gives him Simpson's Reeboks, which have been in Lange's trunk all night. After conducting a quick test on the shoe's red spots, Matheson finds no blood.[52]

Regardless, Lange asks Matheson to turn over the shoes to Fung, who is in charge of booking all of the evidence in the case. Lange wants Fung to take note of the size of the shoes in his report—and to compare them with the size of the shoes that made the bloody prints at South Bundy.

After leaving serology, Lange goes to his office. He sees Vannatter, who arrived at 6:45 A.M., and walks over to his desk. Vannatter, already slugging down black coffee, is organizing paperwork and rereviewing the list of items seized during the search at Simpson's estate.

Vannatter has just completed his two crime reports and two death reports, telephoned the West Los Angeles Division, and obtained two DR numbers, one for each victim—although the entire case will be listed under the main DR number given to Nicole Brown: 94-0817431. This number will now accompany every interview report and each piece of evidence cataloged and booked in this case.

The Robbery/Homicide Division office is oddly somber. No one is joking around; none of the usual wisecracks are going back and forth among the detectives, no gallows humor. The other RHD investigators are leaving Lange and Vannatter alone, allowing them to do their work while offering whatever assistance they can. To an extent, most of the other detectives have been where Lange and Vannatter are right now—in the midst of a big case and a media storm.

Vannatter has asked Detective Bud Watts of the Robbery/Homicide Division to go to the Print Shed, an old dilapidated Quonset hut just south of Parker Center where impounded vehicles are kept, to oversee the collection of the evidence in Simpson's Bronco by Dennis Fung.

As Lange sits at his desk, exchanging data about the two crime scenes with Vannatter, they are suddenly deluged by telephone calls, ranging from the LAPD high command and reporters to potential sources who want to offer up information.

These tips, usually provided anonymously, cause the LAPD to open a "clue book" for what would become 518 clues, 50 of which pointed to a variety of motives and suspects having nothing to do with Simpson. *All* fifty of these tips will also be investigated.[53] Among those clues taken seriously and not-so-seriously include:

- Clue #25: "Person reporting heard dog bark and saw man run across her front yard."
- Clue #92: "Neo-Nazi bikers claim Nicole killed due to interracial marriage."
- Clue #140: "Inmate states he was approached to kill the victims."
- Clue #156: "Waiter at Mezzaluna missing from work (suspect?)."
- Clue #170: "Mezzaluna is a cocaine distribution point and Goldman is supplying."
- Clue #174: "[Person reporting] confesses to killing victims with bayonet."
- Clues #177, #181, and #297: Jason Simpson [O.J. Simpson's oldest son] is the suspect."
- Clue #259 and #317: "Kato did it."
- Clue #262: "[Person reporting] saw a neighbor making a machete."

- Clue #263: "Nicole's family did it."
- Clue #264: "Psychic. Heard a voice. O.J. didn't do it."
- Clue #270: "Informant states the 'mob' committed murders."
- Clue #280: "Informant states Nicole 'laundering' money. Mob 'whacked' her."
- Clue #287: "Psychic. A serial killer involved."
- Clue #326: "Ambulance attendant did it . . ."
- Clue #328: "Two black men out of Houston did murders."
- Clue #337: "Hitman Johnny Reb killed victims."
- Clue #348: "Can prove Simpson didn't commit the murders."
- Clue #356: "Saw a Mercedes Benz follow Nicole from the Mezzaluna."
- Clue #362: "Caller confesses to murders."
- Clue #367: "Simpson didn't do it. [Caller] framed Simpson."
- Clue #368: "Indiana prisoner recruited to kill Nicole."
- Clue #380: "[Person reporting] has videotape. Killer is a male, white."
- Clue #384: "[Person reporting] states, 'This is all my fault.'"
- Clue #401: "Gang member paid $250,000 to kill Nicole."
- Clue #465: "[Person reporting] saw two guys grab Goldman and then attack Nicole."
- Clue #487: "Gang related murder."
- Clue #498: "[Person reporting provides] license number of vehicle involved in murders."
- Clue #499: "[Person reporting has] photo of man who knows real killers."
- Clue #510: "Fuhrman and Kato offered [person reporting] $100,000 to kill victims."

With all of the data and leads pouring in, Lange and Vannatter are already complaining that the LAPD is too slow to provide a separate, private, and secure room—with safe phones and locked file cabinets—for the duration of such high-profile cases. In fact, Lange goes into Captain Gartland's office to make this specific request. Gartland and Lieutenant Rogers, his supervisors, have always run interference for Lange, Vannatter, and the other Robbery/Homicide detectives with the LAPD brass, the district attorney's office, and the media. If there is a political problem, Gartland or Rogers will handle it; if detectives need something, they will help them get it. If investigators have a personal problem, Gartland's and Rogers's doors are always open to them.

Soon after Lange enters Gartland's office, Vannatter joins his partner. Rogers is also present. After quickly briefing their supervisors about the unfolding events since they last talked yesterday—while making their pitch for a secure location to do their work—Vannatter looks at his watch and tells his partner, "We have autopsies."

The two detectives excuse themselves from the meeting and head for Lange's car.

Before going to the coroner's office, they make a quick stop at the Print Shed, where they see Detective Watts and criminalist Fung, who is working on the blood evidence in the Bronco.

Stating the obvious, Vannatter tells Fung, "Dennis, I want everything that even looks like blood collected, taken back to the lab, and analyzed. Get back to us as soon as you can."

Fung nods and continues working as Watts assists.

At 8:30 A.M., Lange and Vannatter arrive at the county coroner's office. The two detectives come in through the back, where bodies are routinely delivered. They show a guard their identification and sign in, a procedure they have become accustomed to after viewing hundreds of autopsies.

They walk into the dressing room and spend about fifteen minutes putting on long-sleeve disposable gowns, foot and head protectors, masks, goggles, and gloves. As he is putting on his gear, Lange remembers the good old days—before communicable diseases and airborne pathogens became of widespread concern—when a detective could just walk into an autopsy room in his street clothes, smoking a cigar or eating a sandwich. Like Vannatter, Lange has trained himself to view murder victims as evidence, even as mannequins, during autopsies, disassociating himself psychologically from them.

Actually, Lange, a U.S. Marine sergeant and combat veteran, had already seen it all, getting his experience as a U.S. Marine combat veteran in the Marble Mountain area of Vietnam. He was a member of the First Battalion, Ninth Marines, nicknamed "The Walking Dead" because of the enormous number of casualties they suffered during the war.

Lange received a Bronze Star for valor in March 1966 during his eleven-month tour of duty. Lange had been decorated for crawling through a minefield to save a South Vietnamese soldier who had stepped on an antipersonnel mine, which blew off his leg. Lange picked up the soldier, along with what was left of his leg, and walked back through the minefield to safety. In the wake of Lange's action, the Vietnamese soldier survived.

After putting on their autopsy-room garb, Lange and Vannatter walk toward one of several preparation rooms. In the hallway just outside the room, a line of bodies—including Ron Goldman's, which is covered with a blood-soaked sheet—are lying on gurneys, ready for posting.

Inside the main autopsy room, the two detectives see that work is being done on all of the other tables: It's a full house today.

Dr. Irwin Golden—whom the two detectives have nicknamed "The Mad Scientist" because of his job, odd appearance, and offbeat sense of humor—greets the detectives. Lange and Vannatter have known Dr. Golden for years and respect him both as an intelligent and extremely competent medical examiner and as a good and decent man. He has probably examined fifteen to twenty thousand bodies during his career.

Golden, who looks a little like Dr. Frankenstein in his surgical wardrobe, teases, "Damn, you guys, you've brought me another high-profile case!" Then all smiles fade as they look at the body before them.

Nicole Brown is completely nude on the last metal table in a row of eight. The dirt and blood have been cleaned from her body.[54] Her massive wounds are now sharply visible.

Lange had spent much of the previous day viewing Brown's body at the crime scene and is familiar with her brutalized condition. Vannatter had only spent a short time at South Bundy and is struck by the severity of her wounds and the fact that she has nearly been decapitated.

While her injuries are being charted and measured by Dr. Golden, the coroner's photographer is taking pictures, as he will continue to do throughout the autopsy. Brown is also being examined for other external injuries to her scalp and hands. As a matter of routine her vagina and rectum are visually inspected for possible rape; there is no evidence of any sexual violence or any recent sexual encounter.

Other than the obvious fatal wounds, Lange and Vannatter see a large contusion toward the back of her head, indicating blunt-force trauma. Both Dr. Golden and the detectives speculate that the assailant struck her before slashing her. Because the bottoms of her feet were clean at the crime scene, Lange believes that she did not get up after being struck down. But defense slash wounds on her hands show that she might have initially tried to ward off her attacker.

Lange and Vannatter are aware of the flood of sick O.J. jokes that are already circulating throughout the country—from Wall Street to Hollywood. They know about the gossipy cocktail-party chatter this case has caused, as well as the kinetic media frenzy surrounding their investigation. And they know that all of that would probably be silenced if the people so enamored with this crime could see this autopsy. This is where the stark results of the act of murder can be witnessed.

Before opening her chest cavity, Dr. Golden slits Brown's breasts and removes her silicone implants—in order to get at the organs beneath them. Then, he makes a Y-incision with a sharp scalpel from each of her shoulders into the center of the breastbone and straight down through the navel to the pubic area. He grabs a flap of her skin, using a scalpel to slice away the flesh that is still attached to the bone. Peeling the skin back, Dr. Golden exposes her entire chest cavity. He takes a large pair of clippers and cuts out her rib cage.

Removing Brown's individual organs, he then weighs and examines each, slicing off cross sections on a carving board and taking fluid samples for analysis.

Because of the large open wound in her neck, Brown had nearly bled out at the crime scene; her body has retained little blood. To obtain a legitimate sample, Golden cuts into her chest and collects what is left. The blood flows downward along the metal table and into a large reservoir. The blood will later be ladled out and placed in jars, which will be labeled.

After her intestines are taken out and analyzed, Brown's stomach is removed and placed in a metal pan. Dr. Golden cuts it open, again weighing and examining the contents. Lange takes notes of his observations. Everyone can see that her last meal consisted of pasta, spinach, and other miscellaneous vegetables. Brown's stomach is full, indicating that she had died very shortly after eating.

When the examination of the stomach contents is completed, they are disposed of in a waste container.

Even though Dr. Golden is speaking and taking notes as he works, Lange and Vannatter are engaging him in constant conversation, asking questions about what he is discovering. And Dr. Golden is asking questions, too: "How did you find her? . . . Was there a lot of blood at the scene? . . . What position was her head in? . . . What else did you see at the scene?" Several times during the course of the autopsy, the county coroner, Dr. Lakshmanan Sathyavagiswaran, appears and asks his own questions of Dr. Golden and the detectives.

Although the photographs from the LAPD/SID Photography Unit have not yet been developed, Dr. Golden refers to the Polaroid shots taken by coroner investigator Claudine Ratcliffe as a frame of reference for the crime scene.

After Dr. Golden completes the internal examination on Brown, he takes a scalpel and begins cutting in back of her ears, along the lower portion of the skull. Then, he cuts in and up to the temporal area on both sides of the head. As with cutting skin from the rib cage, Dr. Golden slices away the galea between her scalp and the skull. After this maneuver, her skin is simply peeled from the back to the front, right over her face, exposing the skull. Once revealed, her skull is examined for injuries. Although the blow to the back of her head is clearly visible, it has not fractured her skull.

Then, a coroner's assistant, using a small handheld electric saw, cuts in basically the same pattern as for removing the skin. When that is completed, he lifts the skullcap, now exposing her brain. He looks for evidence of brain damage and internal bleeding. When he finds none, Dr. Golden snips her brain at its stem and removes it from the skull cavity. He weighs it, examines it from all angles, and slices off portions for further examination.

In his analysis of Brown's specific cause of death, Dr. Golden details four fatal penetration wounds. The most severe is obviously the neck wound that nearly took off her head. In fact, the knife that killed her had actually nicked her spinal column. The front portion of her vertebrae is clearly visible while she is lying on her back. Both carotid arteries are completely severed. Her right jugular vein is nearly totally cut; the other is severely injured.

Because of the possibility of an imprint of a shoe on her back, as well as the lack of blood on the bottoms of her feet at the crime scene, Dr. Golden discusses how this wound could have been inflicted. While the killer had her facedown on the ground, he might have simply placed his foot on her back, pulled her head back with her long blond hair, and slashed her throat from behind.[55]

There are no apparent "taunting" wounds on Brown's body. That is, her killer did not appear to torture her. He killed her quickly and viciously.

However, she has three other serious knife wounds. And, with the use of probes, Dr. Golden can determine which wounds were made with a slashing motion or a stabbing blow and from which direction the knife struck the body. Also, judging from the nature of the wounds, Dr. Golden determines that the killer is right-handed and probably slashed her throat, left to right from behind.

Dr. Golden concludes almost matter-of-factly that Brown's death has resulted from multiple slash and stab wounds, resulting from an "overkill" or "rage killing," as Lange suspected when he first saw her body the day before.

At the end of this autopsy, the coroner's assistants wrap all of her organs in plastic, with the exception of those portions pared off for further examination. Then they restore all of these organs to her open abdominal cavity; her rib cage is put back into place. After her brain, also wrapped in plastic, is placed back into the body, a coroner's assistant fits her skullcap on her head and pulls her skin back away from her face. The assistant then sews her back together.

Dr. Golden's assistant wraps her entire body in heavy plastic, secured with a nylon cord. She is placed on a gurney and wheeled into a cold-storage facility where she will remain, stacked with other bodies, until a mortician, authorized by the Brown family, arrives to take her to a funeral home. Brown's autopsy has taken nearly two hours—after which the table and the surrounding area is washed down and mopped up.

Golden's assistant wheels in Goldman, who is placed on the same table as Brown. There is no coffee break between the two autopsies.

Covered with blood and dirt, Goldman's clothing has been removed, and he has been completely cleaned up. Both detectives notice that he has a tattoo about two inches in height on his outer left shoulder. It almost looks like an abstract, three-dimensional stick man with one leg.

Like Brown, Goldman has a large contusion on the back of his head, which might indicate that he had been struck from behind by the killer.

Although no obvious "taunting-type" wounds appeared on Brown's body, several appear on Goldman's. A long, nonfatal cut is found across his neck. Five nonfatal puncture wounds are discovered on his cheek. In other words, before killing Goldman, the killer tortured him with his knife, inflicting nonfatal sticking and cutting motions that penetrated his skin and must have caused tremendous pain. A series of postmortem wounds indicate that the killer had continued to stab and slash Goldman after he had clinically died. These telltale wounds do not draw blood—because the heart has already stopped pumping.

Numerous slashing and stabbing wounds are obvious on Goldman's body; some even intersect. A cutting wound to the left side of his neck has completely severed his left jugular vein. Two stab wounds penetrated the right side of his chest, perforating his thorax and right lung. A stab wound went into the left side of his abdomen, cutting the abdominal aorta. Another significant injury is a deep stab wound to the femoral artery in his upper left leg, which had caused an enormous amount of bleeding. This is one of four fatal penetration wounds inflicted on him by the killer.

Also, Dr. Golden estimates the time of death as sometime between 9:00 P.M. and midnight—but closer to 9:00—on the evening of June 12. He uses the temperatures of both bodies at the time of their recovery from the crime scene as variables in his equation.

On the basis of his two examinations, Golden believes that the killer used a sharp single-edged knife—at least six inches in length with a thickness of 1/32 of an inch—to kill both victims. Because of the tearing effects of the intersecting wounds on Goldman's body, a ruthless defense attorney could use this phenomenon to claim that *two* killers with *two* different knives might have committed the murders.[56]

However, Dr. Golden and the detectives conclude that there was probably only one killer. This opinion is based primarily on the single set of bloody shoe prints leading away from the two bodies, as well as the similarities of the inflicted wounds on both victims.[57]

Endnotes

52. The actual cause for the red spots on Simpson's Reeboks was not determined. Such testing was not of any importance after blood had been ruled out.

53. Working on the "clue book" and follow-up investigations with Lange and Vannatter were RHD Detectives Rich Crotsley and Ron Ito.

54. Lange later discovered that the blood pattern he had observed on Brown's back—a single, jagged splatter drop about the size of a quarter—had never been collected by the coroner's criminalist, even though Lange had made a specific request that this be done. Although the blood pattern appears in crime-scene photographs, the evidence was lost for serological analysis after a coroner's assistant washed down her body at the morgue.

Lange did note that this pattern on Brown's back was similar to a blood pattern on Goldman's boot, which was analyzed. The analysis indicated that it was a combination of both Brown's and Goldman's blood, which probably was cast off from the murder weapon.

55. The Simpson defense team later created a controversy when one of its expert witnesses, Dr. Michael Baden, disputed the medical examiner's claim that a shoe print was present on Brown's back. Dr. Baden offered a counterexplanation that the discoloration on Brown's back resulted from the "shifting" lividity in her body.

However, no one in the coroner's office, the LAPD, or the prosecution team—who all laughed at this explanation—knew what Dr. Baden was talking about when he referred to "shifting" lividity. After death, a person's blood, due to the forces of gravity, sinks to the lowest part of their body, where it coagulates and becomes fixed after an hour or two hours. (That is how homicide investigators determine whether a body has been moved. For instance, if a dead person lying on his back is found to have lividity on his front, the detective knows that the body has been turned over.) In short, there is no such thing as "shifting" lividity.

56. Although Los Angeles coroner Lakshmanan Sathyavagiswaran later testified that he believed that one person could have committed both murders with a single-edged knife, he could not say so conclusively with a reasonable degree of medical certainty.

57. The Simpson defense team later created a controversy, claiming that there was another type of footprint at the South Bundy crime scene, not accounted for by the LAPD. Defense expert witness Dr. Henry Lee insisted that a series of uniform lines on the walkway of the South Bundy crime scene appeared to be another shoe print, indicating a second killer might have been at the scene.

However, when the LAPD and the FBI returned to South Bundy for another examination in the wake of Lee's testimony, FBI Special Agent Bill Bodziak discovered that Dr. Lee's "shoe-print impressions" were nothing more than trowel marks left by workers on the walkway at the time the tiled areas were poured. Bodziak could actually feel the marks with his fingers.

10

Grunt Work

Shortly before noon, Lange and Vannatter leave the coroner's office for a light lunch at the police academy, which is about three miles away. After eating, they return to the Robbery/Homicide Division, get on the telephone, and continue to goose the crime lab to expedite its blood analysis.

Knowing that blood will make or break their case against Simpson, they spend much of the day running background checks on the two victims, based initially on the information contained on their driver's licenses.[58] Remembering the crime scene, with the lit candles and the soft music, Lange and Vannatter want to understand the relationship between the thirty-five-year-old scantily clad Nicole Brown and the handsome Ronald Goldman, ten years her junior.

After calling only a handful of sources, Lange and Vannatter manage to put together a picture of the relationship between Simpson and Brown, as well as Brown and Goldman.

O.J. Simpson, born on July 9, 1947, and Nicole Brown, born on May 19, 1959, began dating in June 1977. At the time, Simpson was still married to his first wife of ten years, Marguerite, with whom he had two children, Arnelle and Jason. Arnelle was born on the same day that Simpson won the Heisman Trophy in December 1968; Jason was born in 1970. Simpson played three lackluster years for the Buffalo Bills until 1972, when he ran for 1,125 yards. In 1973, he became the first running back in NFL history to run for over 2,000 yards in a single season. Simpson's success on the gridiron and attractive appearance led to roles in motion pictures, like *The Towering Inferno* and a major advertising campaign for Hertz. In January 1977, he had a feature role in the widely popular television mini-series, *Roots*.

In October 1977, while the Simpson-Brown relationship was heating up, Simpson's wife gave birth to their third child, Aaren. Within a year—after Simpson had been traded to the San Francisco 49ers—the couple separated as Simpson grew closer to Brown, who had moved in with him. In August 1979, during the separation and just before Simpson had retired from pro football to become an ABC sports commentator, Aaren Simpson tragically drowned after falling into Simpson's swimming pool at North Rockingham. The following year, according to the detectives' information, the Simpsons divorced.

On February 2, 1985—the same year as his induction into the Pro Football Hall of Fame—Simpson married Brown, and the following October, she gave birth to their first child, Sydney. Three years later, they had a son, Justin.

According to sources developed by Lange and Vannatter, the Simpson-Brown marriage ran hot and cold. Slippage in Simpson's acting and broadcasting career seemed to be accompanied by rumors of increasing physical abuse toward his wife. By 1990, Simpson had left ABC and joined NBC Sports to provide commentary on NFL American Football Conference games.

The Simpsons separated in January 1992, when Nicole moved into a rented home on Gretna Green Way. She filed for divorce a month later, and the divorce became final on October 15 of that year. They maintained joint custody of their children; it was agreed that Sydney and Justin would live with their mother 90 percent of the time.

According to members of Brown's family, the couple had continued to see each other from time to time, even attempting an occasional reconciliation. But when Brown purchased her own home on South Bundy in January 1994, that act appeared to become her declaration of independence from Simpson.

On the night of the murders, as Juditha Brown had told Lange during the early-morning call of June 13, the Brown family had gone to a dance recital for Sydney at the Paul Revere Middle School in Brentwood. Both Nicole Brown and O.J. Simpson were present, but they sat apart and didn't speak to each other.

After Sydney's recital on June 12, the Brown family and some friends went to the Mezzaluna restaurant, where Nicole introduced everyone to Ronald Goldman, a waiter at the restaurant who did modeling on the side and hoped to become an actor someday.

According to Cora Fischman, Brown's friend and neighbor, Nicole had first met Goldman about a month earlier at a local Starbucks coffeeshop. Brown and Goldman became fast friends and, apparently, nothing more—although the detectives realized, of course, that their relationship could have gone further had they not been killed.

The detectives learn that after the Browns returned home from the dinner, Juditha Brown realized she had lost her glasses. She telephoned the restaurant, and an employee, Karen Crawford, found the glasses and placed them in an envelope. Juditha said that she would have Nicole pick them up. After Juditha called her daughter at about 9:40 P.M., Nicole called Goldman, who offered to bring over the glasses on his way home.

After leaving work about ten minutes later—but before going to Brown's house—Goldman, who was driving his girlfriend's car, stopped at his apartment on Gorham Avenue, which is only about a two-minute drive from Nicole's home. He had plans to have a drink with Stewart Tanner, a bartender at Mezzaluna, later that night. Tanner had been the person who had called Goldman on his pager at the crime scene.

Apparently, soon after arriving at Brown's home to deliver the envelope with the glasses inside, Goldman was attacked and murdered, along with Nicole.

Adding to Lange and Vannatter's knowledge of the night of the murders is a typed-up report from Detectives Brian Carr and Paul Tippin of their follow-up interview with Kato Kaelin.

Kaelin told Carr and Tippin that he had first met Nicole Brown in 1992 while skiing in Aspen. She had separated from O.J. Simpson in January 1992 and filed for divorce the following month.

Back in Los Angeles, Brown invited Kaelin, an aspiring actor, to a party at her rented home, then on Gretna Green Way in Brentwood, which was one street west of South Bundy. At the time, Kaelin lived in Hermosa Beach, a small community on the Pacific Ocean near Torrance, which is south of L.A.

Brown and Kaelin became friends. Kaelin, who wanted to move closer to town, asked her if he could rent a guest house in the back of her large residence—where she lived with her two children, Sydney and Justin. She agreed, charging him between $400 and $500 a month. The friendly and affable Kaelin also took care of Brown's children, on occasion, when she was away.

When the Simpson's divorce became final, Simpson, who often visited his kids at Brown's home, also became friendly with Kaelin—after realizing that he and Brown were friends and only friends.

When Brown purchased her home on South Bundy in January 1994, she asked Kaelin if he wanted to rent the spare room at her new house. He agreed, but then changed his mind when Simpson offered him a rent-free bungalow at his estate on North Rockingham. Brown and Simpson were in the midst of an attempted reconciliation, and Simpson did not want Kaelin's presence to complicate matters. When Brown moved to South Bundy, Kaelin brought his things out to Simpson's home.

On June 12—the day of the murders—Simpson told Kaelin that he planned to attend his daughter's dance recital at 5:00 P.M. After the recital, Simpson returned to his home.

Later that evening, sometime after 9:00, Simpson, who was wearing a dark sweatsuit, asked Kaelin if he wanted to accompany him to McDonald's. When Kaelin said he did, Simpson, who insisted that he only had large bills in his pocket, asked Kato for a loan. Simpson said that he wanted enough money to tip the skycap later that night when he went to the airport. Kaelin gave him twenty dollars. (Later, Kaelin revealed that he paid for the food at McDonald's with another twenty-dollar bill, handing it to Simpson at the drive-thru window. Although Simpson claimed to have needed change for the skycap, he returned all of it to Kaelin.)

After they returned from McDonald's, Simpson and Kaelin went their separate ways. Kaelin did not see Simpson again until after he heard the "thumps" on his back wall at about 10:45 P.M. A few minutes later, he went outside to investigate, believing that there had been an earthquake.

At that time, he saw the white limousine at the Ashford Street gate and let the driver onto the property. During their conversation, the driver told Kaelin that he had just reached Simpson on the intercom; Simpson had said that he overslept and was running late. Kaelin asked the driver if he had felt an earthquake during the past few minutes. The driver said he had not.

Simpson came out of the house with his luggage and golf clubs. Both Kaelin and the driver helped load the bags into the limousine—although there was one, Kaelin later said, that Simpson would not allow him to touch. That bag, a half-moon-shaped duffel bag, Simpson insisted on handling himself. Before leaving, Simpson told Kaelin that he would return the following night.

With Kaelin's full account now in the case file, Lange and Vannatter work to establish whether or not the two leather gloves—the left-hand glove at South Bundy and the right-hand glove at North Rockingham—are Simpson's. Also, they are trying to identify the kind of shoes that made the bloody shoe prints found at the South Bundy crime scene.

Marcia Clark remains in hourly telephone contact with Vannatter, who gives her updates about their progress in the case. Although Lange continues to be upset about her involvement, he cooperates fully with her. Like Lange, she is pushing hard for the blood evidence, which will dictate whether or not this case will be filed at all.

After Vannatter's 3:00 P.M. call to Clark, the two detectives receive Dennis Fung's latest property report, which includes:

- Item #18: "Shoes, Athletic, 'Reebok,' white—recovered from Det. Lange at 830 1-14-94."
- Item #19: "Hair and fibers—removed from Item #9." [Item #9 is the bloody right-handed glove found on the south walkway at Simpson's residence.]

Items #20–34 are a list of evidence collected from Simpson's Bronco that day:

- Item #20: "Cloth swatch used to transfer red stain—recovered from the exterior passenger door . . ."

- Item #21: "Cloth swatch used to transfer red stain—recovered from the driver door, interior . . ."
- Item #22: "Cloth swatch used to transfer red stain—recovered from the driver door, interior . . ."
- Item #23: "Cloth swatch used to transfer red stain—recovered from the driver door, interior . . ."
- Item #24: "Cloth swatch used to transfer red stain—recovered from the instrumental panel . . ."[59]
- Item #25: "Fibers, carpet, brown, with red stains—recovered from the driver floor . . ."
- Item #26: "Cloth swatch used to transfer red stain—recovered from the driver floor . . ."
- Item #27: "Cap, plaid—recovered from the driver floor . . ."
- Item #28: "Cloth swatch used to transfer red stain—recovered from the driver seat . . ."
- Item #29: "Cloth swatch used to transfer red stain—recovered on the steering wheel at the 7 o'clock position (wheels straight)."[60]
- Item #30: "Cloth swatch used to transfer red stain—recovered from the center console . . ."[61]
- Item #31: "Cloth swatch used to transfer red stain—recovered from the center console . . ."[62]
- Item #32: "Cloth swatch used to transfer red stain—recovered from the front passenger backrest, front face . . ."
- Item #33: "Carpet, brown, with red stain resembling a partial shoe print—recovered from the driver floor."[63]
- Item #34: "Cloth swatch used to transfer red stain—recovered from the driver wall . . ."[64]

Also, Fung books the evidence he had collected at the South Bundy crime scene the day before, which includes:

- Item #35: "Keys—recovered from the ground . . . north of south walkway edge." (These were the keys for the car Ron Goldman borrowed from his girlfriend.)
- Item #36: "Pager, black, 'Motorola' . . ."
- Item #37: "Glove, leather, with red stain, left-handed—recovered from ground . . ."
- Item #38: "Cap, watchman, blue—recovered from the ground . . ."[65]
- Item #39: "Eyeglasses, within envelope, with red stains—recovered from the ground . . ."

- Item #40: "Ring, metal, white—recovered from the ground . . ."
- Item #41: "Cloth swatch used to transfer red stain—recovered from the tree stump . . ."
- Item #42: "Cloth swatch used to transfer red stain—recovered from the walkway . . ."
- Item #43: "Cloth swatch used to transfer red stain—recovered from the fence . . ."
- Item #44: "Cloth swatch used to transfer red stain—recovered from the fence . . ."
- Item #45: "Cloth swatch used to transfer red stain—recovered from the rail . . ."
- Item #46: "Menu, paper, 'Thai Flavor'—recovered from the ground . . ."
- Item #47: "Cloth swatch used to transfer red stain—recovered from the walkway . . ."[66]
- Item #48: "Cloth swatch used to transfer red stain—recovered . . . west of the west curb . . . north of north curb."[67]
- Item #49: "Cloth swatch used to transfer red stain—recovered . . . west of the west curb . . . north of the north wall."[68]
- Item #50: "Cloth swatch used to transfer red stain—recovered . . . east of the west edge of the rear driveway . . ."[69]
- Item #51: "Cloth swatch used to transfer red stain—recovered from the front gate . . ."
- Item #52: "Cloth swatch used to transfer red stain—recovered from the rear driveway . . ."[70]
- Item #53: "(1) dime and (1) penny totaling 11 [cents]—recovered from the driveway . . ."
- Item #54: "Cloth [swatch] used to transfer red stain—recovered from the front gate . . ."
- Item #55: "Cloth swatch used to transfer red stain—recovered from the walkway . . ."
- Item #56: "Cloth swatch used to transfer red stain—recovered from the walkway . . ."
- Item #57: "Label, 'Bonita Ecuador,' with red stain—recovered from the walkway . . ."
- Item #58: "Hair—recovered with Item #8 [a cloth swatch used to transfer a red stain, recovered from the driveway]."

In his cursory review of the sparsely detailed property report, Lange does *not* notice that Fung failed to collect the blood on the rear gate that leads to the back alley at the South Bundy crime scene.

Other than waiting for the blood-evidence results, Lange and Vannatter's biggest problem at this point is the management of all the information pouring into their office. Because they still haven't received a secure area from which to work, Lange again asks Lieutenant Rogers to plow through the bureaucracy to get them a room where they can work quietly and in private.[71]

In the midst of their paper chase and the continuing barrage of calls, Vannatter receives a telephone tip that Simpson had purchased a knife at Ross Cutlery on South Broadway in downtown Los Angeles. Trying to confirm the story, Vannatter asks Detectives Luper and Watts to drive to the store.

Soon after, Luper and Watts call Vannatter from Ross Cutlery, telling him that Simpson, while shooting a movie at a nearby location, had purchased a German-made "Stiletto" folding knife, fifteen-inches long when fully extended, with a six-inch blade. He bought the knife on May 3, about six weeks earlier. At the time of its purchase, Simpson asked a clerk to have the knife sharpened. Vannatter tells Luper to buy a replica of the knife and bring it back to the office.

Then, Lange asks Detectives Carr and Tippin to track down the limousine driver who had taken Simpson to LAX on the night of the murders. Dale St. John, the owner of the Torrance-based Town & Country Limousine service, had called in voluntarily to give the police the name of his driver, Allan Park.

When Luper and Watts return from the cutlery store, Lange and Vannatter take the knife they purchased. Then, Vannatter asks Luper, along with his partner Detective LeFall, to retrace Simpson's steps—from the time he boarded the plane to Chicago at LAX on the night of the murders to the time he returned the following day. They want the two detectives to search Simpson's hotel room again—which had already been seized and searched by the Chicago police. Luper and LeFall are also to bring back any evidence already found. This includes the bloodstained washcloth and bedding, as well as the broken glass Simpson shattered in the sink, which, he claimed, might have caused the cuts on his left-middle finger. Lange and Vannatter also ask Luper and LeFall to arrange a search of the surrounding area for any evidence of blood, including bloody clothing and perhaps even a knife. A source in Chicago has told Chicago police detectives that he had seen a man fitting Simpson's description walk into a vacant field behind the O'Hare Plaza Hotel.[72]

Widening their net, Lange and Vannatter also assign other detectives to obtain the June 12 passenger list for American Airlines #668, the red-eye flight Simpson had taken to Chicago on the night of the murders, as well as for his return flight, American Airlines #1691, on the morning of June 13. They want statements about the highly recognizable celebrity's demeanor and movements during the trip.[73]

After nearly a thirteen-hour day, both detectives leave the office at about 8:00 P.M., logging in another day with major overtime.

As they are driving home in separate cars and in different directions, Vannatter has little doubt that Simpson is the killer; Lange is still only 90 percent sure because the blood results are still not in. Both detectives realize that they have an extremely strong circumstantial case against Simpson. But they, as well as Marcia Clark and the district attorney's office, want blood, literally, to make this case go.

When both Lange and Vannatter arrive home, they immediately turn on the television news, concerned about what the media is reporting about the case. All of the local reporters covering the Los Angeles police beat know Tom Lange and Phil Vannatter. And, almost without exception, the detectives know them and respect their work.

But now with the Simpson case, a new herd of tabloid reporters are stampeding into the city. And many of them seem to believe that evidence is like a balloon: It's no good unless you blow it up. Suddenly, to some reporters, the rust-stained clothing in Simpson's washing machine has somehow become bloody clothing, or Jason Simpson, O.J.'s oldest son, has become a suspect in the case. Neither of these stories—and so many others like them—have any basis in fact, and yet they are finding their way into print and/or on television. Lange and Vannatter know that an already sensational murder case is about to become surreal.

Endnotes

58. The detectives also ran routine checks on the whereabouts of Jason Simpson, O.J.'s oldest son, and A.C. Cowlings, O.J.'s close friend, at the time of the murders. Both men were investigated and quickly eliminated as suspects.

The LAPD crime lab did find a partial print, linked to Cowling's left hand, on the left running board in Simpson's Bronco. Apparently, Cowlings had been sitting in the driver's seat of the car at some time in the past. Lange and Vannatter could find no relevance to this information and agreed that Cowlings was not under any suspicion. However, they could not rule out his possible complicity *after* the crime.

59. Scientific analysis later determined that this bloodstain was consistent with Simpson's blood.

60. Scientific analysis later determined that this bloodstain was consistent with a mixture of Simpson's and Brown's blood.

61. Scientific analysis later determined that this bloodstain was consistent with Simpson's blood.

62. Scientific analysis later determined that this bloodstain was consistent with a mixture of Simpson's and Goldman's blood.

63. Scientific analysis later determined that this bloodstain was consistent with Nicole Brown's blood.

64. Scientific analysis later determined that this bloodstain was consistent with Simpson's blood.

65. Scientific analysis later showed that the knit cap contained fibers consistent with the carpet in Simpson's Bronco, as well as twelve hairs that were consistent with Simpson's hair.

66. Scientific analysis later determined that this blood spot was consistent with Simpson's blood. In fact, DNA/RFLP testing showed that the frequency that this blood spot found on the walkway could be that of anyone *but* Simpson would be 1 in 240,000.

67. Scientific analysis later determined that this blood spot was consistent with Simpson's blood.

68. Scientific analysis later determined that this blood spot was consistent with Simpson's blood.

69. Scientific analysis later determined that this blood spot was consistent with Simpson's blood.

70. Scientific analysis later determined that this blood spot was consistent with Simpson's blood. In fact, DNA/RFLP testing showed that the frequency that this blood spot found on the walkway could be that of anyone *but* Simpson would be 1 in 170 million.

71. Lange and Vannatter *finally* received their secure room—a real office with locks on the doors and file cabinets—on October 10, 1994. Everyone knew it as simply "The O.J. Room." Lange, Vannatter, and Lieutenant John Rogers had the only keys to this office.

72. A search was later conducted, but nothing of any significance was ever found.

73. All of the passengers contacted by the police who saw Simpson described him as upbeat and pleasant during the flight to Chicago. None of them noticed any cuts on the middle finger of his left hand. One passenger did say that Simpson frequently went to the lavatory during the flight.

11

Blood and More Blood

Wednesday, June 15, 1994

When Vannatter arrives at his office at 7:00 A.M., Lange is already on the telephone with Greg Matheson of the SID Serology Unit, still trying to get an estimate of when the blood analysis will be completed. Matheson says he will get back to Lange within the hour.

When Lange gets off the telephone, Vannatter pulls out the knife that Detectives Luper and Watts received from Ross Cutlery the previous day, telling his partner, "Tom, I'm going to go over to the coroner's office and show this knife to Dr. Golden. We need to find out if it's consistent with the victims' injuries. This might be the kind of murder weapon we're looking for."

Lange is still focused on the blood evidence. He anxiously asks Vannatter, "Phil, what about the blood from the autopsies? Matheson says that it hasn't even been picked up by SID yet."

"Okay, while I'm over there, I'll pick up the blood samples," Vannatter assures his partner. "We're going to need them for the preliminary testing against the evidence samples we've recovered. I'll show the doctor the knife, and then I'll run the blood samples over to serology."

As Vannatter leaves the office, Lange continues assembling his growing case file. He wants it cleared to the district attorney's office by the end of the week so that they can arrest Simpson.

At 8:00 A.M., Vannatter arrives at the coroner's office and immediately proceeds to Dr. Golden's office on the second floor. Handing the medical examiner the knife, Vannatter asks the doctor, "Could a knife like this possibly be the murder weapon?"

Dr. Golden carefully examines the knife, measuring its dimensions, and looks at his notes from the autopsies the previous day. After a few moments of studying the knife, Golden responds, "This could be the type of knife that did it, considering the size of the single-edged blade and the depth of the slashing and stabbing wounds on the victims."

After asking a few follow-up questions, Vannatter continues, "The other thing is: I need to take the blood samples with me. I've got to get them to SID as soon as possible, so we can start the analysis."

"Okay, follow me," Dr. Golden says, getting up from his chair. Vannatter and the doctor walk just down the hall into the coroner's own laboratory. Dr. Golden says to one of the technicians, "Vannatter here wants to pick up the blood samples from the Brown-Goldman autopsies that we did yesterday."

A technician opens a metal upright refrigerator and pulls out two vials of blood, which have been labeled and identified. He places each of the vials in separate envelopes and hands them over to Vannatter.

But, before allowing the detective to walk away, the technician has him sign an evidence inventory form to show that they have been released directly to him, keeping the documented chain of custody intact. After Vannatter signs for the two blood samples, he leaves for Piper Tech, the location of the serology unit, which is less than a five-minute drive from the coroner's office.

It is unusual for a lead detective to pick up the blood at the coroner's office and personally transport it to the police crime lab. However, LAPD policy provides the investigating officer with the power to control the evidence in his or her case.

Because of the intense pressure to complete the blood evidence testing, the intense media interest in this case, and the fact that the police have a prime suspect, as well as his statement, photographs of his cut finger, and a vial of his blood, Vannatter, who believes that he has "a smoking gun" case, decides to expedite matters. Instead of waiting for someone from the SID to pick up the blood whenever he or she gets around to it, Vannatter is handling the chore personally.

Back at Robbery/Homicide, Lange receives the promised call from Matheson. "We're still working on the blood," Matheson tells Lange. "We've started some initial DNA-PCR testing, and those results will be back in a day or two. We can also do some conventional testing, A-B-O-type stuff. This will tell us if we're at least in the ballpark with this guy as a suspect. The more discriminating RFLP testing is not done by our lab. We can't do that here. We have to send it out."

Very simply, other than identical twins, no two people have the same DNA, a "blueprint" molecule with chemically coded information that identifies a person's hereditary composition. DNA has been used both to solve crimes and to exonerate persons wrongly accused. DNA testing can be accomplished with samples of a suspect's blood, body tissue, hair roots, saliva, or semen.

For this investigation, two basic DNA tests will be used: PCR, which is a copying process in which a small sample of DNA may be duplicated and tested; RFLP is more sophisticated, using special enzymes from a larger sample that act as molecular scissors, which can cut out a portion of DNA for testing. PCR is generally used to eliminate someone under suspicion; RFLP testing is much more definitive and can single out a suspect to the exclusion of everyone else in the world.

Vannatter arrives at Piper Tech, signing in about five minutes after leaving the coroner's office. He goes directly to Greg Matheson's office in the serology unit. Matheson, who has just gotten off the telephone with Lange, greets Vannatter and introduces him to Collin Yamauchi, an LAPD/SID blood specialist whom Vannatter has never met before.

Holding up the two envelopes, Vannatter tells Matheson, "Here are the vials of blood from the coroner's office."

"Good," Matheson replies. "Give them to Collin, because he's going to be doing the preliminary work."

Vannatter hands the two envelopes to Yamauchi, saying, "Now, you're going to see that these get booked, right?"

"Yes," Yamauchi responds, "I'll take care of everything."

Yamauchi gives the blood to Dennis Fung at 8:30 A.M., who books them on his growing property report, noting:

- Item #59: "[Vial], containing whole blood, labeled . . . 'Brown, Simpson Nicole'—received from Det. Vannatter."
- Item #60: "[Vial], containing whole blood, labeled . . . 'Goldman, Ronald'—received from Det. Vannatter."

After dropping off the coroner's blood samples, Vannatter returns to his office. As soon as he arrives at his desk, he picks up his telephone and calls Marcia Clark. Vannatter relays to her that, according to Dr. Golden, a knife identical to the one obtained from Ross Cutlery could have been the murder weapon. He also tells her that he has picked up the blood samples from the coroner's office and delivered them to the SID Serology Unit. Clark seems pleased but pushes Vannatter: "Phil, we need the blood results as quickly as possible."

Sensing how impatient she is, Vannatter replies, "Marcia, we need them as badly as you do. We're moving this as fast as we can. When we have the results, you'll have the results. I promise."

To coordinate the activities between the LAPD and the district attorney's office, Vannatter arranges the first organizational meeting among the principals involved in the Simpson case to take place at 1:00 that afternoon.

At noon, an hour before the big meeting between the LAPD and the district attorney's office, Los Angeles attorney Robert Shapiro—who is well known for his defense of Hollywood celebrities like Johnny Carson and Christian Brando—strides into the Robbery/Homicide Division. Ironically, Shapiro had also represented Bruce Roman, a Los Angeles dentist who had been present at the 1989 accidental shooting of Marcia Clark's first ex-husband, Gabriel Horowitz, who survived the wounds but was left paralyzed. No charges were filed in the mishap.[74]

"I am now representing Mr. Simpson," Shapiro announces to the detectives.

Lange and Vannatter, who are joined by Captain Gartland and Lieutenant Rogers, shake hands with the lawyer and ask him what they can do for him.

Shapiro responds, "I would like to offer you the services of pathologist Dr. Michael Baden and criminologist Dr. Henry Lee."[75]

"For what?" Vannatter asks.

"To supplement your investigation. These are nationally recognized forensic experts."

"This is a little premature, isn't it? Your client hasn't even been charged with anything."

"I'm just making the offer," injects Shapiro. "We would like to have a second autopsy performed on both victims."

"Well, our criminalists here at the LAPD do their own work, and we do our own work. And we have no control over what the coroner's office does. If you want a second autopsy, you have to go through them. That's just the way it works."

"I understand," Shapiro replies. "We just want to be cooperative. I'm asking you to use your influence to get approval from the family and the coroner to let Baden do the second autopsy. . . ."

Lange interrupts, "If you want to help us out, you might want to ask Mr. Simpson if he would be willing to take a polygraph test."

"I'll certainly confer with him about that."[76]

Shapiro quickly walks out of the office, as Lange and Vannatter stare at each other momentarily, wondering what that was about.

"No one has ever come in like that before," Lange says.

"He's trying to get ahead of the curve," Vannatter responds. "He's feeling us out."

Soon after Shapiro leaves, Lange, Vannatter, Gartland, Rogers, and four other RHD detectives walk upstairs to the sixth floor to see Commander White, who will host the first organizational meeting in the Simpson case. The gathering is held in "The Chiefs' Board Room," a large and fairly elegant conference room adorned with the pictures of former LAPD chiefs of police. Marcia Clark and William Hodgman of the district attorney's office are waiting for them, as well as Greg Matheson of serology and Michele Kestler, who is in charge of the LAPD/SID's crime lab.[77]

Lange's and Clark's eyes fix on each other after they are both seated in the room. This is the first time they've been in each other's presence since she had blown apart his case earlier in the year. Lange waits for her reaction. She smiles warmly, and he returns the smile. It's strictly business. Without saying a word, they both have agreed to put the past behind them. This is another case. They're moving on.

Bill Hodgman, Clark's supervisor, is widely known among LAPD detectives as a thoroughly professional and intelligent prosecutor. Personally, he has a reputation as a very nice man, perhaps to a fault. A prosecutor's prosecutor who handled the highly publicized case against savings-and-loan financier Charles Keating,[78] Hodgman has spent his entire career trying to do "the right thing" and believes that everyone else, including defense attorneys, should do the same when confronted with certain situations or clear evidence of guilt. Hodgman never plays dirty and expects others to act in kind.

As the meeting opens, Clark immediately wants to know the status of the blood analysis. Matheson explains that four areas of the leather glove recovered from Simpson's home on North Rockingham have now been serologically examined. Two of these areas showed antigenic activity, a mixture of blood from a minimum of two persons.

"Based on the Simpson blood sample we received from the detectives this morning," Matheson says, "Simpson's blood cannot be eliminated after the blood analysis done on the glove."

"How solid is this?" Lange asks.

Matheson explains that his unit has performed a conventional serological test on the glove to make its determination. In other words, the unit was able to determine the blood types on the glove, which is the least discriminating of all known blood tests. That is the best the unit can do in this short space of time.

However, Matheson adds that his unit's serological examination and comparison of the five South Bundy crime scene blood droplets indicates that three of them match Simpson's blood sample. A fourth droplet is inconclusive, and the fifth simply yielded no results.

"What does this mean?" Lange continues.

Matheson replies, "Well, it's just preliminary testing. But it means that by utilizing the DQ Alpha subtyping, we can show, right now, that the blood is Simpson's to the exclusion of ninety-three percent of the population. And, once again, this is just a preliminary test."

Impressed with that news, Lange and Clark start asking about the more sophisticated and discriminating DNA/RFLP testing. Matheson explains that such testing will take more time.

Well acquainted with DNA evidence, Clark articulates her needs to the crime lab, but diplomatically pressures Kestler and Matheson to allow some of the blood evidence to be sent to outside labs, which are better equipped for the more definitive DNA/RFLP analysis.

This first organizational meeting lasts about an hour, concentrating mostly on the blood, hair, and fiber evidence, as well as the location of bloodstains found in Simpson's Bronco.

After the meeting, Kestler quietly complains to Lange and Vannatter that even though the case is under the control of the LAPD until it has been formally filed with the district attorney's office, Clark has been circumventing the two detectives and calling to get information directly from her.

"She's violating procedure," Michele Kestler says. "And I'm having trouble with it. Who is running this case? You or her?"

Lange gives an "I-told-you-so" look at Vannatter and then tells Kestler, "This is our case until we file with the DA. And that won't be until Friday at the earliest. Tell that to Marcia next time she calls you. In fact, tell her to call us."

To ensure that the LAPD keeps control of the case until it is submitted to Clark and the district attorney's office, Lange and Vannatter ask Captain Gartland to call the commander of the SID to review standard operating procedure and to request that the Simpson case receive top priority.

When Lange returns to his desk after the meeting, he sees a fax sent to "Detectives Van Atter [sic] and Lang [sic]" from Robert Shapiro, who repeats his offer "to provide the services of Dr. Michael Baden, pathologist, and Dr. Henry Lee, criminologist, to aid in the investigation of the murder of Nicole Brown Simpson and Ronald Lyle Goldman. . . . I think it is imperative prior to interment, that a second autopsy be performed that may produce evidence relevant to the murders."

Shapiro adds that he would like the detectives "to contact the next of kin for permission in this regard, since I feel it would be inappropriate for me to contact them directly during this period of grief."

Shapiro has sent copies of this letter to Gil Garcetti and Marcia Clark at the district attorney's office; county coroner Lakshmanan Sathyavagiswaran; as well as Captain Gartland and Lieutenant Rogers. Shapiro also directs a second letter to coroner Sathyavagiswaran, requesting "a second autopsy under your supervision." Lange and Vannatter also receive a copy of this letter.

"What the hell does this guy have up his sleeve?" Lange asks Vannatter.

Vannatter laughs, "Did someone charge Simpson already, and we don't know about it yet?"

The LAPD will not comply with Shapiro's request.

That afternoon, Lange receives Carr and Tippin's written report of their interview with Simpson's limousine driver, twenty-four-year-old Allan W. Park.

Based on the detectives' work, Lange writes in his growing murder follow-up report:

Park responded to the Simpson residence to pick up O.J. Simpson. He arrived at 2225 hours on 6-12-94. Park had been advised to pick up Simpson at 2245 hours. Consequently, he was 20 minutes early. After his arrival, Park drove up to the Rockingham gate of the Simpson residence. He observed no vehicles parked at the curb. Park then drove the limo north-bound on Rockingham to the Ashford gate where he attempted to contact anyone inside the residence with the gate phone. No one responded. At approximately 2250 hours, Park observed a male black . . . walk up the driveway from the direction of the Rockingham gate "at a fast pace" and enter the residence. At that time, Park again attempted to raise someone inside the house. A male voice, he identifies as O.J. Simpson, responded stating, "I'm sorry, I overslept, I just got out of the shower. I'll be down in a minute." A short time later, O.J. Simpson emerged from the residence carrying two black nylon duffle [sic] bags. Additionally, there was a golf bag on the walkway at the front of the house. Brian Kaelin was standing in the front yard. As Simpson exited the residence, Kaelin started towards an additional dark colored bag which was lying in the driveway closest to the Rockingham gate. Kaelin stated he would pick up the bag. However, he was stopped from doing this by Simpson, who retrieved the bag. All three bags, plus the golf bag, were loaded into the limo.

Park went on to state that Simpson was sweating profusely and complained of the heat several times while en route to the airport. The air conditioner was on and Simpson had the rear window down.[79]

When Lange finishes writing this section of his report, he exclaims to Vannatter, "This is a terrific witness! Everything he's saying is consistent with what we have, plus he's giving us a lot more. The person walking across the driveway must be Simpson."

"It all fits perfectly," injects Vannatter. "Park says that he gets no response from inside the house until just before eleven o'clock. Then, the mystery man enters, the lights come on, and the phone finally gets answered. Allan Park can seal Simpson."

"And he's telling us that Simpson's sweating profusely," continues Lange. "He wants the window open, even though the air conditioner is on. I mean, it's all coming together, Phil."

"But the biggest thing of all is that bag that Kaelin offered to pick up, Simpson insisted on handling himself. Where is that bag? There's no accounting for it."

Lange theorizes, "Maybe if we find that bag, we'll also find his bloody clothes and, possibly, the murder weapon, too."

"Unless," Vannatter adds, "the bag's already been disposed of—with all that stuff in it."

Soon after, Vannatter receives a call from Jill Shively, who lives in Brown's neighborhood. She gives him an amazing story, which will be written up in an interview report, stating:

On Sunday, 6-12-94, witness was en route to the Westward Ho Market on San Vicente across from the Mezzaluna Restaurant. Witness was eastbound approaching Bundy, the light was green for east/west traffic. Witness observed a white Ford Bronco northbound on Bundy run the red light and almost collide with a light grey Nissan, 2-door, who was westbound on San Vicente. The driver of the Nissan was a male white, 18/25, clean shaven, looked like a college student. Both the Ford Bronco and Nissan stopped. Witness recognized the driver of the Bronco to be O.J. Simpson. Witness had stopped at the intersection also. Witness observed Simpson lean out of the open driver's door window and yell at the driver of the Nissan. Witness heard Simpson yell, "Get out of the way, move, move, get out of the way." [She said,] "O.J. was angry." The driver of the Nissan got out of the way and continued driving westbound. Simpson drove northbound on Bundy at a high rate of speed. Witness continued to the store.

Witness specifically remembers that this all occurred just before 11:00 p.m., because she thought the Westward Ho Market closed at 11:00 p.m. Witness had to get to the market before it closed.

Witness frequents the Brentwood Village area and has seen both O.J. and Nicole in the neighborhood many times.

Vannatter genuinely believes that she had an encounter with Simpson on the night of the murders.

At about 6:30 P.M.—after nearly a twelve-hour workday—the two detectives knock off for the evening, hoping to put their case together the following day for submission to the district attorney's office on Friday. After clearing their case, they will arrest O.J. Simpson.

Endnotes

74. Before this incident, Roman, a lay minister with the Church of Scientology, had presided over the marriage of Clark and her second husband, Gordon Clark. Although not a member of the Church, she had met Gordon in 1979 while attending Scientology meetings with Horowitz. Marcia Clark left Gordon Clark in 1993.

75. Michael Baden has worked as a New York City medical examiner; Henry Lee runs Connecticut's state police lab. Both men are extremely well known and respected.

76. According to Lawrence Schiller's *American Tragedy*, Simpson had already taken a polygraph test the previous day, Tuesday, June 14, at the request of attorney Robert Shapiro. Skip Taft, Simpson's business attorney, accompanied Shapiro to the examination; Robert Kardashian brought Simpson. The test was conducted at the office of Edward Gelb, one of the most respected polygraph operators in the United States.

Because Gelb was out of the country, Dennis Nellany, who worked with Gelb, performed the test on Simpson. "Half an hour later," Schiller wrote on page 32, "Simpson comes out alone. He's wound up, talking a blue streak: It was very emotional. Every time he heard Nicole's name, his heart started to pound. The test was very hard to get through. Difficult, very tough."

Schiller continued, "Simpson scored a minus 22, Nellany says. . . . Minus 22 means Simpson failed virtually all of the questions about the murders."

77. Also present was David Conn, another deputy district attorney who headed the Special Trials Division. He had been pulled off the prosecution's upcoming retrial of Erik and Lyle Menendez, the brothers who murdered their parents in their Beverly Hills estate, to work on the Simpson case. However, after a few weeks on the Simpson detail, he returned to the Menendez case.

78. Los Angeles Superior Court Judge Lance A. Ito was the presiding judge during the Keating case. In late 1996, Keating's conviction was reversed by the state court of appeals.

79. Later, detectives interviewed Park again. During this interview, Park added that while waiting for Simpson, he had driven his limousine back and forth between the two gates on North Rockingham and Ashford. When asked whether he had seen a white Bronco parked near the North Rockingham gate, Park replied that he did not remember seeing one—

although he clearly remembered seeing the Nissan 300ZX parked near the Ashford gate.

When Simpson finally climbed into the limousine, Park exited the property through the North Rockingham gate. When he stopped at the gate, he remembered seeing a car parked on the street nearby that he had not seen earlier, which could have been the white Bronco.

12

Timeline

Thursday, June 16, 1994

At 7:00 A.M., Lange calls Greg Matheson and discovers that the friction between SID crime lab chief Michele Kestler and Marcia Clark has nearly reached the point where it could become explosive. In anticipation of receiving the case from the LAPD within the next twenty-four hours, not only is Clark circumventing the detectives at Homicide Special, she is now actively trying to take the blood work away from the SID.

"Damn it!" Lange exclaims to Vannatter. "Clark is just chomping at the bit! She can't wait to get this case away from us!"

"What can we do?" Vannatter asks, still defending Clark. "She's going to get the case pretty soon anyway."

"We can sit on this case and not file it until we've turned over every rock," Lange suggests. "We still have plenty to do. This case is ours until we file it. The minute we file, we lose control. Already, Clark and the DA's office are trying to shove us off to the side. Phil, either we control the investigation or Marcia Clark does!"

"Let's talk to Gartland," Vannatter suggests.

The two detectives walk into Captain Gartland's office and explain the situation between Clark and the SID. Gartland responds, "I thought I handled that yesterday when I called the SID commander."

"Well, apparently there are still problems between Kestler and Clark," Lange replies.

"Are you ready to file your case?" asks Gartland.

"We could be ready by tomorrow morning," Lange explains, "but we still don't have the final blood analysis yet."

"Then don't file until you do," Gartland suggests. "If the blood is Simpson's, file your case; prepare to make your arrest. If it's not, then make Clark and the DA's office wait until you have what you want. If they cause trouble, I'll back you guys up. That's what I'm here for. I don't want to see this case filed until we have it solid. Do you have any preliminary indication that Simpson's blood was at Bundy or the victims' blood was at Rockingham?"

"Not yet," Lange responds.

"When you get that," Gartland says, "clear your case."

Lange and Vannatter return to their desks and continue working on their murder follow-up report, which is what they will file with the district attorney's office—whenever they decide to file it.

During the course of the day, Lange receives several telephone calls from Matheson, giving him additional preliminary results to their blood testing of both the glove and the Bronco. After the final conversation, Lange immediately transfers his notes to the murder follow-up report, writing:

> On 6-16-94, detectives were contacted by L.A.P.D., S.I.D. Serology supervisor Greg Matheson regarding the . . . right handed leather glove found at the residence of O.J. Simpson. Further DNA typing of this item revealed that the glove contains bloodstains that could include both victims' blood as well as that of O.J. Simpson. All of the blood could not have come [from] O.J. Simpson.

Lange immediately gives the news to Vannatter, who smiles and says, "Do you mind if I call Marcia?"

Nodding back, Lange says, "It's still preliminary, but I think it's sufficient until the DNA/RFLP testing gets done in the weeks ahead. It's still not definitely his blood at Bundy or the victims' blood on the glove at Rockingham—but the indications are there. So, go ahead, Phil. Call her. She's definitely going to have this case pretty soon."

Vannatter reaches Clark at her office and gives her the details about the blood analysis.

Delighted, Clark exclaims over the telephone, "Goddamn it, Phil, we've got him!"

"We should be filing the case sometime tomorrow morning."

"Come in really early," she says to Vannatter, "and we'll do the paperwork. We'll get the warrant for you."

With their concentration on questions of evidence addressing Simpson's means and opportunity, Lange and Vannatter have focused less during these early days of their investigation on motive. However, Simpson's possible motive appears to emerge from a shocking police report, filed on January 1, 1989, by Officer John Edwards of the West Los Angeles Division. This came into their hands after a follow-up request by Vannatter, who had obtained some preliminary information about this incident while writing his search warrant on June 13.

According to Edward's handwritten report, which was faxed to the Robbery/Homicide Division at 5:04 P.M. on Thursday, June 16:

I responded to a 911 emer r/c at O.J. Simpson's home, 360 N. Rockingham, on 1-1-89 0330 hrs. Upon arrival, I pushed the electronic gate speaker box button out front. A female answered (housekeeper). She said that everyone was fine and that police were not needed. I told her that I must speak with and see the woman that dialed 911, and I would not leave until I did.

About that time, Nicole Simpson came running out of some bushes near the house. She was wearing only a bra and sweat-type pants, and she had mud down the rt leg of the pants. She ran across the driveway to a post containing the gate release button. She collapsed on the post and pushed the button hard several times.

She was yelling during this time, "He's going to kill me. He's going to kill me." As she said this, the gate opened, and she ran out to me. She grabbed me and hung on to me as she cried nervously and repeated, "He's going to kill me."

I asked her who was going to kill her. She replied, "O.J." I did not know this was O.J. Simpson's home, but at this point I felt she might have meant O.J. Simpson. I asked her, "Do you mean O.J. Simpson, the football player?" She said, "Yes." I asked her if he had a gun. She said he's got lots of guns. (The question had been for my protection since she had mentioned he was going to kill her.)

I could see clearly that her face was badly beaten with a cut lip, swollen and blackened left eye and cheek. I also noted a hand imprint on her left neck.

When I asked her what happened to her face, she replied, O.J. had slapped her & kicked her.

I saw that she was shaking, so I had my partner [Patricia Milewski] put her uniform jacket on Nicole. Then I had her sit in back of the police veh. As she was giving the crime info to my partner, she kept saying, "You never do anything about him. You talk to him then leave. I want him arrested. I want him out so that I can get my kids." She also made the statement that police have come 8 times before for the same thing.

I had only worked WLA for a few months and was unaware of any reports on the Simpsons or radio calls at the home.

About this time, O.J. Simpson arrived at the closed gate inside his yard. At first, he did not speak directly to me, but yelled for about 30 seconds towards Nicole seated in the police car.

He yelled, "I don't want that woman sleeping in my bed anymore. I got 2 women, and I don't want that woman in my bed anymore."

When he slowed down, I told him Nicole wanted him arrested for beating her. He blew up again and yelled that he did not beat her up. He just pushed her out of the bedroom and nothing more.

I again told O.J. that Nicole wanted him arrested for beating her, and that I could clearly see physical evidence on Nicole that confirmed she had been beaten.

I then told O.J. I was going to have to place him under arrest for beating Nicole. He yelled back, "The police have been out here 8 times before and now you're going to arrest me for this? This is a family matter. Why do you want to make a big deal of it? We can handle it."

O.J. was wearing a bathrobe only so I told him to go, put some clothes on, then come outside. I told him when my supervisor gets here, I'm going to have to arrest [him]. O.J. went inside.

In approx 2 min, the housekeeper came out thru the gate and walked directly to the police veh. She opened the rear door and started pulling on Nicole and saying, "Nicole, don't do this. Come inside now."

I pulled the housekeeper back and closed the door. I told her to leave. She was interfering with a police invest and could be arrested. She left.

About 3 min passed and O.J. peeked over his wall, now dressed. He again complained that I was the only one to come to his house that made a big deal of this. I told [him] again that I was going to have to arrest him based on Nicole's injuries, and that the law required me to arrest him.

Sgt Vinger drove up and O.J. disappeared from the wall. As I explained the situation to Sgt Vinger, I saw O.J. drive out of another driveway in a [black] Bentley. He sped off [southbound] Rockingham, 35–45 mph. We were out of our cars at the time and faced in awkward directions. We drove [southbound] after O.J., but never saw him again. We fanned out throughout the nearby streets with 5 units but could not locate him. Red lights & sirens not used during chase due to distance.

Nicole was still in our police car and wanted to go back to her kids. She had already signed the crime rpt, but refused medical treatment or photos of her injuries downtown.[80]

During our search for O.J., I had driven down Bundy at Wilshire. I told Nicole we could take quick photos at WLA [Division] then take her home. She agreed to that.

I took 3 photos of Nicole's injuries and had my partner check her for any additional injuries.

I then took her home. Within 15 minutes, I got a call from the station that Nicole called, saying O.J. came back. I went back over to 360 Rockingham but parked 3 houses up, waiting for O.J. to drive out again. After approx 45 min, I had the station call her at home. She told the station that O.J. had left again before I got there.[81]

In trying to establish motive, Lange and Vannatter now suspect that Simpson's physical abuse of his wife might have led to her murder. They know that they must investigate any other incidents before and/or after the 1989 episode described in Officer Edward's report.

During the early evening on Thursday, Lange and Vannatter crank into high gear, assembling their paperwork and evidence for filing with the district attorney's office. Planning out the following day, they want to obtain the arrest warrant, call Robert Shapiro, and arrange to pick up Simpson.

Lange and Vannatter again sit down with Captain Gartland and Lieutenant Rogers. The detectives present their summary of events for June 12 that, they believe, led to the murders of Nicole Brown and Ronald Goldman:

2:18 P.M.: According to his cellular phone records, O.J. Simpson called Nicole Brown's house, talking to someone, perhaps his daughter, for three minutes and nine seconds. During Lange and Vannatter's interview with Simpson on June 13, he seemed to indicate that he had called his wife's home later that night to speak with his daughter. However, there is no toll record of that local call. If this call was made, Simpson probably made it from the telephone inside his home—instead of his cellular phone.

4:45–5:00 P.M.: Nicole Brown attended her daughter's dance recital at Paul Revere Middle School in Brentwood. Simpson arrived a few minutes late. He brought flowers for his daughter.

6:30–6:45 P.M.: The recital ended. After the recital, Brown and other family members—including her mother and father—and friends went to dinner at the Mezzaluna restaurant in Brentwood. During Simpson's June 13 interview with Lange and Vannatter, Simpson claimed that he had been invited to the dinner but declined. In fact, according to other witnesses, he had left the recital upset because he had *not* been invited to the dinner. As the others go to the restaurant, Simpson left for his home on North Rockingham.

7:00 P.M.: Simpson returned to his home.

7:20 P.M.: Kaelin asked for and received permission to use Simpson's Jacuzzi. Kaelin later indicated that during this conversation, Simpson complained about the provocative clothing his ex-wife and her women friends wore at his daughter's recital, adding that his relationship with Brown was over.

8:40 P.M.: Simpson went to Kaelin's room, claiming that Kaelin had forgotten to turn off the water jets on the Jacuzzi. Kaelin insisted that he had.

Circa 8:45 P.M.: Brown, Justin, Sydney, and Sydney's friend left Mezzaluna and went to a Ben & Jerry's ice cream shop across the street from the restaurant.

9:00 P.M.: Brown, her two children, and Sydney's friend arrived at Brown's home at 875 South Bundy Drive. Soon after, the friend's mother picked up her daughter.

9:10 P.M.: Simpson, wearing a dark sweatsuit, again went to Kaelin's room. This time he asked to borrow twenty dollars to tip the skycap at LAX, claiming that he only had large bills. Kaelin gave Simpson a twenty-dollar bill.

9:15–9:30 P.M.: Simpson and Kaelin went to a McDonald's in

Brentwood in Simpson's Bentley, using the drive-thru.[82] Kaelin paid for the food with another twenty-dollar bill. Simpson neither obtained change for the twenty-dollar bill Kaelin had given him, nor did he ask Kaelin for smaller bills from the change he received for the food.

9:35-9:45 P.M.: Simpson and Kaelin returned from McDonald's. Kaelin went to his bungalow to eat and did not see Simpson again for nearly ninety minutes.

9:37 P.M.: Brown's mother, Juditha, called Mezzaluna restaurant to report that she had lost her eyeglasses. After a brief wait on the phone, an employee, Karen Crawford, informed Juditha that she found them outside in the street.

9:40 P.M.: Juditha Brown reached her daughter to tell her about the glasses. They talked for about two minutes.

9:43 P.M.: Nicole Brown then called the restaurant and spoke to her friend, Ron Goldman. Goldman offered to drop off the glasses after his shift. Mezzaluna manager John DeBello told Goldman that he didn't have to make "a special trip" to Brown's house, but Goldman insisted.

9:50 P.M.: Goldman, who had plans to meet a friend later that night, left the restaurant in a red Toyota—borrowed from his friend, Andrea Scott—and headed for his apartment to change his clothes. Soon after, Goldman went to Brown's home, parking on the north side of Dorothy Street, facing west near the alley.

10:03 P.M.: Simpson tried to reach Paula Barbieri on his cellular telephone, but he could not locate her.

10:15-10:20 P.M.: Pablo Fenjves, a screenwriter who lives behind Brown's condominium, first heard Brown's Akita's "plaintive wail." The dog's name is "Kato."[83]

10:25 P.M.: Allan Park, a limousine driver, arrived twenty minutes early at North Rockingham to take Simpson to LAX for his flight to Chicago. He parked at the Ashford Street entrance of Simpson's home.

10:30-10:40 P.M.: Park moved back and forth between the North Rockingham and Ashford Street gates. He did not notice Simpson's white Bronco parked on North Rockingham.

10:35-10:40 P.M.: Park rang Simpson's buzzer. No one answered. He noticed that one light was on upstairs, and it was dark downstairs.

10:40-10:50 P.M.: Jill Shively supposedly saw Simpson when he crashed a red light and nearly hit another car at the corner of South Bundy and San Vicente Boulevard.

10:45–10:50 P.M.: Kaelin, while on the telephone with his girl-friend, Rachel Ferrara, heard noises on his back wall and wrongly believed that there had been an earthquake. A few minutes later, he went outside with a dim flashlight to investigate.

10:53–10:55 P.M.: Park, who had continued to ring Simpson's buzzer, called his boss to say that Simpson was not at home. While on the telephone, he saw Kaelin at a distance on the other side of the house with a flashlight.

10:53–10:55 P.M.: Park saw a tall person in dark clothing walk across the driveway and quickly enter Simpson's house. The downstairs lights immediately went on.

10:55 P.M.: Brown's neighbor, screenwriter Steven Schwab, while walking his dog, noticed the white Akita, wearing no tags, barking and walking aimlessly. Its paws were bloody, but the dog had no injury. Schwab took the dog to his own home. He later gave the dog to his neighbors, computer-hardware repairman Sukru Boztepe and his wife, Bettina Rasmussen.

10:55–10:56 P.M.: Park rang the buzzer again. This time, Simpson answered. He explained that he had overslept and just stepped out of the shower. In the meantime, Kaelin opened the Ashford gate and waved Park into the driveway.

11:00–11:02 P.M.: Simpson exited his house with four pieces of luggage—a garment bag, a leather travel bag, a half-moon-shaped duffel bag, and his golf clubs. Kaelin saw Simpson for the first time since they returned from the McDonald's.

11:03–11:04 P.M.: Kaelin helped Simpson load his luggage in Park's limousine. Simpson insisted on putting the half-moon-shaped duffel bag in the car himself, refusing to allow Kaelin to handle it. Kaelin also told Simpson about hearing the three "thumps," adding that he was going to look around when he saw the limousine driver. Because Kaelin's flashlight didn't work very well, Simpson tried to find him one before leaving. Unable to find it quickly and telling Kaelin that he was running late, Simpson left without giving him another flashlight.

11:05–11:10 P.M.: Park, with Simpson in his limo, pulled out of the driveway, heading for LAX. While stopped momentarily at the North Rockingham gate, he noticed a car parked to the north that he had not seen earlier.

11:20–11:25 P.M.: Simpson called and asked Kaelin to set the alarm at his estate. However, Kaelin neither had a key to the main house, nor did he know how to turn on the burglar alarm.

11:45–11:55 P.M.: Noticing how restless the Akita was, Sukru Boztepe and Bettina Rasmussen took the dog for a walk.

12:10 A.M.: The Akita led Boztepe and Rasmussen to Brown's condominium. The dog stopped and looked into the dark walkway. In the moonlight, through all the foliage, they noticed blood trickling down the tile of the walkway on the street side of the gate. At the bottom of the steps, they saw Brown's dead body.

After reviewing the possible timeline, Gartland asks, "How do you think these murders occurred? Do you have any theories yet?"

Lange replies, "Judging by the evidence and the possible direction of attack, we have three or four, maybe even five different scenarios. The knit cap and gloves gives us a lying-in-wait aspect. The killer's there in the dark—perhaps looking through a window at Nicole and took his opportunity when she walked outside to meet her visitor."

Vannatter continues, "Or maybe he came out from the side where Goldman was attacked. Or maybe he was up on the patio, behind the hedge, and ambushed them while they were together at the bottom of the steps. He hits her in the back of the head first and knocks her unconscious. Then he goes after Goldman, kills him, then returns to Nicole to finish her off."

"Obviously, he would've had to have taken them out one at a time," adds Lange. "Goldman might've walked onto the scene while he was killing her; then he had to kill him. Maybe the killer came in from the front walkway and attacked them while the gate was open. Or maybe he walked up on them from the rear gate where he apparently parked his car. At this point, we don't know for sure. Maybe we'll never know."

The detectives are also struck by the continuous contact Simpson had with Kaelin, which even Kaelin had found unusual. Had Simpson used Kaelin to establish his alibi?

After their meeting with Gartland and Rogers, Lange and Vannatter walk across the street and go to the eighteenth floor of the Los Angeles Criminal Courts Building to visit Patti Jo Fairbanks, a senior administrative aide with the prosecutor's office.

Fairbanks helps them type up their follow-up murder report and the formal complaint against Simpson. The final package includes these items, along with the death reports, crime reports, analyzed evidence reports, property reports, and police interview reports, among other documentation. When these materials are organized, Fairbanks makes six copies of the entire package, ready to be placed in loose-leaf notebooks, which will eventually be distributed to prosecutors and Simpson's defense attorney.

Driving home north on the 405, both Lange and Vannatter are mindful of the burial service that has been held for Nicole Brown that day in Mission Viejo, about ninety minutes south. Both detectives in their own separate cars wonder whether O.J. Simpson attended. Since the LAPD has no surveillance on him or at the service, they assume they will get their answer on the television news, which is now blanket-covering this case.

Despite her own busy schedule, Rita Vannatter already has the television on when her husband walks into their house. As she sets the kitchen table, the detective sits in his favorite chair in the den, watching the evening news, and sees Simpson with his two small children at his ex-wife's burial service.

As part of the Simpson media frenzy of the day, a man who appears to be O.J. Simpson, returning from Nicole Brown's service, runs into the North Rockingham home with his arms over his face. As the television cameras follow the man, Vannatter's attention zeroes in on an off-duty LAPD cop caught on the videotape, who appears to be moonlighting as a security guard for Simpson.

Vannatter knows the officer, who works on the Harbor Division's day watch. They had been classmates at the LAPD Academy. Seeing his old friend running interference, like a pulling guard, Vannatter says to his wife, "Jesus! Look at this! He's an L.A. cop, and he's guarding a murder suspect!"[84]

Endnotes

80. Later, at 6:00 that evening, Nicole Brown Simpson was treated at St. John's Hospital for bruising and soreness to her head. She had told a doctor that her injuries resulted from a bicycle-riding accident—instead of a clear-cut case of physical abuse.

81. Simpson was charged by the city attorney's office, not the LAPD. He pleaded "no contest" to one count of misdemeanor spousal battery and was sentenced to 120 hours of community-service work and two years' probation. Because Simpson was never arrested by the LAPD, no record of his crime and punishment appeared in the police department's computer system.

This matter will be further discussed in Part Two.

82. Since early in the investigation, rumors have circulated that Simpson and Kaelin met a reputed drug dealer during the trip to and from McDonald's. An allegation to this effect was made to the police, but it was completely unsubstantiated. Simpson and Kaelin did *not* meet a drug dealer at McDonald's or anywhere else that night.

83. Fenjves had originally testified that he heard the dog wail at 10:20 P.M. On the stand, he changed that time to 10:15 P.M. Fenjves also testified that he heard the same dog between 11:00 and 11:40 P.M. However, Brown's neighbor, Steve Schwab, had taken the dog away at 10:55 P.M.

84. To evade the media, Simpson had given reporters a head fake after Brown's burial. He swapped clothes with Al Cowlings, who then went to Simpson's estate on North Rockingham in Simpson's limousine, taking the press with him. Simpson accompanied Robert Kardashian in Cowlings's white 1993 Bronco, and he spent the night at Kardashian's home in Encino.

The LAPD sergeant Vannatter saw on television helped to engineer this ruse. This officer later became the subject of an investigation by the LAPD's Internal Affairs Division. The results of this probe have not been announced.

13

The Aborted Arrest

Friday, June 17, 1994

Officially, Lange and Vannatter file Case No. BA097211 with the Los Angeles County District Attorney's Office at 7:20 A.M. The case is no longer theirs. It is now under the control of the DA. From this moment on, they will follow the prosecutors' orders.

Meeting in Patti Jo Fairbanks's office, Lange and Vannatter walk Marcia Clark through the case and their evidence. Clark, who is now in charge of this case and its investigation, says, "Okay, let's finish writing up the arrest warrant so that you can pick up Simpson." Even though the district attorney's office now owns this case, the cops still have to make the arrest.

Lange picks up Fairbanks's telephone and calls Simpson's attorney, Robert Shapiro, and tells him, "Mr. Shapiro, we are getting a warrant for Mr. Simpson's arrest. We want to pick him up this morning, and we want your full cooperation. Like you, we want to avoid a media circus. If possible, we'd like to sneak him in through a back door." Without mentioning a specific time, Lange says he wants this done as soon as possible.

Shapiro, usually an extremely articulate man, appears to be at a loss for words. Apparently, this news has taken him completely by surprise. He hasn't expected that Simpson would be arrested so soon. When he finally does speak, he immediately tries to buy some time, appealing to Lange to allow him to bring his client to Parker Center. He asks for an 11:00 A.M. deadline.

Lange talks to Clark, among others, and they do not appear to have any problem with the arrangement. "Okay," Lange tells Shapiro. "Bring him to the Robbery/Homicide Division at eleven o'clock."

Shapiro replies, "I'll call you back to make the final arrangements after I get hold of Mr. Simpson."

The four-page arrest warrant is completed and approved by Los Angeles District Attorney Gil Garcetti. Vannatter and Clark leave Lange behind in Fairbanks's office and proceed to Municipal Judge Elva Soper's courtroom in the same building.

Lange calls Captain Gartland and Commander John White. Lange tells them what he and Shapiro have just discussed.

"Alter that plan just a little," White replies. "We've been talking to the DA's office, too; and we want Simpson to turn himself in at the jail in back of Parker Center."

Lange, who would prefer a quiet arrest and booking, knows that the danger of White's order, orchestrated in concert with the district attorney's office, is that the media will have close access to the scene of the arrest. Suddenly, Lange realizes: The LAPD's high command really wants a dog-and-pony show. Lange has no choice but to follow orders—just like Captain Gartland and Commander White.

Lange calls Shapiro again and gives him the change in plans, saying that Simpson must surrender at the jail in back of Parker Center. Shapiro replies that Simpson is extremely depressed, adding, "Detective, you know he's bigger than me. I can't handle him when he's like this."

Assuming that Shapiro is still stalling, Lange tells him to hurry. He reminds the attorney that if Simpson has not surrendered by 11:00 A.M., the LAPD will come and get him.

At 10:15, after his second conversation with Shapiro, Lange reports back to Gartland, who has just ended his own telephone call with the attorney. Gartland tells Lange that Shapiro said that they would be a little late. According to a written record Gartland is keeping, Shapiro explained that "Simpson was saying goodbye to his mother and children and was taking care of personal business with his personal attorney. Shapiro stated that a doctor was attending Simpson and that Simpson had been sedated. He would be leaving in 15 to 20 minutes."[85]

Gartland is not happy with the delay, but apparently knows that the LAPD brass has insisted that the arrest be made in front of the media. Gartland seems as frustrated by this decision as Lange.

Vannatter and Clark are escorted by the bailiff into Judge Elva Soper's chambers.

"What do we have today?" asks Soper, a respected judge whom Vannatter and Clark have known for years.

"Judge, we have a warrant for the arrest of O.J. Simpson," Vannatter replies. "And we need your signature. The warrant charges Simpson with two counts of murder."

Soper has no immediate reaction to the request, accepting the paperwork and reading through it carefully.

After finishing, she pauses momentarily, saying, "You know, I feel like I could cry, because I'm a USC graduate, and this is O.J. Simpson."

But at 10:25 A.M., along with Vannatter and Clark, Soper signs the warrant—which authorizes that Simpson be arrested and held without bail. After the arrest, Simpson will be promptly arraigned at a brief hearing.

Vannatter heads for the county clerk's office with the warrant to have it certified. Asking Vannatter to bring her a copy, Clark peels off and returns to the district attorney's office.

After the warrant is certified and duplicated, Vannatter goes to Marcia Clark's office and hands her a copy. She is preparing to take her case to the county grand jury, which will begin hearing testimony today, even before Simpson is arrested.

After leaving Clark, Vannatter rejoins Lange in Fairbanks's office. Lange tells Vannatter about the LAPD's decision and the plans for Simpson's arrest. Of course, Vannatter is just as upset as Lange.

"It's going to be a goddamn zoo out there," Vannatter says. Both detectives know that there is nothing they can do, because the decision comes from the LAPD brass.

Shortly before 11:00 A.M., the two detectives decide to go to Gartland's office and wait for Simpson and Shapiro to arrive. As Lange and Vannatter walk outside the courthouse toward Parker Center, they see that the media and a crowd of curious spectators have nearly surrounded Parker Center. A half dozen extremely loud helicopters are flying in circles overhead at varying altitudes, drowning out everything and everybody. They are joined by other choppers, including a LAPD helicopter, which is providing additional security.

Lange immediately fears that two or more of them will collide, with the wreckage falling on the burgeoning crowd below. Vannatter agrees with his partner's concerns and says to Lange, "This could be a real disaster."

Lange and Vannatter are also worried about Simpson's personal security. Looking at all the high ground around police headquarters, they even fear that a sniper might take a shot at Simpson. But, within minutes, they notice that the police chopper flying above has moved away from the area over police headquarters and begins to cruise over the tops of buildings, looking for possible snipers with long-range rifles.

The LAPD high command has already called in its uniformed Metro Division, the department's specialists in tactical operations, to handle the security problems. They are primarily concentrated in the parking lot in back of Parker Center where Simpson is to surrender.

Eleven A.M. comes and goes. No Shapiro. No Simpson.[86]

At 11:05, Shapiro again calls Gartland, who is now with Lange and Vannatter. Gartland later writes in his notes, "Shapiro called a second time and stated that Simpson is now talking to his children and is still working on his will. Two doctors, two friends, and Simpson's personal attorney [are] present, along with Shapiro."

Forty minutes later, at 11:45 A.M., "Shapiro called again," Gartland writes, "and indicated that he was having a difficult time getting O.J. to leave the location. He quoted Simpson as saying, 'I won't be getting out, what's the hurry getting in.'

"Shapiro then indicated that there would be two cars bringing Simpson to Parker Center, a black Isuzu with four occupants and a white Bronco driven by O.J.'s bodyguard, A.C. [Cowlings] and occupied by Shapiro and Simpson. He estimated a 30-minute ride because they were in the area of the 101 and 405 Freeways."

Gartland tells Shapiro—with Lange and Vannatter standing nearby—"Hey! We've got to get this guy in here! We've got to quit screwing around! Get him in here now or we're coming to get him!"

Twelve-fifteen P.M. comes and goes. Simpson is still a no-show. Lange and Vannatter realize that the plan conjured up by the

LAPD and the DA's office is backfiring. Seeing the media crowd still getting larger, Lange angrily says to Vannatter, "This is ridiculous! We look silly! If we had been allowed to do this the way we wanted—go out and pick him up—we wouldn't look so damn stupid!"

Vannatter responds to Lange by saying, "Simpson's been pulling our chain! He's going to do what he wants to do! What's he going to try to pull next?"

Both detectives leave Gartland and go to Commander White's office in Operations Headquarters.

At 12:35, after receiving a quick briefing from the detectives, Commander White, now equally furious, calls Shapiro at his office. A receptionist answers, but says that Shapiro is not in. When White says that he needs to reach Shapiro immediately, the receptionist connects him with Shapiro's personal secretary. Explaining that he must reach Shapiro right now, White is transferred to an unknown location. The phone rings a few times and is answered by a man identifying himself as Dr. Saul Faerstein. White asks him if Simpson and Shapiro are there. The doctor replies that they are. The commander then demands that he give him their location, but Faerstein refuses. When White tells him that he might be in violation of the law, Faerstein hands the telephone to Shapiro.

"Where are you?" White yells into the receiver. "Where's Simpson?"

Again, Shapiro pleads with White for more time and offers to put Simpson's doctor back on the telephone. The doctor explains that Simpson is extremely depressed, and they fear a possible suicide attempt.

Shapiro tells White that Simpson is "making a will because he said he will be in prison for the rest of his life. He [is]also saying good-byes to friends." Once again, Shapiro asks for more time.

"No go!" White replies firmly. He demands that Shapiro give him their location.

When Shapiro balks, White responds, "Well, if you don't tell me, let me advise you that you're harboring a fugitive at this point. We're tired of waiting, and we're not waiting any longer. So if you don't tell me where he is, you'll be in violation of the law yourself, Mr. Shapiro. You, sir, are out of time. What is your location?"

After this very serious threat is delivered to Shapiro, White learns that Simpson is at the home of attorney Robert Kardashian, a longtime friend, in Encino.[87]

At 12:50 P.M., on White's orders, the Robbery/Homicide Division detectives call Lieutenant Tony Alba, the day-watch commander of the West Valley Division, and ask him to send some patrol officers, as well as a supervisor, to Kardashian's home to arrest Simpson. Lange and Vannatter also send Detectives Paul Tippin and Brian Carr to the house.

Within minutes, Lange hears that Alba, who has personally gone to the location, has also dispatched two black-and-whites, code 2 (sans red lights and sirens).

Soon after, Lange and Vannatter receive a preliminary, unconfirmed report from the police group in Encino: Simpson appears to have left the scene with his friend, A.C. Cowlings.

Among those present at Kardashian's house and seemingly as baffled as the police are Shapiro and Kardashian, as well as criminalist Dr. Henry Lee, pathologist Dr. Michael Baden, Dr. Saul Faerstein (who is Simpson's personal physician), and UCLA professor Dr. Robert Huizenga. To the police, all of them plead complete ignorance of the whereabouts of Simpson and Cowlings.

On orders from Parker Center, Alba establishes a sign-in log at 1:30 P.M., preventing anyone from entering or leaving Kardashian's residence without being questioned. Also, Alba and his officers begin a room-to-room search for Simpson.[88]

Officers learn that Simpson's girlfriend, Paula Barbieri, who had been with Simpson earlier that morning, has also just left Kardashian's house with her talent agent, Tom Hahn. Lange and Vannatter immediately send Detective Ron Phillips and uniformed officers to Hahn's home in the Hollywood Hills.

After locating and interviewing Barbieri, Phillips reports to Lange that she knows nothing about Simpson's whereabouts. She is spending the afternoon talking business with Hahn, who had gone to Kardashian's home to pick her up at about 11:30 A.M. She had spent the previous night there with Simpson. Phillips adds that Barbieri believes Simpson is "suicidal."

After talking with Phillips, Lange informs Vannatter what he has just heard.

And, then, everything collapses.

At 1:40 P.M., a detective in the Robbery/Homicide Division office fields a telephone call and immediately tells Lange and Vannatter: "That was Tony Alba on the line. Simpson's gone. He's running. He's taken off with A.C. Cowlings."

"Goddamn it!" Vannatter yells loud enough for everyone in the room to hear.

Immediately, they receive another call, telling them that Simpson and Cowlings are fleeing in Cowlings's white 1993 Bronco, which is almost identical to Simpson's 1994 Bronco. Simpson is wearing a yellow golf shirt, faded blue jeans, and white Reeboks. Cowlings is dressed in a black shirt, black pants, and black shoes.

Although Vannatter has not doubted Simpson's guilt since finding the drops of blood in his driveway on Monday—leading from the Bronco to his front door—Lange has remained only 90 percent sure. He has wanted to see the more sophisticated DNA evidence. But hearing that Simpson has fled, Lange no longer harbors any doubts. Lange and Vannatter are now of the same mind: Simpson is their man, and he's on the loose.

Vannatter calls into the police department's computer system to collect information on Allen Gordon Cowlings, who is six feet five, 235 pounds, brown hair, and brown eyes. He turned forty-seven years old yesterday. He has had no known arrests, convictions, failures to appear, or accidents.

A few minutes later, Lange and Vannatter receive word from the West Los Angeles Division that Simpson has called Lou Brown, who is now at his murdered daughter's home. Simpson has told him that he is en route to South Bundy; Brown then called the police. Immediately, the division's watch commander has dispatched black-and-whites to the condominium. Vannatter also asks the Orange County Sheriff's Office to send units to the cemetery where Nicole Brown had been buried yesterday.

Soon after, Lange receives a report from Lieutenant Alba's officers that the LAPD's dragnet at Kardashian's house has discovered at least one apparent suicide letter written by Simpson.

Endnotes

85. In his book, *The Search for Justice*, Shapiro wrote on page 38: "O.J. made endless phone calls; he needed to put his affairs in order, he wanted to talk to his kids, to his mother. By 9:30, [Dr. Robert] Huizenga and his nurses were taking blood from both of O.J.'s arms simultaneously. Henry Lee, who needed body samples that would address his investigation, was pulling out O.J.'s hair and scraping his skin. Michael Baden, in the process of painstaking pathological examination, was taking pictures of his body."

86. In *The Search for Justice*, Shapiro wrote on pages 38–39: "By eleven, although we were getting close, we still weren't ready to leave, and everyone's nerves were getting a little raw. At the center of it all was O.J. He had written and sealed some letters, addressed to family and friends. Now he was sitting in his underwear, methodically arranging custody of his children and power of attorney over his personal and business affairs. . . ."

87. In *The Search for Justice*, Shapiro mistakenly claimed on page 39 that he had this conversation with Tom Lange. In fact, he had been speaking to Commander White, the chief of detectives, according to both Lange and official LAPD records.

88. On page 55–61 of his book, *American Tragedy*, author Lawrence Schiller detailed Kardashian's conversations with Simpson before the police arrived. Kardashian admitted to the author that he knew Simpson had a gun. However, there is no record that Kardashian ever notified the West Valley Division's police officers that Simpson was armed.

14

O.J. on the Run

Just before 2:00 P.M., acting on the orders of Deputy Chief Bernie Parks, who heads the LAPD's Office of Operations under LAPD Chief Willie Williams, Commander David Gascon, the department's official spokesperson, holds a nationally televised press conference. With Vannatter standing close by, Gascon, obviously furious but restrained, tells reporters: "I have an official announcement from the Los Angeles Police Department.

"This morning, detectives from the Los Angeles Police Department, after an exhaustive investigation which included interviews with dozens of witnesses, a thorough examination and analysis of the physical evidence both here and in Chicago, sought and obtained a warrant for the arrest of O.J. Simpson, charging him with the murders of Nicole Brown Simpson and Ronald Lyle Goldman.

"Mr. Simpson, in agreement with his attorney, was scheduled to surrender this morning to the Los Angeles Police Department. Initially, that was eleven o'clock. It then became eleven-forty-five. Mr. Simpson has not appeared.

"The Los Angeles Police Department right now is actively searching for Mr. Simpson."

The gasp from the audience of journalists is felt and heard throughout the room and on television.

"Mr. Simpson is out there somewhere," Gascon concludes. "And we will find him."

During Commander Gascon's news conference, Lange is at his desk in the Robbery/Homicide Division, watching everything on a television set that is propped up near the ten-foot-high ceiling in the northeast corner of the room. He is in disbelief.

After Gascon's dramatic statement, nearly every telephone in the division begins ringing. It's like Jerry Lewis's telethon on Labor Day. Other detectives, working on their own important investigations, are pressed into service on the Simpson case.

Oddly enough, even though the scene appears chaotic, there is some semblance of order. After all, every man and woman in this room is trained to function under extreme pressure. Despite the incredible chaos, they all seem to be performing well, together and individually. They are fighting to make the best of a horribly embarrassing, potentially dangerous, and tragic situation. Lange is already starting to fear that somebody is going to wind up dead.

After the press conference, Vannatter, Deputy Chief Parks, and Commanders Gascon and White come to the Robbery/Homicide Division. Along with Lange, they meet with Captain Gartland and Lieutenant Rogers. They need to decide what to do, how to do it best, and who to contact.

Their first order of business is to set up a command post right there at RHD. Lange and Vannatter are placed in charge. The two detectives quickly arrange for notifications to be issued to the airlines, the border patrol, the FBI and U.S. Customs Service, the Mexican police, and all ports of exit and entry. An FBI special agent, Bob Rattleman, who has already heard the news, walks into the RHD office and offers to help arrange for the unlawful flight to avoid prosecution warrant.

Also notified is the Orange County Sheriff's Department, which writes in its log:

> LAPD . . . Robbery/Homicide reported O.J. Simpson has been declared a fugitive & requested our assistance. LAPD felt Simpson was headed into Orange County & requested we respond to [the Browns' address] where the family of the former Mrs. Simpson has gathered. LAPD also requested we respond to the

Ascension Cemetery in Lake Forest. LAPD considers O.J. Simpson suicidal.

The telephones at RHD continue ringing nonstop. Tipsters from all over southern California, who have just seen the press conference on television, are reporting "O.J. sightings."

A master log is kept by Paula Donahey, the chief clerk-typist in the Robbery/Homicide Division. Among the most memorable "sightings" logged in by the detectives:

- "O.J. can leave the area by boat."
- "Jermaine Jackson had O.J. flown out of area."
- "Psychic from Florida states he [O.J.] is hiding at [a local dry-cleaning store]."
- "Caller states she saw a well-built black man with sunglasses in a new black Mercedes Benz going north on Highland Avenue . . . , resembled O.J."
- "Anonymous caller—whereabouts of O.J.—San Diego, Point Loma Hotel Posada Best Western Inn. O.J. has a friend who rented a room in friend's name between 9:00/11:00 A.M. . . . Unknown tipster said he saw O.J. there today."
- "Anonymous caller—O.J. owns two condos at Monarch Beach in Orange County. . . . Caller said O.J. may be going there."
- "Operator #514 . . . stated male called from pay phone . . . at corner of Vanowen and Woodman [and] saw O.J. pumping gas into his Rolls Royce at 1540 hours—76 station."
- "[Female source] called . . . saw O.J. in a white Rolls Royce going north towards Sun Valley."
- "[A Los Angeles sheriff's deputy] received anonymous call from male in Atlanta, Georgia. O.J. observed at Winner's Restaurant . . . , wearing white linen suit and dark glasses."
- "[Anonymous source] on 215 Freeway southbound . . . saw white pickup, small Ford Ranger with lumber rack . . . [a man] looked like O.J., wearing burgundy polo shirt, dark pants and possible sunglasses. Stopped at side of road and entered a black Fiero. [W]as done very casually, headed towards San Diego."
- "Male caller—observed a large bluish-green car going south on Pacific Coast Highway near Corona Del Mar with possibly O.J. in it. Large black man with sunglasses . . ."
- "Male called and stated that he saw O.J. and his old teammate [male black] sitting in a French restaurant . . . located on Santa Monica Blvd between Fairfax and Crescent Heights."

- "O.J. at Latuna Motel, Studio City."
- "[Male source] says O.J. either with Magic Johnson or Magic knows where he is."
- "Psychic . . . lives in New England. Feels O.J. is hiding in a white or gray house. The house is on the left hand side if one looks down from the hilltop. O.J. is maybe dead inside. She never felt this strong before."

Even a bounty hunter calls in, asking whether a reward for Simpson's capture has been established and how much it is.

At 5:00 P.M., Lange and Vannatter's attention is again diverted to the television in the Robbery/Homicide Division. With no prior notification, they see Robert Shapiro on the screen.

"What now?" Lange says, looking at his watch and knowing that he, Vannatter, and their wives have to get to a retirement dinner for their close friend, Officer Russell Young of the Bunco Forgery Division.

From his office, Shapiro reads a prepared statement to the press: "O.J., wherever you are, for the sake of your family, for the sake of your children, please surrender immediately. Surrender to any law-enforcement official at any police station, but please do it immediately."

"This is a bad dream," Vannatter says with considerable frustration.

After Shapiro steps away from the podium, Robert Kardashian steps up and reads one of Simpson's letters, found at Kardashian's home:

"To whom it may concern:

"First, everyone understand, I have nothing to do with Nicole's murder. I loved her, always have and always will. If we had a problem, it's because I loved her so much.

"Recently we came to the understanding that for now we were not right for each other, at least not for now. Despite our love, we were different and that's why we mutually agreed to go our separate ways.

"It was tough splitting for a second time but we both knew it was for the best. Inside I had no doubt that in the future we would be close friends or more. Unlike what has been written in the press, Nicole and I had a great relationship for most of our lives together. Like all long-term relationships, we had a few downs and ups.

"I took the heat New Year's 1989 because that was what I was supposed to do. I did not plead no contest for any other reason but to protect our privacy and was advised it would end the press hype.

"I don't want to belabor knocking the press, but I can't believe what is being said. Most of it is totally made up. I know you have a job to do, but as a last wish, please, please leave my children in peace. Their lives will be tough enough. . . .

"I think of my life and feel I've done most of the right things. So why did I end up like this? I can't go on. No matter what the outcome, people will look and point. I can't take that. I can't subject my children to that. This way, they can move on and go on with their lives. . . .

"I've had a good life. I'm proud of how I lived. My mama taught me to do unto others. I treated people the way I wanted to be treated. I've always tried to be up and helpful, so why is this happening?

"I'm sorry for the Goldman family. I know how much it hurts. . . .

"At times I have felt like a battered husband or boyfriend, but I loved her. Make that clear to everyone. And I would take whatever it took to make it work.

"Don't feel sorry for me. I've had a great life, great friends. Please think of the real O.J. and not this lost person. Thanks for making my life special. I hope I helped yours.

                                        "Peace and love, O.J."

"He's going to kill himself," Lange says with complete despair. "That is a good-bye letter. This guy is actually going to kill himself."

"It's a con," Vannatter insists, believing Simpson is absolutely diabolical. "He even has his own people conned. Simpson loves himself too much. He won't do it."

"Don't you think it's a suicide note, Phil?"

"No, it's an admission of guilt. He never once said that he's sorry that his ex-wife is dead. Not once. He's only sorry about being under so much stress. I don't think for a moment that this guy cares about anyone but himself. He'll *never* commit suicide."

In the midst of this, Lange receives a call from Patti Jo Fairbanks in the district attorney's office. She has an official from a cellular telephone company on her other line. The executive tells her—and she relays the information to Lange—that Simpson has been making calls on his cellular phone.

Lange learns that his calls have been roughly made up and down the 405 freeway. Simpson does not appear to be moving in one direction; he and Cowlings seem to be just riding around.

Lange has another detective call the Orange County Sheriff's Department again, placing it on alert. The patrol watch commander there says in his log:

> 1725: LAPD Homicide said they have been tracing cellular phone calls being made from a white Bronco thought to contain O.J. Simpson and a friend, Al Cowlings, who is now wanted for aiding a fugitive. The last call came from S/B I-5 at the El Toro "Y" at 1646 hrs. The vehicle, belonging to Cowlings, bears license 3DHY503. Control One was contacted and a red broadcast was made. Info was also relayed to San Diego County via Control One.

Lange stays on the telephone with Fairbanks and continues to receive reports about Simpson's calls. Whenever he receives any information, he immediately relays it to Orange County.

Thirty minutes later, the Orange County Sheriff's Department sends out a report:

> 1755: LAPD Homicide said they have traced 3 more cellular calls from the vicinity of the El Toro "Y". Area units were advised, and Regional Air is en route. It is felt the suspects may be at a restaurant or gas station in the area. Dana Point DET unit was redirected to the El Toro area to assist.

One minute after that bulletin goes out, the first credible report of a Simpson sighting is received. Simpson has been seen on the freeway just north of El Toro by a young couple, who had heard the news of Simpson's flight on their car radio. They spotted Simpson and Cowlings on I-5 and called the police from an emergency phone box just off the freeway. They gave the police a description of the Bronco and its license plate number.

Immediately after receiving this information, the LAPD authorizes an updated all-points bulletin.

Arranging a conference call, Vannatter and Marcia Clark, who has already been presenting her case to the grand jury that afternoon, telephone Los Angeles Superior Court Judge Charles Horan, asking that the judge authorize a telephonic arrest warrant for Allen Gordon Cowlings for harboring a fugitive. It is issued at 6:26 P.M. Cowlings's bail will be set at $250,000, assuming that he is captured alive and not killed.

At 6:33 P.M., as Lange is getting ready to make another call, he hears a loud commotion in the office. Someone close to him shouts out, "Hey, O.J.'s on the tube!"

Lange jerks his head up toward the television screen, where numerous detectives are now standing. Lange sees a live-camera shot, focusing in on a white Bronco with dark-tinted windows on the freeway.

Lange cannot believe his eyes as he stands up slowly from his desk. "Is that Simpson?" he asks another detective.

"That's him!" The detective replies.

Baffled, Lange asks, "How did they find him?"[89]

As the detective shrugs, Lange continues, "Where's this television broadcast going out to?"

"It's on network television, Tom! The whole country's getting it!"

"This is unreal!" Lange says out loud, rubbing his head and face with considerable frustration, fearing that someone is going to get killed. "This just is not happening! It has to be a bad dream!"

The entire office seems hypnotized by the scene unfolding on television. For a few seconds, everyone is just watching in disbelief. No one is making a sound. Everything just stops.

In the midst of the near-deafening silence, someone yells out, "He's coming our way! O.J.'s heading back towards Los Angeles!"

Suddenly, everyone in the Robbery/Homicide Division office seems to be in motion, jetting around the room, reaching for telephones and grabbing paperwork.

In the midst of this, Lange's phone rings. An official with the Orange County Sheriff's Department is on the line. He tells Lange that A.C. Cowlings, the driver of the car, has refused to pull over and stop when deputies turned on their overheads and sirens—

even when they pulled beside the car and pointed their guns at him.[90]

However, as Lange can see on television, Cowlings has turned on his blinkers and slowed down to a maximum speed of forty to forty-five miles an hour. Clearly, Cowlings is not employing any evasive action—at least not at this point. Escape is now an impossibility.

"Our patrolmen are in their cars on the freeway, right behind O.J. Simpson," the sheriff's official tells him. "They can see inside, and he has a gun to his head."

Lange shouts to the sheriff's official on the phone, "He has a gun? Tell your men to stay with the car but hang back! Do not try to take him! I repeat: Do not try to take him!"

The official adds, "We've just received a communication with Cowlings. Simpson threatens to kill himself if we move in. He's asking us to let him get to his home in Brentwood."

"Just stay with him!" Lange continues. "Don't take him! We'll take over when he gets into L.A.!"

Lange and Vannatter receive immediate confirmation of this report: Cowlings has called 911 on his cellular phone and said, "This is A.C. I have O.J. in the car. Right now . . . we're okay. But you got to tell them, just back off. He's still alive, but he's got a gun to his head. . . . Let me get back to the house."

Seeing that this entire predicament could climax at the Simpson estate, Captain Gartland orders the LAPD Metro Division to dispatch its negotiation and SWAT teams to Simpson's home on North Rockingham.

The already cluttered RHD office appears to fill with the LAPD high command—chiefs and assistant chiefs, deputy chiefs, commanders, as well as a variety of captains and lieutenants—who converge on the room, trying to become part of the decision-making process. Other than Captain Gartland, who is constantly receiving reports from both Lange and Vannatter, the others, although meaning well, seem to be in the way of all the detectives' activities swirling around them.

When Simpson and Cowlings cross the border into the city of Los Angeles, LAPD helicopters take over for those being flown by the Orange County Sheriff's Department. However, the Orange County patrol cars, as well as those from the highway patrol, do not relent, even though LAPD black-and-whites have now joined in the slow-speed pursuit.

Watching this scene develop, Lange picks up the telephone and calls his wife, telling her, "Linda, I don't think we're going to make it to Russ Young's retirement party tonight."

Endnotes

89. Television coverage started after a local television station received a tip-off about Simpson's whereabouts from an employee of a cellular phone company in southern California. Like Lange, the tipster was receiving minute-by-minute updates of Simpson's position on the basis of the calls being billed to Simpson, who subscribed to the company's phone service. The tipster's source was his wife, who also worked for the company. She also gave her husband Simpson's telephone number. He called and talked to Simpson on at least two occasions during the chase.

Later, the company conducted an internal investigation of the affair, learned what the husband and wife team had done, and fired both of them from their jobs for their unauthorized use of the firm's computer system.

90. Orange County Deputy Sheriff Larry Pool, en route back to sheriff's headquarters, spotted Cowlings's white Bronco driving northbound and, again, getting onto I-5. They were just outside Tustin, a small community southeast of Santa Ana. Using his car radio, Pool reported in and was quickly joined by Sergeant J. Sewell, Deputy R. Gunzel, and Res. Deputy L. Santoni. At that point, the chase began.

15

"I'm begging you"

Now mentally thrashed, Lange stands by his desk watching this debacle unfold on national television. He tries to figure out what his next move will be. He pounds his fist on a stack of papers as crowds of people—stopping their cars and running toward the freeway—begin to form a parade route for Simpson and Cowlings. The number of choppers overhead starts to resemble a film clip from *Apocalypse Now.*

Vannatter is fed up with the increasingly carnival-like atmosphere. He says to Deputy Chief Bernard Parks, "Chief, we ought to stop this thing! It's turning into a circus! We should put police cars in front of him, and block the freeway, and stop him! This guy's got a gun, and who knows what he's going to do! This is very dangerous! Somebody's going to get killed!"

Parks replies, "Phil, I agree with you. But they have asked to go back to the Rockingham location. And we will have that secured."

Like Vannatter, Lange is concerned that Simpson, who has a gun, could jeopardize not only his own life but the lives of Al Cowlings, the helicopter pilots overhead, the people stopping along the freeway, and especially the police officers involved in the chase. Lange fears the obvious: What happens to the officers who approach the Bronco if they force it to pull over?

Soon after, Vannatter receives word that twenty-three SWAT officers and four sergeants, headed by Sergeant Michael Albanese, have been deployed and will soon be in place at Simpson's home. The vehicle assault team is en route. Four sniper locations will also be established. A two-man negotiating team, headed by Peter Weireter, and "one full element" of well-trained Metro officers will be waiting inside Simpson's residence.

While Vannatter and Commander Parks discuss the situation, Lange comes to believe that the solution to everything is to get Simpson to throw his gun out of the car. But how can Lange, sitting helplessly in his office at the Robbery/Homicide Division, arrange that?

Suddenly, Lange realizes that he has Simpson's cellular phone number, which he has obtained from Patti Jo Fairbanks while they were tracking his location through his calls.

Lange calls Simpson's number, but the phone clicks off. He tries again. Another miss.

On Lange's third attempt at about 7:26 P.M., Simpson picks up.[91]

Amidst the whining sound of sirens in the background on the phone and the television in front of him, Lange says, "O.J.? O.J.? This is Tom Lange from the police department. Remember me?"

"Yeah, man," Simpson replies. "How are you doing, Tom?"

Lange, who is still watching the Bronco chase on television, just starts talking, hoping to make a personal connection with Simpson, who sounds scared, tired, and/or drugged.

At this point, Lange has only one simple goal: to get Simpson to throw his gun out of the car.

They talk for a few minutes. A couple of detectives who hear about Lange's contact with Simpson are already starting to pass him notes, offering advice as to how to keep Simpson on the line and how to keep him talking. "Remind him about his kids. . . . Tell him that his mother wants to see him again. . . ."

Then Lange's phone goes dead. Simpson has either hung up or is out of his cellular area.

Word quickly spreads around Robbery/Homicide: Lange has reached Simpson. Everyone in the room becomes very quiet; many crowd around Lange's desk. Vannatter, who has been frantically making calls on his own telephone, puts down his receiver. He wants to listen to his partner's side of the conversation.

Lange calls back. Once again, Simpson answers. They continue their conversation until the phone goes dead.

A little nervous, Lange is thinking to himself, "What the hell am I doing in the middle of this?"

As Lange calls again, a technician from the LAPD's sound lab, who has just heard that Lange has reached Simpson, sprints into the office with a tape recorder and a telephone hookup.

This time, just as Simpson answers, the technician switches on the recorder. Once again, the sound of numerous whining sirens is in the background.

SIMPSON: . . . Just let me get to my house. Please.

LANGE: Okay. We're gonna do that.

SIMPSON: I swear to you, I'll give you me. I'll give you my whole body.

LANGE: Okay.

SIMPSON: I just need to get to my house where I lived with Nicole.

LANGE: Okay. We're gonna do that. Just throw the gun out the window.

SIMPSON: I can't do that.

LANGE: We're not gonna bother you. We're gonna let you go up there. Just throw it out the window. Please. You're scaring everybody. [Pause] O.J., you there?

SIMPSON: This is for me. This is not to keep you guys away from me. This is for me.

LANGE: I know that. Nobody's gonna hurt you.

SIMPSON: This is for me.

LANGE: Okay, it's for you. I know that. But do it for—

SIMPSON: This is for me *for* me. That's all.

LANGE: I know that. I know that. But do it for the kids too, will you?

SIMPSON: How?

LANGE: Think of your kids.

SIMPSON: How?

LANGE: Please. Just toss it out. You're scaring everybody, man.

SIMPSON: Aw, I'm not gonna hurt anybody, you know that.

LANGE: I know you're not gonna hurt anybody, but—

SIMPSON: —But I need it for me.

LANGE: —I know you're not, man.

SIMPSON: I'm just, I'm just gonna go with me.

LANGE: Please, you're scaring everybody though. You're scaring them.

SIMPSON: Aw, just tell them I'm all sorry. You can tell them later on today and tomorrow that I was sorry. And that, I, I'm sorry that I did this to the police department.

LANGE: Listen I think you should tell them yourself.

SIMPSON (moaning): —aah huh—

LANGE: And I don't want to have to tell your kids that.

SIMPSON: —aah—

LANGE: Your kids need you.

SIMPSON: I've already said good-bye to my kids.

LANGE: Listen. No. We're not gonna say good-bye to your kids.

SIMPSON: I already have.

LANGE: You're gonna, you're gonna see them again.

SIMPSON: —aah—

LANGE: You want to see them again. Please. You're scaring us. You're scaring them. Please, man.

SIMPSON: Hey, you've been a good guy to me.

LANGE: Thanks.

SIMPSON: And let me tell you. I know you're doing your job.

LANGE: I appreciate that.

SIMPSON: You were honest with me right from the beginning, just saying you're doing your job. I know you do a good job.

LANGE: Okay, thank you. But there's a lot of people that love you. Don't throw it all away.

SIMPSON: Aah—

LANGE: Don't throw it all away.

SIMPSON: I can't take this.

LANGE: Oh, yes, you can. Yes you can.

SIMPSON (sobbing): I can't.

LANGE: You got your whole family out here.

SIMPSON: Aah—. I can't take this.

LANGE: They love you, man. Don't throw this away.

SIMPSON: Aah—

LANGE: Don't do this. They love you.

SIMPSON: Aah—

LANGE: Don't do it, O.J. It's gonna work itself out.

SIMPSON: Aah—

LANGE: It's gonna work. It's gonna work. You're listening to me. I know you are. And you're thinking about your kids right now, aren't you? Aren't you?

SIMPSON (still moaning): Aaaaoh—

LANGE: They're thinking about you. They're thinking about you.

SIMPSON: Aah—

LANGE: So is your mother. Your mother loves you. Everybody loves you, don't do this.

SIMPSON: Aoooh—

LANGE: I know you're thinking.

SIMPSON: Aoooh—

LANGE: Man, just throw it out the window.

SIMPSON: Aaaahh—

LANGE: And nobody's gonna get hurt.

SIMPSON: I'm the only one that deserves—

LANGE: No you don't deserve that.

SIMPSON: I'm gonna get hurt.

LANGE: You do not deserve to get hurt. You do not deserve to get hurt.

SIMPSON: Aaahh—

LANGE: Don't do this.

SIMPSON: All I did was love Nicole. That's all I did was love her.

LANGE: I understand.

SIMPSON: I love everybody. I tried to show everybody my whole *life* that I love everybody.

LANGE: We know that. And everybody loves *you*.

SIMPSON: Aaah—

LANGE: Especially your family. Your mother. Your kids. All your friends. A.C.

SIMPSON: Aooh—

LANGE: Everybody does. Don't do this. Just put it down or throw it out the window.

SIMPSON: Aah—

LANGE: And this will all go away. It's gonna be a lot better tomorrow, believe me.

SIMPSON: Aah—

LANGE: Please. We'll let you go up to the house, but we need you to throw it out the window.

SIMPSON: Yeah, yeah—

LANGE: We'll let you go up there but we need you to throw the gun out the window. Please.

SIMPSON: Aaah, aaah—. A.C. will take it from me when I get home.

LANGE: But if you throw it out the window they're not gonna have to do that.

[Sound of sirens ends]

LANGE: Okay? Hello. O.J.? You still there? [To others at RHD:] Lost him under the freeway there.

[Phone rings twice]

LANGE: Ringing again, came back.

[Automated message: We're sorry, you have reached a number that has been disconnected or is no long—]

LANGE: O.J., it's Tom again. How you holding up?

SIMPSON: Aaaaooooooohhh—

LANGE: Hey, it's gonna be better tomorrow. Get rid of the gun. Toss it. Please.

SIMPSON: Aaah—

LANGE: Too many people love you man. Don't give it all up. Don't hurt everybody. You're gonna hurt everybody.

SIMPSON: Aah—. I'm just gonna . . . leave.

LANGE: No. Don't.

SIMPSON: I'm just gonna go with Nicole. That's all I'm gonna do. That's all I'm trying to do.

LANGE: Hey, listen. Think about everybody else, right?

SIMPSON: I just need somebody on the freeway. I couldn't do it in a field. I went to do it at her grave. I want to do it at my house.

LANGE: You're not gonna do anything. Too many people love you.

SIMPSON: Aah—

LANGE: Your kids. Your mother. Your friends. A.C. Everybody. You've got the whole world. Don't throw it away.

SIMPSON: Aah—

LANGE: Don't throw it away, man. Come on.

[Sound of sirens ends.]

LANGE: O.J.? [To those at RHD:] Help. Lost him again.

[Brief pause]

LANGE: O.J., it's Tom again. How are you doing?

SIMPSON: Not ba—. You just call them at my house. I know that they're all over the place with guns and stuff.

LANGE: They're not gonna do—

SIMPSON: You just let them know I'm not coming there to hurt any of them.

LANGE: Okay. They know that and they don't want to hurt you.

SIMPSON: Okay? It was just the first date I ever had with Nicole. The very first date I ever had with her. The first night we ever went out.

LANGE: Yeah?

SIMPSON: We went to that house. It was all in shambles. I had just bought it. But that's not, that's where we went.

LANGE: Okay.

SIMPSON: It was our first date, first night we were together.

LANGE: Ah-haa.

SIMPSON: That's all. And I tried to go to be with her down there at—.

LANGE: Yeah?

SIMPSON: But you wouldn't let me. And I just want to go to, go to my house.

LANGE: Okay.

SIMPSON: That's where we were. And that's where we were happy. . . .

LANGE: I like talking to you. Is that all right?

SIMPSON: Aaah—

LANGE: Will you keep talking to me?

SIMPSON: Aah—. Man, you deserve whatever you get.

LANGE: Well, thank you.

SIMPSON: You've been a good guy, man.

LANGE: Thanks . . .

SIMPSON: I know you're just doing your job like you told me.

LANGE: Yes. Yes. And nobody's gonna hurt you either.

SIMPSON: And, and, and, and man, I appreciate it.

LANGE: Okay.

SIMPSON: You know? I'll c—

[Sound of sirens ends]

LANGE: You still, are you there? Hello?

[Brief pause]

LANGE: It's okay, I'm back.

SIMPSON: I'm here. . . .

LANGE: All right. Listen.

SIMPSON: You did your job well.

LANGE: I think you are too, all right?

[Transmission breaking up]

LANGE: You there? Hello? Yeah, I'm losing you a little bit. Hang on the line. I want to talk to you.

SIMPSON: I'm here.

LANGE: Okay, I'm still here. Just getting a little interference here. Can you hear me?

SIMPSON: I am sorry. Okay?

LANGE: That's okay. There's nothing to be sorry about.

SIMPSON: [Inaudible]

LANGE: You're breaking up just a little, but hold on. Don't hang up. Don't hang up. It'll come back.

[Sound of sirens ends]

LANGE: Hello? You there? Hello?

[Phone ringing. Automated message: We're sorry, you have reached—]

SIMPSON: Yeah?

LANGE: It's Tom again. You guys are getting close, huh? Hello? I'm losing you. O.J., are you still there? Hello? Juice, you still there? Talk to me. Hello? Hello? Juice? Hello? Hello?

[Phone ringing. Automated message again.]

LANGE: This is Tom again.

SIMPSON: Aah, Tom. Aah—

LANGE: You guys gonna, you going up there, man, or what do you want to do?

[The Bronco goes onto the Sunset Boulevard exit ramp and turns left on Sunset.]

SIMPSON: I'm just pulling up to my house, Tom.

LANGE: You gonna go up there?

SIMPSON: Where?

LANGE: You gonna go to the house?

SIMPSON: That's where I told you we were—. You know, you just let them all know, you let the police know, you let them all know. I wasn't *running*—

LANGE: I know you weren't running. I know you weren't running.

SIMPSON: —I was trying to go, I was trying to go to Nicole's grave.

LANGE: I know you weren't running.

SIMPSON: We went there, and now I ca—

LANGE: I know you weren't, man. But you got everybody scared.

SIMPSON: Yeah.

LANGE: You got us all scared with a gun, man.

SIMPSON: Aah—. And I'm sorry I made the police look bad by not showing up. I didn't mean to do that.

LANGE: No. Hey, we don't care. That's, that's not a problem. You know what, you know what the important thing is here? Is that you don't hurt everybody and break their hearts.

SIMPSON: I'm not going to hurt anybody.

LANGE: You're gonna break somebody's heart, is what you're gonna do.

SIMPSON: I know, if I hurt somebody. I'm not gonna hurt anybody.

LANGE: And I'm, I'm talking your mother and I'm talking your kids. Don't do this.

SIMPSON: Aah—

LANGE: Just toss it man. Come on.

SIMPSON: Aah—

LANGE: Everything's gonna be—

SIMPSON: You know I'm not gonna hurt, you've been around me even the few days you've been around me, and you know I'm not gonna hurt anybody.

LANGE: I know you. That's where you're right, I do know. And you're better than that. You're not gonna do this. You're not gonna do it. A.C. is there with you?

SIMPSON: I'm just gonna hurt me.

LANGE: Just stop. Please, man. And throw it out. Please? Please. So I can talk to you again, all right?

SIMPSON: Aaah— . . .

LANGE: Please. Hey you want me to beg you? I'm begging you.

SIMPSON: Don't beg me.

LANGE: I'm begging you.

SIMPSON: It's like a bad dream.

LANGE: You want me to beg you?

SIMPSON: No!

LANGE: All right. Then do it. Come on.

SIMPSON: Oooh—

LANGE: Come on. You're scaring the hell out of those people. They're, they're they're being stupid out there. I can see them on the TV.

SIMPSON: Aah—

LANGE: Come on. Just tell A.C. to pull over, will you?

SIMPSON: No.

LANGE: Please.

SIMPSON: No.

LANGE: Don't do this to your kids. Don't do this to your mom. Don't do this to everybody who loves you.

SIMPSON: Aah—

LANGE: Come on.

SIMPSON: Aah—

LANGE: Please? Come on.

SIMPSON: Aah—

LANGE: I want to talk to you again.

SIMPSON: Aaah—

LANGE: We gotta talk, all right? Man to man, all right?

SIMPSON: Aah—

LANGE: Listen, you've been a man all your life.

SIMPSON: Aaah—

LANGE: You know, don't stop now, O.J. Don't give in now.

SIMPSON: Aaah—

LANGE: *Juice!* Don't give in now. You've been a man all your life. You're admired. Don't give it up.

SIMPSON: Aaah—

LANGE: You're listening to me, and you're thinking. I know you're thinking.

SIMPSON: Ooh—

LANGE: You're tired too, aren't you? Huh?

SIMPSON: I'm so tired.

LANGE: I know. I know.

SIMPSON: I just want to be with Nicole.

LANGE: You don't need to be with Nicole. You need to be with your family and with your kids. . . .

SIMPSON: Aah—

LANGE: All right? That doesn't need to be done now. You need your kids and your kids need you. Don't do this to them. You're hurting everybody man.

SIMPSON: Aah—

LANGE: You're being selfish with your kids, man. Don't do it. They *love* you. And so does everybody else. You're gonna break your mother's heart. Don't do it.

SIMPSON: Aah—

LANGE: All right? Please. Just have A.C. pull over and just toss that gun out and everything's gonna be okay. It's gonna be better tomorrow.

SIMPSON: [Inaudible] He's taking me home.

LANGE: I know he's taking you home. But will you please toss that gun? We're gonna let you go home. But please toss the gun. Because you're gon—, you're scaring everybody. Okay?

SIMPSON: I will *not* point it at anyone.

LANGE: I know you're not gonna point it.

SIMPSON: Aah—

LANGE: But you're still scaring them. How about this? We let you go home, let you pull right inside. All we need to see is that gun come out the window.

SIMPSON: I'm *not* gonna point it at anyone.

LANGE: I *know* that man. I know that. But you're scaring them anyway. . . .

SIMPSON: Ooh—. I want to [Inaudible].

LANGE: —But you're scaring everybody. Just toss it [out] the window and drive right in. Okay?

SIMPSON: Ooh—I just want to see my home.

LANGE: You will. You will. You want to see your kids though too, don't you? Huh?

SIMPSON: I've got pictures with me.

LANGE: You've got pictures?

SIMPSON: With me.

LANGE: Okay, but how about the real thing? And your mom? All right?

SIMPSON: Aah—

LANGE: How about the real thing? They need you. Don't do this to them. Don't do this to them.

SIMPSON: Aaah—

LANGE: You're gonna break their hearts. They're young yet. Come on!

SIMPSON: Aah—

LANGE: How about Arnelle? Did you think—. Have you thought of Arnelle yet?

SIMPSON: Huh?

LANGE: Have you thought of Arnelle yet. She needs you.

SIMPSON: Aaah—

LANGE: They all need you, man. Come on. You're gonna break their hearts. Don't do this. Juice?

SIMPSON: Yeah?

LANGE: Toss it. And drive right in.

SIMPSON: Aaah—

LANGE: Just toss it.

SIMPSON: Aaah—

LANGE: Just tell A.C. to toss it.

SIMPSON [as the Bronco turns right off Sunset Boulevard and onto North Rockingham]: Aaah—. Almost home.

LANGE: Okay. You're gonna get home. But your kids need you. Okay? They want you too. All right? Nobody's gonna hurt you, and you don't want to hurt anybody, right?

SIMPSON: I ain't gonna hurt nobody.

LANGE: I know, I know you're not, man. I know you're not gonna do that. I know you're not. And nobody wants to hurt you, right? Huh? When's the last time you saw the kids?

SIMPSON: Aah—

LANGE: Huh? When did you see the kids last, Juice?

SIMPSON: A.C., pull me in my dri—, driveway.

LANGE: I know, I see you. I see you. Please, toss the gun.

SIMPSON: Aah—

LANGE: Juice, just toss it. Come on man.

SIMPSON: Aah—

LANGE: Just toss it. Please? All right? Juice just, just toss the gun.

At this point, 7:57 P.M., Simpson, now parked in his driveway, drops his telephone. Although Lange continues to plead with Simpson to throw out his gun, Simpson is no longer on the other end. However, the line is still open, and the tape picks up much of the tense drama that unfolds:

[Sounds of frantic inaudible voices.]

COWLINGS [as Simpson oldest son, Jason, rushes the Bronco]:- Jason get back![92]

SIMPSON: [Sobbing, still with his gun to his head]

COWLINGS: O.J., please! Don't you get——. O.J.! No! No! Don't run away from here!

SIMPSON: Oooh—

COWLINGS [hysterically]: O.J.! I'm begging you! *Don't do it, O.J.!* It isn't worth it! For your kids! And, me, O.J.! O.J. don't! Don't! Don't! [Inaudible] Don't just leave, man! Don't make me fi——. They got you, O.J.!

SIMPSON: Aah—

COWLINGS: Please! Listen to me! Listen to me, O.J.! Listen to me!

SIMPSON: Fuck off!

COWLINGS: [Inaudible] Please! I beg of you man! O.J. No! No, O.J.! O.J.! O.J.! Think about the babies!

SIMPSON: Oooh—

COWLINGS: Hey! They lost their mother, O.J.!

SIMPSON: Ooh—

COWLINGS: Please, O.J.!

SIMPSON: Oooh—

COWLINGS: O.J.!

COWLINGS: Please put it down, O.J.! Please lay the gun down!

COWLINGS: O.J., don't do this!

SIMPSON: Ooh—

COWLINGS: Think of all of them, O.J.! Right now they can't handle it, O.J., anymore! They can't handle it, man! Don't do it, O.J.!

SIMPSON: They'll be okay.

COWLINGS: O.J.! They [the police] can kill you! You're the Juice, man! Don't make them go over the edge, O.J.! [Inaudible]

SIMPSON: Ooh— [Brief unintelligible words to Cowlings, then]

I'm not gonna hurt nobody! I'm not gonna hurt Nicole Simpson!

SIMPSON: [sobbing heavily, apparently yelling out to the LAPD negotiator]: I'm not gonna hurt you guys!

COWLINGS: No one's going to look down on you! I know you hurt, buddy! I know you're hurting!

SIMPSON: This is all a fucking dream!

COWLINGS: [Inaudible]

SIMPSON [moaning]: Noooh—

[Brief inaudible words exchanged between Simpson and Cowlings]

SIMPSON [to LAPD negotiator Pete Weireter, who is situated between the Bronco and Simpson's house]: No. No . . . Tell them I'm not confused! Tell them I'm not going to hurt anybody!

WEIRETER: What about the gun?

SIMPSON: O.J. is not going to point it at anybody.

COWLINGS: Let me talk to him. Where's his mother? [screaming] *Where's his mother?*

[Cowlings is taken out of the picture by the police. Simpson is now dealing directly with Weireter.[93]]

SIMPSON: Oooh—

WEIRETER: O.J., please.

SIMPSON: Tell these guys I ain't gonna hurt nobody. Tell them I'm not gonna hurt nobody. Would you tell them that?

[Simpson listens to Weireter, speaking inaudibly from outside the car.][94]

SIMPSON: Nicole and I did this house together.

[Weireter continues inaudible comments.]

SIMPSON: I want them out of here. I want Arnelle and Jason—

[Lange still watches everything unfold on television and continues to plead with Simpson to pick up the telephone. A soft murmur of inaudible conversation goes on for several minutes.]

SIMPSON [shouting out to the police officers]: You guys, I would ne—, I would never point anything at you guys! I would *never* point anything at you guys! Never! *Never* want to point anything at you guys!

WEIRETER: [Inaudible]

SIMPSON [still shouting out]: No, they don't have to put them down! You don't have to put them down! I just want you to know I would *never ever* hurt any of you guys! I'd never point *anything* at you!

Seconds later, Lange's phone goes dead.[95]

As of this moment, all of the information Lange and Vannatter are receiving is coming exclusively from what they are seeing and hearing on television.

Finally, at 8:45 P.M., the light in Cowlings's Bronco goes on and the door opens. Although Simpson, holding framed pictures of his family, is slow to come out, he finally emerges.

Then, after taking a few steps, Simpson collapses into the arms of the waiting police officers.

Endnotes

91. In his book, *The Run of His Life,* Jeffrey Toobin wrote on page 108: "At about 7:15 P.M., when A.C. and O.J. were still wending their way to Brentwood, Detective Tom Lange had reached Cowlings on the cellular phone in the Bronco. In their conversation, Cowlings confirmed that he was heading to O.J.'s home and that Simpson remained suicidal."

Toobin is wrong on this point. Lange *never* spoke with Cowlings during the Bronco chase. Lange called Simpson's cellular phone number, not Cowlings's, and talked directly to Simpson.

92. According to the Metro Division's log, Robert Kardashian managed to get inside Simpson's house during the Bronco chase. When LAPD negotiator Pete Weireter discovered that Simpson and Kardashian were friends, he used a willing Kardashian for background intelligence on Simpson. Also, Kardashian introduced Weireter to Simpson after the Bronco arrived at the North Rockingham estate. According to the log, Weireter's intent was "to have a familiar voice once the [negotiating] process is in place."

With people everywhere outside Simpson's gate, along with all of the black-and-whites and the noise level of the helicopters, the Metro log chronicled that the police "could not have scripted a crazier scenario."

The log added that when Jason Simpson charged the Bronco, "Kardashian immediately ID's Jason as OJ's son. . . . [Jason is] cuffed and secured in the house."

93. According to the official Metro log, the problems with Cowlings— who appeared to be losing control of himself, and, thus, jeopardizing the situation—began moments earlier: "A.C. takes an aggressive role— claims OJ had a gun to his head and is going to commit suicide. From inside—we can see OJ slumped over cradling what appears to be pictures with a revolver under his chin."

Then, negotiator Weireter tried to open negotiations with Simpson via Cowlings. However, Cowlings, according to the log, was "an unwanted third party negotiator. A.C. refused to get close—anticipating his arrest. A.C. walking back/forth appears to be out of control—efforts to temper his behavior while establishing dialogue with O.J. A.C. ultimately becomes part of the background."

94. The official Metro log continued that Weireter, via a second cellular phone in the car, gained "voice to voice with O.J.—issues regarding his safety. Telephonic dialogue with O.J.—regarding his image and safety. [O.J.] requests voice to voice—wanting to see who he was talking to."

95. According to the official Metro Division log, the cellular phone, which negotiators used to communicate with Simpson, also went dead. "A.C. delivers cell phone battery and is out of the picture. Back on the phone—overtures that he wants to surrender. Dialogue regarding the surrendering process. Issues of safety and wanting to surrender in his home. Issues regarding a call to his mother."

The log cites that Simpson had an overwhelming fear for his safety, believing that he could be "swooped upon" by Metro's SWAT team.

16

The Aftermath

Total relief and euphoria sweep across the Robbery/Homicide Division at the moment of Simpson's surrender. The ticking time bomb everyone in the office has been sitting on for nearly eight hours has been defused. Although there isn't any spontaneous cheering, Lange and Vannatter quietly receive congratulations from their colleagues—handshakes and pats on the back. The crisis has passed. Cool heads have prevailed.

The two detectives quickly receive word that both Simpson and Cowlings are being brought back to Parker Center—this time with an armed escort. Simpson is in a car driven by Robbery/Homicide Detective Addison "Bud" Arce, accompanied by LAPD negotiator Pete Weireter and RHD Detectives J. R. Kwock, who is Arce's partner, and Jerry Stephens.

Metro officers are bringing in Cowlings. Stephens's partner, Detective Mike Berchem, who is working with Metro, seizes Cowlings's Bronco and everything in it.

Lange and Vannatter get on the telephone, making the required notifications to their superiors, as well as voicing relief to their own families. Then, at a little after 9:00 P.M., they officially shut down their makeshift command post in the division's office.

Lange and Vannatter go downstairs to the city jail in back of Parker Center—the location where attorney Robert Shapiro had promised and failed to surrender Simpson at 11:00 A.M. When

Arce's car pulls in, they see Simpson—still wearing a blue jacket, yellow golf shirt, and blue jeans. Now handcuffed, Simpson is brought into the building, saying nothing but acting somewhat haughty. Sensing this, Lange and Vannatter view his attitude as more fear and embarrassment than anything else.

However, Simpson's cool veneer cracks when Vannatter, after reading his Miranda rights, says sarcastically, "O.J., you missed your appointment today—big-time." Turning deeply sincere, Simpson replies almost tearfully, "You know I'm sorry, Vannatter. I'm really sorry. I'm really sorry I caused you all these problems."

Vannatter believes that Simpson is actually on the verge of a mental collapse. Standing in the entrance to the city jail, the detectives ask Simpson if he's sick or injured, knowing that the dispensary where Simpson's blood had been drawn on June 13 is in an adjacent room. Simpson shakes his head, indicating that he is neither sick nor injured.

Hearing that Metro has just arrived with Cowlings, who has been taken to the Robbery/Homicide Division, Vannatter leaves Lange and Simpson prior to the booking process and returns to his office to deal with Cowlings.

Without any conversation at all, Lange walks with Simpson, who will be held without bail, up to a counter where a civilian booking officer works. A thick, clear-plastic barrier separates the booking officer from the suspect and the arresting officer. Simpson is sternly ordered to empty his pockets and to remove all other personal items. He complies and places them in a metal dish. The officer runs Simpson through the preliminary paperwork of the booking process, asking him a series of perfunctory questions.

Although Simpson's driver's license is seized, the booking officer asks him his name and address, among other pro forma questions. When asked for his occupation, Simpson replies, "Entertainer."

After the initial processing, Lange takes Simpson into a small padded room where Simpson is strip-searched. In front of another booking officer, Simpson removes all of his clothing. Allowing himself to be examined, he raises his arms over his head and slowly turns completely around. He opens his mouth and sticks his tongue out. He shows the bottoms of his feet. Then, he turns around, bends over, and spreads the cheeks of his buttocks, allowing the officer to inspect him, making sure that nothing is concealed.

With this humiliating act now completed, Simpson puts his own clothes back on. His arraignment is not scheduled until the following day—after which he will be transported to the county jail and placed in his prison fatigues, an orange jumpsuit.

Until the arraignment, Lange, still fearing that Simpson might try to commit suicide, requests that Simpson be isolated in the city jail, apart from the other prisoners. He asks that prison guards stand close by on a suicide watch.

In Cowling's Bronco, detectives find Simpson's travel bag, the same bag the police had seized—and Vannatter inspected—on Monday, June 13. Inside the travel bag, detectives find his passport, his treasured NFL Hall of Fame ring, a disguise kit,[96] a variety of credit cards, toilet articles, a change of underwear, and two sets of keys. These items are booked as evidence.

Later, Detective Mike Berchem gives Lange the other items found in the Bronco: Simpson's Smith & Wesson .357 magnum, a Motorola cellular telephone, a piece of paper with the handwritten name of the mortuary that handled his ex-wife's funeral, and six live rounds of ammunition, which were found in the magnum.[97]

When Lange finishes his work downstairs, he joins Vannatter up in the RHD office. Vannatter is sitting with Al Cowlings in the same interrogation room where they had interviewed Simpson earlier in the week. Vannatter reads Cowlings his Miranda rights.

Cowlings waives those rights, agreeing to talk to Lange and Vannatter without an attorney present. Appearing to be completely cooperative, Cowlings also seems totally spent and exhausted.

First, Vannatter tells Cowlings to empty his pockets, and Cowlings complies. Among other items, Cowlings drops a wad of money, totalling $8,750, on the table. Cowlings tells the detectives, "O.J. gave me over eight-thousand dollars. He wanted me to give the money to his kids, Jason and Arnelle."[98]

As the detectives talk to Cowlings, they quickly grow to like him. Without a doubt, he has been a loyal and devoted friend who would do anything for Simpson. Both officers recognize that Cowlings has just proven that by placing his life on the line for him.

"Tell us how you became involved in this?" Vannatter asks.[99]

"I guess it started last night," Cowlings replies. "O.J. needed to get some rest and didn't want to be hounded by the media. So he asked me to pretend to be him. O.J.'s security guys rushed me into the house . . ."

Vannatter interrupts, "Was one of those security people a LAPD cop?"

"Yeah, I think so. I think there was one."

Vannatter was referring to the off-duty sergeant with the Harbor Division he remembers seeing at Simpson's residence the previous night on television after Brown's funeral service.

"Okay, go ahead," Vannatter says.

"So, anyway, O.J. goes to Bob Kardashian's house over in Encino to spend the night. . . . The next morning, I went over to Kardashian's to be with O.J. and the others—Bob Kardashian, Bob Shapiro, and some of the doctors."

Lange asks, "Did you know that we had a warrant for Simpson's arrest?"

"Yeah, I knew about it," Cowlings admits. "O.J. was very upset about it. He was crying. While I was with him this morning, he wrote some letters."

"Did you know what they said?" Lange continues.

"No, I never read them. He didn't tell me what he wrote. I did think he wanted to kill himself."

"What else was going on in the house?" Vannatter asks.

"I remember that the doctors came and examined him. They took some blood and hair samples from him."

"Then what?"

"During the early afternoon, O.J. and I were alone downstairs and everyone else was upstairs. He just kept crying. He was looking at Nicole's picture. That's when he asked me to drive him to her grave at the cemetery in Orange County."

Vannatter asks, "Did anyone tell you that uniformed officers were on their way to Kardashian's house to pick up Simpson?"

"No. No one told me that," Cowlings answers emphatically. "I knew about the warrant. I knew that O.J. was going to be arrested for murdering Nicole. But, when he asked me to drive him to the cemetery, I agreed to do it. I just agreed. He's my friend. So we just walked outside. I don't think anyone upstairs knew when we left. We just split. We were gone. We left in my Bronco."

"Knowing that you would be breaking the law?" Vannatter asks. "Knowing that you would be harboring a fugitive?"

"I'm a loyal friend," Cowlings replies sincerely. "And O.J. is my friend."

Lange continues, "Did you believe that he was still going to kill himself?"

"While we were on the road, O.J. showed me a gun, a .357 magnum, that he had wrapped in a towel. That's when he started talking about killing himself."

Vannatter inquires, "Where did you go?"

"To the cemetery. We went to Nicole's grave at the cemetery in Orange County."

"How long were the two of you at the cemetery?"

"Not long," says Cowlings. "There were a couple of uniforms in a police car, and we thought they might be looking for us. We hid my car in an orange grove. But while we were at the cemetery, O.J. started talking again about suicide. I thought for sure that he was going to kill himself. So I just started talking to him. I told him that I was going to drive him back to his home."

Asks Lange, "So you went back up the freeway towards Los Angeles?"

"Right."

"Why didn't you stop when the Orange County sheriff's office put on their lights and wanted you to stop?"

"Because I was afraid that O.J. was going to kill himself. After the police got on our tail, that's when O.J. climbed in the back, and put the gun to his head."

Vannatter then asks, "Do you think O.J. murdered his wife and her friend?"

Cowlings replies sharply, "We never talked about that."

"A.C.," Lange presses, "do you think he did it?"

Cowlings pauses momentarily, drops his head, and says quietly, "I don't know. You have a lot of evidence."

After their half-hour interview with Cowlings, the detectives have him taken downstairs to be processed and booked. He is charged with harboring a fugitive. Of the $8,750 he walked in with, he is permitted to keep only eight dollars while in jail. The rest is booked as Cowlings's personal property, as per LAPD policy, even though the money is Simpson's.

When Lange and Vannatter return to their office, several Robbery/Homicide detectives who had participated in the Simpson adventure get together to exchange reports and to draw up a common log of the day's events.

At the end of this long and bizarre experience, Lange is physically and emotionally drained. Vannatter is so tired that he is ready to curl up on the floor and just go to sleep right there rather than face the long drive home.

Tomorrow is Saturday, a day they would normally sleep in. But after today's events, they know they will be back on the job bright and early. They still have plenty of work to do, considering that, among other things, they do not have a murder weapon, and they have not found the clothing Simpson wore on the night of the murders.

While organizing his files, Lange receives a telephone call from a friend who has just returned from Officer Russell Young's retirement dinner that night. Lange laughs when he hears that everyone watched the Bronco chase on a television in the banquet room, adding that one of the speakers had presented Young with an NFL football on Lange's behalf—a clear reference to Lange's role in the Simpson case.

As Lange and Vannatter get ready to go home for the evening, Captain Gartland steps out of his office.

Gartland says sternly. "I want to talk to both of you. Bring your coffee cups in."

"What's this about?" Vannatter asks his partner as they walk into Gartland's office. Once inside, they see their immediate supervisor in Homicide Special—Lieutenant John Rogers, who had assigned them this case five days earlier—seated at a long table. Gartland opens his desk drawer and pulls out an unopened bottle of Irish whisky.

Then, he takes everyone's coffee cups and pours them a drink.

With a little smile, the legendary Will Gartland proudly raises his cup, toasting his men and saying softly, "Here's to you guys."

With the whole world watching, the Los Angeles Police Department, facing a potentially humiliating and tragic situation, had performed with remarkable restraint and compassion, sparing and perhaps even saving the life of a murder suspect.

Everyone returned home safely tonight, including O.J. Simpson.

EVIDENCE DISMISSED

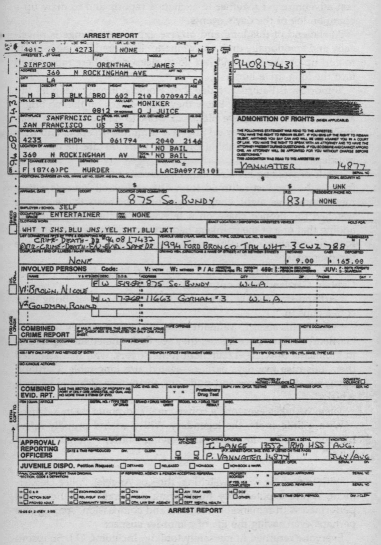

PAGE NO.	TYPE OF REPORT				BOOKING NO.	CR NO.
2	ARREST				4013970	94-08 17431

ITEM NO.	QUAN.	ARTICLE	SERIAL NO.	BRAND	MODEL NO.	MISC. DESCRIPTION (EG. COLOR, SIZE, INSCRIPTIONS, CALIBER, REVOLVER, ETC)	DOLLAR /A...

SOURCE OF ACTIVITY:

Detectives investigating the double homicide of victims Nicole Brown and Ronald Goldman.

OFFICERS' OBSERVATIONS:

Information and evidence developed by detectives from crime scene and witness interviews led to the involvement of O.J. Simpson as a participant in the crime.

ARREST:

The suspect was arrested at his residence after he was pursued from the Orange County area.

BOOKING:

Advised by Detective III F. D. Lange #13552 and Simpson booked at Jail Division for 187 P.C. (Murder).

Endnotes

96. Sales receipts showed that Simpson purchased the disguise kit from Cinema Secrets Beauty Supply, Inc., in Burbank on May 27, sixteen days before the murders.

In *The Search for Justice*, Robert Shapiro wrote on page 47: "The explanation was simple: The mustache-and-beard disguise had been ordered by [Simpson] weeks before (using his own name and address, the police easily discovered, which hardly pointed to subterfuge) so that he could take his children on a planned trip to an amusement park without being recognized. . . ."

97. A controversy over Simpson's .357 magnum served as the impetus for an investigation by the LAPD's Internal Affairs Division. Detectives learned that Simpson's gun had originally been purchased in or about 1988 by a supervisor at the LAPD Academy. Simpson's .357 was among five weapons bought by this supervisor for an executive of the Los Angeles Raiders, who then gave them to five friends, including two members of the football team. One of these players gave his gun to Simpson. The IA investigation concluded that the supervisor had not broken any law at the time of the purchase.

98. On November 30, 1994, prosecutor Christopher Darden told Lange that a security guard from a Brentwood bank had called him. The guard alleged that on June 17, 1994, at approximately 12:30 P.M., he had escorted Simpson's assistant, Cathy Randa, and Simpson's business attorney, Skip Taft, to a safe-deposit box at the bank. The guard observed them remove several stacks of new one-hundred-dollar bills. It remains unclear whether this was a portion of the cash Simpson had given to Cowlings before the Bronco chase.

99. The following is a recreated conversation, based on an interview report with Cowlings and Lange and Vannatter's recollections of their discussion with him.

PART TWO

Evidence Presented

17

Tug-of-War

June 19–September 23, 1994

In the wake of the Friday arrest of Simpson two days earlier, Phil and Rita Vannatter invite Tom and Linda Lange to their home in Valencia for a Sunday barbecue. Actually, this informal get-together turns into a little party, celebrating the fact that everyone had walked away from the sixty-mile Bronco chase alive. There are no funny hats or expensive champagnes at this gathering, just a lot of good feelings.

Sitting on a couple of lawn chairs by Vannatter's rose garden in the backyard, the two detectives honestly believe that they have developed clear evidence of Simpson's motive, means, and opportunity. Additionally, the overwhelming physical evidence makes this case appear more solid than any they had ever seen before in their long careers with the LAPD. With confidence now running high, the two detectives feel prepared for the anticipated legal maneuvering by the defense that will follow.

At his arraignment on Monday, June 20, O.J. Simpson, accompanied by Robert Shapiro, appears haggard and somewhat pathetic. Lange and Vannatter are stunned by his appearance. He looks like a broken man. At first, they wonder how fast his attorney will try to negotiate a plea-bargain arrangement with the district attorney's office. Head down and speaking almost in a whisper when asked how he pleads to the double-murder charge, Simpson simply replies, "Not guilty," as expected. Municipal Court Judge Patti Jo McKay orders that he continue to be held without bond.

On Wednesday, June 22, two days after Simpson's not-guilty plea, the Los Angeles City Attorney's Office helps the county's prosecution team go for Simpson's throat by releasing the tape of a desperate 911 call Nicole Brown made on October 25, 1993.

"Can you get someone over here now?" a terrified Brown asked the police dispatcher. "He's back. Please. . . . He's O.J. Simpson. I think you know his record. Could you just send somebody over here?" Throughout the call, Simpson can be heard in the background, screaming with such rage that most of his words are virtually unintelligible.

Two days after the tape's release, on Friday, June 24—and *because* of the release—Superior Court Supervising Judge Cecil J. Mills ends the county grand jury's investigation of the case, insisting that pretrial publicity has potentially interfered with Simpson's right to a fair trial. Consequently, no indictment will be handed up. Instead of a simple indictment, the decision about whether Simpson will have to stand trial is going to be made by a municipal court judge in the wake of a full-blown preliminary hearing.

Suddenly, the Simpson case doesn't seem like the cakewalk Lange and Vannatter expected. But the detectives remain confident. Los Angeles District Attorney Gil Garcetti has described the case they've put together as "a mountain of evidence." They assume that this delay will simply give Simpson more time to make a deal.

But another complication has already occurred. Jill Shively, whose story about an encounter with Simpson at the intersection of South Bundy and San Vicente on the night of the murders Lange and Vannatter still believe, had impeached herself as a witness during her June 21 appearance before the twenty-three-member grand jury. When Marcia Clark asked her whether she had shared her story with anyone other than the police and the grand jury, she replied that she had told only her mother and a small number of friends.

However, that same night, Shively appeared on the tabloid television show *Hard Copy*, telling the entire country of her alleged moment with Simpson. The question of whether she had done the interview before her grand jury appearance was answered when she waved her grand jury subpoena into the camera. Furthermore, she had received $5,000 for the interview.

On Thursday morning, Clark questioned Shively again before the grand jury. Shively admitted that she had not revealed her monetary deal with *Hard Copy*.

As a result, Clark, who was livid, told the grand jurors before the case was taken away from them, "Because it is our duty as prosecutors to present only that evidence in which we are 110 percent confident as to its truthfulness and reliability, I must now ask you to completely disregard the statements given and the testimony given by Jill Shively in this case. . . . I cannot allow her to be part of this case at this time now that she has proven to be untruthful. . . ."

Vannatter, in particular, is upset that Shively has been removed from the case, but he trusts Clark and realizes that she's doing the right thing. However, *both* Lange and Vannatter are already growing concerned with the press coverage of this case. Now, through checkbook journalism, the media is starting to buy off witnesses with lucrative fast cash.

Later, an employee of Ross Cutlery admits that he and two fellow employees have split a $12,500 fee from the *National Enquirer* in return for telling the story about their sale of the Stiletto knife to Simpson a few weeks before the murders. Consequently, none of them will be called as witnesses during the criminal trial.

On Thursday, June 30, the preliminary hearing begins with Municipal Court Judge Kathleen Kennedy-Powell presiding on the bench. The proceedings appear on national television, allowing the public to watch for themselves the American justice system in action. Broadcasting the hearing daily, Court TV and CNN have never before experienced such high ratings, surpassing even the murder trial of the Menendez brothers.

Even as the hearing gets under way, the Simpson defense team begins to demonstrate its ability and willingness to employ questionable tactics in this case. On Friday, July 1, Shapiro turns over his taped interviews with Kato Kaelin and Allan Park to the prosecution as part of the defense team's discovery requirements. The problem is that neither Kaelin nor Park allegedly knew that they were being tape-recorded during the interview, a violation of California law. Upon listening to these tapes, police detectives and prosecutors discover that Shapiro had left the tape running after his conversation with Park had concluded. The tape picked up

Shapiro and Skip Taft, who was also involved in the conversation, expressing concerns about Simpson's alibi, which included discrepancies in his story.

Another unsettling event makes the detectives think that the defense team is coming after them. It happens during a return to the South Bundy crime scene on Sunday, July 3. Lange is aware that someone is videotaping his every move. Apparently directing the filming is Bill Pavelic, a former LAPD officer who is now working for the Simpson defense. Lange remembers Pavelic from a dispute they had years earlier.[100]

Accompanying Pavelic is a potential defense witness who claims that, on the night of the murders, he saw two men running from the crime scene.[101] Lange and Vannatter talk to this witness and quickly discover that his story is nothing but a figment of his imagination. After a routine background check, the detectives learn that this same witness has made earlier claims to possess key information in the Polly Klaas murder investigation in northern California, as well as the gangland slaying of Mafia boss Paul Castellano in New York.

For the most part, such witnesses do nothing more than waste the detectives' time—as they and other Robbery/Homicide detectives must run down every lead that comes into their office. Both Lange and Vannatter now believe that Simpson's defense team wants nothing more than to force the detectives to chase ghosts.

In the midst of the preliminary hearing, Phil Vannatter becomes embroiled in a major controversy. While on the witness stand on July 6, he is grilled by Robert Shapiro about his decision to enter Simpson's property—along with Detectives Lange, Phillips, and Fuhrman—on the morning after the murders. The defense team claims that their actions were illegal and violated Simpson's Fourth Amendment rights against unreasonable search and seizure.

Although the detectives' reasons for entering the area are numerous, the defense concentrates on one in particular—the red speck Fuhrman had found above the door handle on the driver's side of Simpson's white Bronco.

"I observed what I thought was blood," Vannatter testifies. "It was a small spot, an eighth or a quarter of an inch."

Vannatter concedes that he needed a flashlight and his eyeglasses to see the red speck, which was later confirmed as blood by SID criminalist Dennis Fung. The defense tries to play upon this admission, distorting what has actually occurred by making it seem that Fuhrman had spotted this little speck from nearly a block away. However, the prosecution fails to make it clear that when Fuhrman discovered the blood, the Bronco was already a focus of attention because Fuhrman had seen a package—with the words, "Orenthal Productions"—in the cargo bay. After that discovery, Fuhrman had simply continued to examine the car, which was when he found the speck of blood.

Vannatter continues, "I think seeing the blood was the trigger that caused me to make the decision to go over the fence. . . . I made a decision that we should go in there and check to see if everything was okay. We were within five minutes of a very, very brutal murder scene. I was concerned that this could be a second murder scene, whether someone was stalking Mr. Simpson and his wife. I didn't really know at that point what I had or what I was looking for."

Vannatter explains that the detectives came onto Simpson's property because they were concerned for his safety—not because he had suddenly become an actual suspect in the murders on South Bundy.

On this point, Marcia Clark supports the detectives in open court, saying, "They had to do something to assure themselves that any people inside were safe. Had they not gone in, we would justifiably have accused them of being derelict in their duty. We would have said they were incompetent. The search was reasonably undertaken for the protection of life."

On July 8, following six days of testimony, Judge Kennedy-Powell rules that Simpson must stand trial. The decision has already been made by Garcetti to hold the trial in downtown Los Angeles rather than in a courtroom in Santa Monica. And both Lange and Vannatter agree with the district attorney's rationale. The facility in Santa Monica is quite small and, during the previous January, had suffered earthquake damage. Garcetti prefers the downtown location because it is more convenient for the prosecutors and the police, who, for the most part, are located downtown. Garcetti believes that any jury selected in either venue would vote to convict Simpson on the basis of all the evidence that has been collected. Garcetti insists that he can try this case anywhere and win.

Soon after the preliminary hearing ends, Johnnie L. Cochran, a prominent and stylish Los Angeles attorney who drives a Rolls-Royce and had once worked in the district attorney's office, joins Simpson's defense team. Two weeks earlier, two other prominent attorneys had joined the fray for the defense: legal magician F. Lee Bailey, who had defended Dr. Sam Sheppard (the prototype for the 1960s television series and 1993 movie, *The Fugitive*), Patty Hearst, and the Boston Strangler; and longtime cop critic Alan Dershowitz, whose clients included Claus von Bülow, Leona Helmsley, and Mike Tyson.

With their famous and high-priced abilities to use smoke and mirrors in the courtroom, Cochran, Shapiro, Bailey, and Dershowitz, along with several other lesser known lawyers, are dubbed by the press as "The Dream Team." But to Lange and Vannatter, these lawyers are simply "The Rat Patrol."

The tug of war between the prosecution and the defense begins quickly. The prosecution wants a sample of Simpson's hair for analysis, but the defense team balks. After a hearing on the matter, the court makes its decision on July 8, ordering that "at least 40, but not more than 100 hairs" may be removed from Simpson's head to compare with hair evidence found at the two crime scenes. It is a minor victory for the prosecution but one that required considerable time and effort. It is already becoming clear that Simpson might be prepared to match the county of Los Angeles dollar for dollar in this legal battle.

On Tuesday, July 12, Lange, along with Detective Jim Harper and an SID criminalist, arrive at the Los Angeles County Jail and are escorted to Simpson's cell to take the hair samples.

Isolated from other prisoners, Simpson is confined to a spartan pale blue nine-by-seven-foot cell in the midst of a small ward in which he is the only inmate. Adorning his living space is a stainless steel sink, a toilet with no seat, and a metal bed. In a common area outside the cell, Lange sees a television set, a variety of news and sports publications, and a basket of fresh fruit, as well as a table and chairs; a pay phone is also nearby. Lange can't help but think how dramatic this transition—from cushy elegance to imprisonment—must be for Simpson.

Even though they have become well acquainted since June 13—

dramatically culminating with Lange begging Simpson not to shoot himself during the June 17 Bronco chase—the two men say virtually nothing to each other. Lange has his job to do, and Simpson has been ordered by the court to cooperate, which he does. The scene is strictly business, almost clinical, with each of them wearing their best game faces.

The only thing Simpson does say to Lange is, "I hope when you find something for me, you don't throw it under the table." In other words, Simpson has asked the detective not to bury information that could clear him. "Count on it," Lange replies.

Learning from the hair-sample experience that she will have to fight for every inch in this case, prosecutor Marcia Clark starts to anticipate problems—but begins to drive those around her crazy in the process. Four days after receiving Simpson's hair sample, Lange is having dinner in Burbank with an old friend when he receives a message on his pager from Patti Jo Fairbanks in the district attorney's office. He calls Fairbanks back, and she tells him that two friends of Nicole Brown are at Nicole's home on South Bundy, helping to remove furniture. While performing this task, one of them discovers a red stain on one of the children's bedposts.

"Marcia wants a complete investigation of this red stuff," Fairbanks tells Lange. "She wants to know if it's blood."

"Patti," Lange replies to his friend, "tell Marcia that we've gone through this before. The killer never came in the house. His bloody shoe prints go right past the front door."

Fairbanks gives Lange's message to Clark, but she refuses to relent. Fairbanks calls Lange back, saying, "Marcia wants a criminalist, a photographer, and an investigative team dispatched to Nicole's house to impound the bed. . . . Sorry, Tom. She wants it done at once."

"Okay," Lange says reluctantly, knowing that the district attorney's office is now calling the shots in his case. "Call Nicole's house and tell those guys to keep the bedpost secure until the SID man gets there." Lange calls the crime lab and asks for a criminalist to go immediately over to the South Bundy crime scene. Knowing that this is just another wild-goose chase, Lange doesn't bother to go himself.

The following day, as Clark and the prosecution team eagerly wait, the SID Serology Unit—after conducting a battery of tests and measurements—issues its final report on the red stain: raspberry syrup.

Lange sees that Clark is starting to get panicky. And her sudden celebrity status in the wake of the televised preliminary hearing has already caused her relationship with the LAPD—even with her loyal friend, Phil Vannatter—to chill.

In the past, whenever Vannatter wanted to speak with Clark, he would simply walk into her small and cluttered office on the eighteenth floor of the Criminal Courts Building overlooking South Central Los Angeles. Now, after receiving flowers, telegrams, and letters from anonymous admirers all over the country, Clark starts to insist that Vannatter schedule an appointment before coming to her office.

Vannatter, who has been one of Clark's biggest fans and has enjoyed her new star status, feels somewhat slighted, especially since he's the one who brought her into this case on the day after the murders. Actually, the message sent by Clark's snub really has less to do with the hurt feelings of one detective than it does with the more practical issue of access. The loose relationship between Vannatter and Clark has always worked to their mutual advantage in their previous cases. Now, Clark is placing limitations on her availability.

At Simpson's formal arraignment on Friday, July 22, a new O.J. Simpson, standing tall and confident, appears at the hearing. This time when asked how he pleads, he replies defiantly and forcefully, "Absolutely, one hundred percent not guilty." Lange and Vannatter, who are working on another case at the time, are not present at the hearing but hear about it soon after. They can't believe that Simpson is going to fight this out.

That same day, Judge Mills announces that Judge Lance A. Ito will preside over the case. Judge Ito's wife is Margaret York, a respected captain in the LAPD—who, along with her partner, Helen Kidder, served as inspirations for the popular long-running television series, *Cagney and Lacey*. Lange and Vannatter know both women as the first female police officers in LAPD history to work homicide cases.[102]

A few days later, Deputy District Attorney Christopher Darden joins the prosecution team. Darden had formerly worked on the district attorney's team that investigated officer-involved shootings and police misconduct. Because of his job, he occasionally had some problems with a few of the detectives in the Robbery/Homicide Division. However, both Lange and Vannatter had become acquainted with the prosecutor through their close friend, RHD Detective Addison "Bud" Arce, who knew Darden to be a stand-up guy and a good attorney.

Prior to becoming part of the Simpson prosecution team, Darden had been handling the harboring case against A.C. Cowlings, which the district attorney's office indefinitely postpones on July 29. Both Lange and Vannatter view Cowlings as an honest and loyal friend who has been used by Simpson. Neither detective wants to see Cowlings prosecuted; nor do they believe that any jury would convict him on the harboring charge.

As for the Simpson case, Marcia Clark needs all the help she can get. The tabloids seem to be working her over, later even exploiting her child-custody battle with her second husband and publishing a topless photograph of her on the beach years earlier with her first husband. Early on, Lange and Vannatter see the pressure getting to Clark, who breaks down crying in front of the detectives. As a result of all the media attention and her own legitimate concerns, Clark receives armed protection from a team of investigators from the district attorney's office.

While the LAPD and the district attorney's office remain hell-bent on keeping Simpson in jail, O.J. suddenly offers a $500,000 reward for information leading to the "real killer or killers" of his ex-wife and Ron Goldman. Clearly, Simpson is getting ready to fight for his freedom. At this moment, there is no known talk of a possible plea bargain.

In mid-July, the LAPD and the prosecutors get a brief look inside the defense team. Writer Jeffrey Toobin publishes a remarkable article in *The New Yorker*, revealing that Detective Mark Fuhrman will become the key to the defense strategy.[103] Fuhrman had testified during the preliminary hearing, telling the court about his discovery of, among other things, the bloody right-hand glove on Simpson's estate during the early-morning hours after the murders.

After reading the story, both Lange and Vannatter are surprised to learn that the defense is going to play "the race card," claiming that Fuhrman is a longtime racist. In the course of researching his story, Toobin had supposedly obtained the detective's personnel file and, in particular, a psychological analysis of the detective in the wake of his request for a stress pension from the LAPD during the early 1980s. These documents reportedly detailed Fuhrman's disturbing pattern of behavior. The department had allegedly turned down Fuhrman's request for an early retirement but kept him on the force. Toobin insists that he discovered the documents independently—as opposed to having it spoon-fed to him by the defense, which had obtained them via Bill Pavelic.

According to Toobin's article, Simpson's defense team will also allege that Fuhrman might have planted the right-hand glove he found at Simpson's estate. During his testimony at the preliminary hearing, Fuhrman had inadvertently referred to the left-hand glove already discovered at the South Bundy crime scene as "them," which helps form the basis for this charge.

Lange and Vannatter, having been present at Simpson's home when Fuhrman found the glove on the morning after the murders, simply laugh off the thought that Fuhrman had planted evidence. The reasons are quite simple: Fuhrman had been the seventeenth police officer listed on the crime scene sign-in log, nearly two hours after the first officers arrived. During the interim, other officers had established a secure perimeter while viewing the existing evidence on and around the two bodies. They only saw a left-hand glove. *Not one of them saw a right-hand glove.*

Fuhrman—who was not permitted to touch any evidence until a police criminalist arrived—would have had to enter the secured perimeter, see a glove that sixteen other police officers never saw, remove it without being seen by anyone, conceal it, and then plant it where Kato Kaelin had heard the noise against his back wall—not knowing whether another suspect would turn up in the interim. In short, Fuhrman simply did not have the opportunity—let alone a motive and means—to plant the right-hand glove at North Rockingham.

Although Lange and Vannatter feel that they can dispel the planting theory, they are unaware of Fuhrman's alleged racism. The only information they have about his past is that he had been recently turned down for a transfer to the Robbery/Homicide Division's Officer-Involved Shooting Section for reasons they neither knew nor cared about.

In the midst of the furor over Toobin's article, Fuhrman's

personal attorney, who has been retained in the wake of the preliminary hearing, says, "The only people calling Mark Fuhrman a racist are the attorneys for the defense. We're going to fight back. By the end of the trial, the entire world will know that Mark Fuhrman is not a racist." In a prepared statement, LAPD spokesman David Gascon adds that Fuhrman "enjoys the full respect, support, and admiration of the chief of police and the [LAPD's] management staff."

Ever since Simpson's initial arraignment on June 20, the media has smelled blood and flocked not only to the prosecutors but also to Lange and Vannatter for inside information about the case. In the opinion of the two detectives, who aren't talking to the press, the playing of "the media card" by both the prosecution and the defense had already developed into a dangerous game. Both detectives plead with District Attorney Gil Garcetti and Marcia Clark to push Judge Ito to issue a gag order on all parties involved in the case.

"Listen," Lange tells Clark in a conversation in her office, "we need a gag order, because this media thing is already out of control. We've already lost one of our witnesses who got paid off by *Hard Copy*, and the guys at Ross Cutlery who took money from the *National Enquirer*. There's no reason to think that it's not going to happen again and again. And, now, this Toobin guy is giving credence to the defense theory that we planted evidence. I think we need to prevent Simpson's lawyers from putting their own spin on evidence and witnesses that haven't even been introduced yet in court. And a gag order is the only way I know to do that."

"That might be true, Tom," Clark replies, "but I think the bigger problem is controlling the leaks over at the LAPD."

"What leaks?" Lange asks.

"From what I'm hearing, the leaks are coming from the crime lab," says Clark. "That's why I want to get all of the blood evidence away from SID and give it to Cellmark and the other DNA specialists."

"That's hard to believe," Lange replies. "I can't imagine Michele Kestler or Greg Matheson leaking information to the press. These people are pros."

Clark says, "Tom, I'm not saying it's them, but it's somebody over there."

Lange continues, "Marcia, there're always rumors about leaks. Hell, we hear there's a leak in the DA's office. The fact is that people are talking about this case. And most of the talk is based on 'overhears'—somebody overhears something walking past your desk or mine or anyone else involved in this case. I mean, look what's coming out: half-truths. Look at that story about the bloody clothes in Simpson's washing machine. That's just another reason why I'm asking you to push for the gag order."

But whenever Lange brings up the subject of a gag order in any of his personal meetings with the key prosecutors, he sees the ambitious looks on their faces. The DA's office knows that this is not just a routine criminal case. Rather, this is a once-in-a-lifetime phenomenon that catapults legal and political careers.

It finally dawns on Lange: A gag order? On the lawyers? No way!

However, within the police department, LAPD Chief Willie Williams issues an interdepartmental memorandum on Friday, September 23, requiring all officers to sign a two-page agreement promising not to reveal any information about the Simpson case.

Consequently, for the duration of the trial, the only people required not to talk about the case—or to defend their roles in it—are those who will be the principal targets of the defense: the cops.

Endnotes

100. Pavelic had been a LAPD detective with the Southwest Division, working juvenile crimes. Years earlier, Lange had a run-in with him over a case they both worked. The investigation involved a sexually abused eight-year-old girl who had been found in a San Pedro park by the harbor, beaten and choked to death. She had been placed in a green trash bag, which was covered with a flammable substance and set on fire.

Because the little girl had initially been reported missing and her family lived in the Southwest Division's jurisdiction, Pavelic conducted the investigation. However, after her murdered body was found, Lange and his then partner, Fred Miller, were assigned the case by Homicide Special.

Pavelic bristled at Lange's slow, deliberate, and methodical manner of conducting the investigation. Pavelic, who has a reputation as being confrontational, simply wanted the investigation conducted one way while the Homicide Special detectives decided to do it another way.

While Pavelic was busy filing complaints against Lange and Miller with his supervisor and even Captain Gartland at Robbery/Homicide, Lange and Miller collected their evidence. They discovered blood in the bathroom of the girl's home; and they found the same type of garbage bag, flammable substance, and even matches in the family's car.

In the end, the Homicide Special detectives presented their case against the girl's mother and uncle and the mother's boyfriend. All of them were charged, convicted, and sentenced to life in prison.

After an informal internal LAPD review of Pavelic's complaint, the alligations were deemed unsubstantiated.

101. Pavelic was also responsible for interviewing Rosa Lopez. A housekeeper for one of Simpson's neighbors, Lopez claimed to have seen, among other things, O.J.'s white Bronco parked on North Rockingham at the time of the murders. The defense planned to use her as its key alibi witness. However, during her testimony outside the view of the jury, Lopez self-destructed with a remarkable number of conflicting and false statements.

Pavelic had initially tape-recorded an interview with Lopez on July 29, 1994. For reasons unknown, Carl Douglas, an attorney on Simpson's defense team, denied in open court that any such interview had taken place with Lopez. Later, Douglas was forced to recant that claim.

102. Lange and Vannatter respected both Kidder and York. The women detectives had investigated a series of prostitute murders in Highland Park during the early 1980s and came to work at the Robbery/Homicide

Division on loan from the Northeast Division. Lange knew Kidder and became acquainted with York through her. Vannatter met York and Kidder through a teammate on the LAPD shooting team who was close to both women. Lange and Vannatter knew Kidder and York to be quiet and professional, keeping to themselves and doing their work well.

After being promoted to captain, York was placed in charge of the LAPD Internal Affairs Division, the position she held at the time of the Simpson trial.

103. Toobin's story is based on his "off-the-record" conversations with Robert Shapiro, who is not named as his primary source in the article.

18

Collecting Additional Evidence

June 21, 1994–January 20, 1995

While the prosecution wrangles in and out of court with the Simpson defense team, Lange and Vannatter continue doing their jobs and collecting new evidence. On Tuesday, June 21, Detective Dennis Payne files a report of an interview he has just had with Robert Heidstra, Nicole Brown's neighbor on Dorothy Street. Lange and Vannatter receive a copy of Payne's report, which indicates:

Mr. Heidstra stated that he walks his two dogs on a nightly basis at approximately 2200 hours. His route of travel always consists of the same streets although the direction he takes varies. On the night in question, Sunday evening, June 12, 1994, he left his apartment with the dogs at about 2215 hours. He walked east on Dorothy to Westgate, then north on Westgate to Gorham. He turned left on Gorham and walked west to Bundy Drive. He turned left on Bundy and began walking south. He indicated that Bundy Drive has a large curve in the roadway at that location and because of that curve he was unable to see the front of [Brown's home]. Mr. Heidstra stated he walks the same route every day and is familiar with the dogs in the various residences as well as the exterior of the various residences themselves.

Shortly after turning south on Bundy Drive, Mr. Heidstra

heard the sound of the Akita dog owned by Nicole Brown. . . .
[The dog began] to bark furiously. The barking was non-stop and
the dog appeared agitated. Mr. Heidstra is familiar with the
sound of the bark of the Akita as it barks frequently whenever
Mr. Heidstra passes the location with his two dogs.

Believing the dog might possibly be loose and a danger to him
and his dogs, Mr. Heidstra changed his route of travel and
turned in an adjacent alley which paralleled Bundy Drive and
which would take him back to Dorothy Street. As he reached the
alley, he heard a male voice loudly cry, "Hey, Hey, [Hey]," then
the sound of a large metal gate closing. It was his opinion the
sounds came from the Brown [home], as that residence is the
only one in the area with a large metal security gate. He then
heard the sounds of two men loudly arguing, but he was unable
to discern what they were saying specifically. All the while, the
Akita continued to bark, non-stop, and, in fact, continued to bark
until about 2300 hours.

As Mr. Heidstra reached Dorothy Street, he looked west and
observed a large white vehicle, which he indicated was shaped
similarly to [his own] Chevrolet Blazer, . . . on Dorothy Street, at
the intersection of Bundy Drive. The white vehicle turned
[right], south on Bundy Drive and drove from the location at a
high rate of speed.

Heidstra believes that he has been an earshot witness to the
murders, which he estimated occurred at about 10:35. Both Lange
and Vannatter believe Heidstra to be an extremely important
witness. They hope this witness keeps his integrity and doesn't sell
his story to some tabloid newspaper or television show.

On Wednesday, June 22, Lange interviews Lou and Juditha
Brown at their residence in Dana Point. Also present during the
interview are Denise and Dominique Brown, Nicole's sisters, who
have children of their own and live with their parents. Tanya, a
fourth daughter, is not in attendance.

Their home is just a short walk from the ocean. The family lives
in a large and beautiful one-story residence within the bounds of a
gated and guarded development of upscale homes. Nicole's children, Sydney and Justin, have been living with the Browns since
June 15—when O.J. Simpson asked them to be their temporary

guardians. Almost immediately after Lange arrives at the Browns' home, Lou Brown, Nicole's father, asks a houseguest to take the two young children to play on the beach.

The scene inside the Browns' comfortable home is somber during the three-hour interview. Pictures of family members, including their late daughter, Nicole, appear to be everywhere. Lou Brown is stoic and composed. Lange senses that he cannot accept the idea that Nicole is dead, and that Simpson murdered her. Juditha is hesitant to accuse. However, their daughters are burning mad. There doesn't seem to be any doubt in the minds of the younger Brown women: O.J. murdered Nicole.

Juditha Brown explains that her daughter, Nicole, had continued dating Simpson on and off since their 1992 divorce. "While they appeared to be happy when they were out together," Lange writes on his notepad as members of the Brown family speak, "it was the opposite when they were alone. . . . O.J. was very jealous of Nicole. Denise Brown stated that Nicole tried 'to make it work' with O.J. but confided to her sisters that 'He drains me. He has nothing to say, but he calls all the time.'"

Juditha then recalls several alarming conversations she had with her daughter, as well as with Simpson. For instance, several months earlier, Simpson had told Juditha, "The only woman I want in my life, and I can't have, is your daughter." Juditha adds that the month before the murders, Nicole had said that Simpson had told her, "If I ever see you with another man, I'll kill you."[104]

Also, three weeks before the murders, Nicole had told Juditha, "He's following me again, Mommy. I'm scared. I go to the gas station, [and] he's there. I go to the Payless shoe store, and he's there. I'm driving, and he's behind me."

Then, Denise Brown, Nicole's sister, reveals to Lange that Nicole had told her two weeks before her death that Simpson had been continuing his threats. Nicole confided to her, "I need to get a recorder or put this down on paper." She also told Denise that, after their most recent breakup, Simpson had said, "I have no reason to live now."[105]

After recounting the events of the day of the murder, Sunday, June 12—at Sydney's dance recital and afterward at the Mezzaluna restaurant—Juditha repeats that Nicole had introduced the family to waiter Goldman, whom Nicole had identified as "my friend."

No one in the family believes that Nicole had been dating him. It was the first and, obviously, last time the Browns had either met or seen him.

Lange senses that Juditha feels horrible about leaving her glasses behind at the restaurant. Had she not forgotten them, Goldman probably would not have gone over to Nicole's condominium that night, and he might be alive today.

Before Lange leaves the Browns' home, Juditha also tells him that Nicole had complained less than two weeks before the murders that an extra set of two keys to her house was missing. Each key fits both Nicole's front door and front gate. Nicole believed that Simpson had stolen them.[106]

Within days after Lange's interview with the Brown family, while examining the items on the official property report seized from Cowlings's Bronco on the night of Simpson's arrest, Lange and Vannatter focus on a second set of two keys found in Simpson's possession at the time of his arrest, which were still unidentified. They wonder if there is a connection with Brown's missing keys.

Talking to other sources, Lange and Vannatter learn that on June 8, four days before the murders, Brown had attended a personal intervention for a close friend, Faye Resnick, who was badly strung out on cocaine. While at Resnick's home, Brown was still concerned about her missing set of two extra keys. Resnick stayed with Brown for a short period of time and left on Friday, June 3. While at Resnick's home, Brown went through Resnick's purse to see if she had the keys. Resnick did not have them. And that concerned Nicole even more, because she feared that Simpson really might have taken them.

The two detectives open their official investigation of the extra set of keys shortly after Lange's June 22 interview with the Browns. Earlier, Lou Brown had told Lange that on Friday, June 17, he had changed the locks on her condominium and discarded the old locks and keys. Consequently, the old locks no longer exist, so the keys Simpson had cannot be checked.

However, Lange and Vannatter obtain Nicole Brown's original key from Cora Fischman, one of Nicole's neighbors, who kept an extra set in case of an emergency. Using this key, Lange and Vannatter have a lock constructed which that key will fit.

Then, while a drum roll plays in their heads, the detectives take the two keys in Simpson's possession and insert them in the newly constructed lock.

Both keys fit the lock perfectly. In fact, they are identical keys that would have fit all of the residential doors at Nicole Brown's home, as well as her front gate.

In other words, Simpson had two identical keys to Nicole's front gate and front door in his possession at the time of his arrest. To Lange and Vannatter, this is even more damning evidence against Simpson.

Still hoping to find the murder weapon, Lange and Vannatter send RHD Detective Vic Pietrantoni to Connecticut on Friday, June 24, to conduct a detailed interview with a limousine driver who had worked as Simpson's chauffeur for one day on Thursday, June 9, just three days before the murders.[107]

According to the chauffeur, Simpson had been in Shelton, Connecticut, attending a board of directors' meeting of the Forschner Group, a manufacturing company that markets the popular Swiss Army–brand knives and watches. Simpson was a member of the Forschner board.

As part of the directors' activities that day, board members visited a warehouse where Forschner kept its inventory. The driver took Simpson to this location at about 1:10 P.M. When Simpson returned to the limousine twenty minutes later, he was carrying two white plastic bags with handles.

Simpson showed the driver the contents of both bags. One contained several watches; the other contained about ten knives, three of which were between twelve and sixteen inches long, fully extended. In fact, Simpson—who said that he would be giving these items away as gifts—offered one of the knives to the driver. The driver politely asked for a watch instead, and Simpson obliged.

While in the car, Simpson took one of the knives from its cardboard box and started waving it around in the backseat. The driver could see Simpson in his rearview mirror. While performing this macabre dance, Simpson remarked, "This could hurt someone real badly. It could kill someone. It's real sharp."

After telling Detective Pietrantoni this story, the driver agreed to take a polygraph examination, conducted by the Connecticut State Police. The driver passed the test. Excited, Pietrantoni calls Lange and Vannatter and gives them the news. All three of the detectives are sure that Marcia Clark and the prosecution team will want to use this witness.

Armed with another search warrant written by Vannatter, the LAPD conducts a second search of Simpson's North Rockingham estate on Tuesday, June 28, 1994, now sixteen days after the killings. Among other things, they are trying to find a dark blue sweatsuit Simpson had possibly worn on the night of the murders as well as the actual murder weapon.[108]

Although they do not find either the sweatsuit or the weapon,[109] several intriguing items are seized and booked as evidence, including a script, call sheet, and videotape from the television-pilot film, *Frogmen.*

The film, in which Simpson had a starring role, depicts the lives and loves of a group of Navy SEALs. The movie has not yet aired but apparently was being considered as a possible weekly series.[110]

On August 12 and again on September 2, the LAPD searched Simpson's business office at 11661 San Vicente Boulevard, suite 632. During the first visit, the police discovered a three-page document regarding Simpson's physical abuse of Nicole Brown. However, for procedural reasons, the detectives were blocked from seizing it by one of Simpson's attorneys and a court-appointed master who supervised the search. When the detectives came back the second time with the authority to seize the document, Simpson's assistant, Cathy Randa, admitted that she had already shredded it.

On Friday, August 26, while Lange is at Keystone Tow in Van Nuys, scientific testing is continuing on Simpson's Bronco. The detective watches as the passenger seat of the vehicle is carefully removed by the SID. Crime lab technicians are specifically conducting further testing into the amount of blood contained in the vehicle. Using the substance Luminol, a sophisticated but toxic spray-on chemical that makes blood glow in the dark, the technicians find several additional locations of blood evidence in the Bronco. They are quickly collected and cataloged by a SID criminalist.

Meanwhile, viewing the inside of the car, Lange sees a small light bulb, which is loose and rolling around under the area where the passenger seat has been. Lange looks up at the ceiling of the car and notices that the cover for the interior light is missing, as well as its bulb. He then preserves the small bulb for fingerprint analysis.

Clearly, someone has removed the light bulb, which lights up when one of the car's doors is opened. The crime lab later reports that the bulb contains no fingerprints but fits the ceiling-light socket perfectly and is still serviceable.

Lange remembers his early days as a patrol officer, working the night watch in a radio car. He would always remove the overhead bulb and place it under the seat so that he would not be illuminated—and made an easy target—when he got out of his police car after stopping someone.

Lange believes that Simpson might have reached for the bulb under the passenger seat after the killings, rubbing his bloody clothes up against the seat and the console. Lange thinks, this might explain how the mixture of both victims' blood wound up on the passenger side of the console.

The following day, Saturday, August 27, Lange and Detective Ron Phillips give defense attorneys a walk-through of the South Bundy crime scene. The lawyers from both sides in this looming legal battle are polite to each other but hardly friendly. Simpson's lawyers appear totally unprepared. None of them bring any notes, charts, or pictures of the area—all of which have been supplied to them in advance by the prosecution. In fact, one member of the defense team, Carl Douglas, who questions Lange, seems to believe that the bodies were found near the front door of Brown's condominium, instead of by the front gate. And defense investigator Bill Pavelic has been under the impression that Detective Fuhrman first saw the bodies while looking out of a window in Brown's home.

Because of their total lack of background—or even interest—in the crime scene, at least on this day, Lange wonders why everyone is even bothering with this exercise. Then, outside in the street, he sees Johnnie Cochran holding a press conference. Lange and the other detectives realize that they have apparently been called out on a Saturday afternoon for a show-and-tell photo opportunity with Cochran.

On Friday, September 9, Gil Garcetti announces that he will *not* seek the death penalty in the Simpson case. Both Lange and

Vannatter have mixed feelings about this, but they understand Garcetti's reasoning. Prosecutors have certain criteria that determines whether or not they will seek capital punishment in a murder case. While a double murder qualifies, the DA's office also considers the accused's past criminal history. Clearly, Simpson is neither a career criminal nor a serial killer and, technically, he has no criminal arrest record—even though spousal abuse charges were filed against him in 1989. To just about everyone but his ex-wife, he had been a model citizen. In short, Simpson's alleged crime, although heinous, did not fulfill the requirements of the DA's office to seek the death penalty.

On Sunday, September 11, prosecutor Bill Hodgman and Detective Bert Luper accompany Lange to Chicago to conduct interviews with witnesses who had seen and talked to Simpson on the night of the murders—with the help of Ken Berris and Mike Fleming of the Chicago Police Department.

One of their first stops is the O'Hare Plaza Hotel, which has been closed for renovation for several weeks. There are no guests there—although there have been guests, even in Simpson's room, since O.J. checked in and out on June 13. Having made an appointment to meet with the hotel's management, the visitors from Los Angeles are escorted directly to room 915, Simpson's small suite on the morning of the murders.

Lange sees two of the hotel's standard drinking glasses in the bathroom where Simpson claimed to have cut or reopened a wound on the middle finger of his left hand. With considerable force, Lange pushes one of the thick glasses into the sink and watches as it rolls around without breaking. Lange takes both glasses for booking in Los Angeles. He believes that there is no way that Simpson accidently broke a glass in the sink. Instead, Lange insists, Simpson broke it intentionally to explain the cut on the middle finger of his left hand. Earlier analysis of the glass in the sink indicated no traces of blood—although Chicago detectives found blood on Simpson's washcloth and bedding. Lange believes that these bloodstains have come from the cuts Simpson had already received on the middle finger of his left hand at the crime scene.

After their examination of the suite, Hodgman and the detectives interview the hotel's front-desk clerk who was on duty when

Simpson checked out—after receiving the news of his ex-wife's death. With other people waiting in line, Simpson created somewhat of a scene, demanding that the clerk find a bandage for the cut on the middle finger of his left hand. The detectives and Hodgman believe that Simpson was simply trying to establish an alibi for the cut on his finger.

Among other interviews in Chicago, the three men talk to a Hertz employee who had driven Simpson to the airport for his trip back to Los Angeles. The Hertz man says that when he picked up Simpson at the hotel, the ex-football star was sitting on the curb with his large travel bag open. He adds that he couldn't help but notice "how empty" Simpson's large travel bag appeared to be.

Lange wonders out loud to Luper and Hodgman whether something else had previously been in it—such as the half-moon-shaped bag, seen by Kato Kaelin and Allan Park, that Simpson took with him to Chicago but has never been seen again. This larger travel bag is the same bag that police detectives seized when Simpson returned to his estate at about noon on June 13, and the same bag found in Cowlings's Bronco after the Bronco chase on June 17.

When Lange asks the Hertz man about Simpson's demeanor on the morning of June 13, he replies that Simpson was visibly upset, but that Simpson did not explain why.

On Friday, September 30, Lange picks up Dominique Brown, Nicole's sister who works at a local stock brokerage firm, at her office in Newport Beach and takes her to Marie Callender's, a nearby restaurant, for lunch. Dominique is a petite, attractive, and intelligent woman who has an eye for fashion. While they talk, Lange shows her a photo display of a variety of Bruno Magli shoes. Testing by the FBI has shown that one of these rare and expensive styles of Bruno Maglis had made the bloody shoe prints at the South Bundy crime scene. But neither the LAPD nor the FBI can place them on Simpson's feet.[11k]

Lange's photographs show two particular styles of shoes—one is low-cut; the other has a higher top. The photos display both styles in a variety of colors.

Without knowing which pair of Bruno Maglis has made the bloody shoe prints—or any mention of their significance to the Simpson case—Dominique points to a black low-cut pair of shoes on the display, saying that she had seen Simpson wearing them around Easter 1994. It is the right choice, according to the FBI's analysis.

After making that selection, Dominique continues to examine the photo display and points to the official Bruno Magli logo, saying, "I've seen that before, too. Nicole owned a pair of Bruno Magli pumps."

Lange is unaware that Bruno Magli makes women's shoes. When he expresses some skepticism about this, Dominique replies, "Sure, they do. I have those shoes. In fact, I'm wearing Nicole's shoes." When Dominique sees the surprise on Lange's face, she takes off one of her shoes and hands it to him, showing him the Bruno Magli logo that she has just seen in the photo display. "Nicole," she adds, "bought them in New York."

Since the preliminary hearing, the prosecution has obtained photographs from the FBI of O.J. Simpson broadcasting from a January 1991 NFL game for NBC Sports. Simpson is wearing what appears to be the same pair of Aris Isotoner leather gloves found separately at the South Bundy and North Rockingham crime scenes. The prosecutors will be using this evidence at trial.

Lange and Vannatter have been working overtime, trying to link the bloody gloves found at the two crime scenes to Simpson. Significantly, the LAPD could not find the gloves pictured at the 1991 football game during their two searches of Simpson's home. After making contact with the world headquarters of Aris Isotoner in New York, they discover that the company has sold only a few pairs of this particular style of gloves—all of them through Bloomingdale's flagship store in Manhattan.

Collecting several hundred of Nicole Brown's credit-card receipts from three different accounts, Lange and Vannatter discover that she had purchased two pairs of gloves at Bloomingdale's in New York City on December 18, 1990. The detectives gain the cooperation of Brenda Vemich, a Bloomingdale's employee, who confirms that the expensive Aris gloves Brown purchased were part of the same shipment sold by the department store under its exclusive contract with the Aris company in 1990.

Vemich also gives the detectives a copy of Brown's actual sales receipt, which is still in the department store's files. She had made the purchase with her American Express credit card. However,

Bloomingdale's has erred, writing the wrong stock number down on the sales receipt; thus, the number on the receipt does not exactly match the actual gloves Brown had purchased.

In order to clear up the mistake, Vemich tells Vannatter that he should talk to Richard Rubin, Aris's general manager, who knows everything there is to know about the gloves the police are interested in. Vannatter calls Rubin in New Jersey and convinces him to fly to Los Angeles to look at the pair of gloves found at the South Bundy and North Rockingham crime scenes.

When Rubin sees the gloves, he remarks, "You have no idea how rare those gloves are." Only three hundred pairs of this particular style had been manufactured. Rubin also corrects Bloomingdale's stock-number mistake on Brown's receipt, which was off by one digit. In fact, Rubin says, Nicole Brown had purchased two pairs of "Aris Lights" for about $55 each, with the same style, size, and color as the gloves found at the two crime scenes.[112]

Endnotes

104. On June 28, RHD Detective Dennis Payne interviewed Robin Greer, a close friend of Nicole. According to Payne's report: "Ms. Greer stated that the root of the problem between Nicole and Simpson was attributed by Nicole to his constant 'philandering.' She worried about his constant affairs, and feared that he might eventually infect her with AIDS. Ms. Greer stated Nicole would hear of one of Simpson's trysts [and] confront him with her knowledge, which would enrage him. Nicole mentioned to Ms. Greer that Simpson would physically assault her during some of these arguments. . . .

"After Nicole moved out, she told Ms. Greer that Simpson would stalk her, and on one occasion, lurked outside her Gretna Green Way address, watching her kissing her new boyfriend 'Keith' while both were seated on the couch in the front room. She stated the neighbors observed Simpson loitering about the area and called police."

Although Simpson's stalking story was introduced at the criminal trial, Greer was not called to testify.

105. On May 8, 1994, a month before the murders, Nicole Brown had drawn up her will, simultaneously severing her communications with Simpson.

106. Rosa Elvia Alonzo, who had worked as Nicole Brown's housekeeper since December 1993, later confirmed the missing keys scenario to Detectives Bert Luper and Cliff LeFall. The detectives wrote in their report: "[Alonzo] stated Ms. Brown had a habit of leaving her keys (key ring with many keys, including house and car keys) on a hook in the kitchen. These keys were found missing between 6-4-94 and 6-5-94."

107. Pietrantoni's interview with the limousine driver followed Officer Bill Parker's initial telephone conversation with the driver on June 22.

108. In late June, Vannatter also directed a street search for the murder weapon, taking dozens of recruits from the LAPD Academy, organizing them in groups of ten with an RHD detective in charge of each. All of the groups walked the various possible two-mile routes from the South Bundy crime scene to the North Rockingham crime scene, checking everything from vacant lots to the sewers. No weapon was ever found.

109. The day after the June 28 search of the North Rockingham estate, defense attorney Gerald Uelmen claimed to have found the knife Simpson purchased at Ross Cutlery in a box inside a vanity cabinet in Simpson's bedroom.

Lange and Vannatter have insisted that this cabinet was thoroughly examined during the search. Upon "finding" the knife, Uelmen, who didn't touch it, and his colleagues on Simpson's defense team arranged for a retired judge to supervise the recovery of the knife, which was then placed in a sealed envelope and given to Judge Kathleen Kennedy-Powell. Not knowing its contents, the judge displayed the envelope in open court, allowing everyone to speculate what was inside.

110. Lange screened a small portion of this film in progress, which did not include sound. He did *not* see the scene in the movie that the tabloids later claimed depicted Simpson grabbing either a man or a woman from behind and slashing his or her throat. The producers of the film, the police added, were not very cooperative with the investigation.

111. Simpson denied ever owning a pair of Bruno Maglis, calling them "ugly" shoes. However, during the wrongful death civil suit filed against Simpson by the Brown and Goldman families, the *National Enquirer*, directly or indirectly, supplied the plaintiffs with a photograph, allegedly depicting Simpson at Rich Stadium in Orchard Park, New York, on September 26, 1993, at a game between the Buffalo Bills and the Miami Dolphins, wearing that exact style of Bruno Magli shoes.

On the witness stand, Simpson claimed that the photograph was a fabrication. His testimony was supported by his own expert witness, Robert Groden, who was attacked on the stand by Peter Gelblum, one of the attorneys for the plaintiffs.

Soon after Simpson and Groden made their claims, a new set of pictures, taken by another photographer, were revealed from that same NFL game, reportedly showing Simpson wearing the same pair of Bruno Maglis.

112. Also, according to her sales receipt, Brown had purchased a pair of shoes at the time she bought the gloves at Bloomingdale's. As with the gloves, the brand name of the shoes is not specified on the receipt; therefore, the detectives have to go through the same process to determine whether she had purchased her Bruno Maglis at the same time—or whether she had purchased a pair of Bruno Maglis for Simpson.

Once again, RHD Detective Vic Pietrantoni, who is working closely with Lange and Vannatter, conducts the investigation, but he determines that the shoes Brown purchased at Bloomingdale's were *not* Bruno Maglis.

19

The Investigation of
Domestic Abuse

September 6–September 9, 1994

On Tuesday, September 6, Lange and Vannatter head over to Marcia Clark's office to interview D'Anne Purcilly-LeBon, a close friend of Nicole Brown until the summer of 1993. She insists that Simpson had forced his ex-wife to stop seeing her for reasons he never explained. Purcilly-LeBon recounts to the detectives how in 1993, Brown had told her while they were walking on the beach at Monarch Bay, "Everywhere I go, he shows up. I really think he's going to kill me."

The summer of 1993 was the last time she saw Brown alive. However, Purcilly-LeBon tells the detectives that while at Brown's funeral, she heard Juditha Brown ask Simpson, "Did you kill my daughter?" Simpson simply stated to his former mother-in-law, "I loved her. I loved her."

Juditha Brown, who later confirmed this to Lange during a telephone call, just walked away from him.

The following day, Wednesday, September 7, Lange and Vannatter meet with Kris Jenner and her husband, Olympic decathlon gold medalist Bruce Jenner, who offered to come to Marcia Clark's office. Kris Jenner, the ex-wife of Robert Kardashian and a close friend of Nicole Brown, had received an odd and unexpected telephone call from Simpson three days after the murders. When Kris Jenner started to grill him about the bloody glove the police had found on his property, Simpson replied sarcastically, "I wish they would have put that in your backyard."

As for her friendship with Brown, Kris Jenner explains that Simpson had brought Brown, whom she had never met before that time, to her wedding to Kardashian in 1978. Simpson was still married to his first wife, Marguerite.

Soon after, Nicole and Kris became close friends. Jenner tells Clark and the detectives that Brown had often complained about Simpson's infidelities—even after their 1985 wedding. In 1990, Brown told Jenner, who had encouraged her friend to leave him, "I can't leave. . . . If I leave, he'll kill me!" Nicole also complained about how Simpson had been physically abusing her.

In 1993—the year after the Simpsons divorced and while the two women were jogging—Brown repeated to Jenner, "Sooner or later, he's going to kill me!" In fact, Brown wanted Jenner to help her make a tape recording, discussing her concerns about Simpson's violent temper. She wanted to place the tape in a safe-deposit box.

On September 9, Lange and Vannatter interview Los Angeles deputy city attorneys Mary Clare and Robert Pingel and city domestic violence worker Matthew St. George—all three of whom had spoken to Nicole Simpson about the beating Simpson had given her on New Year's Day 1989 at their home on North Rockingham. They tell the detectives that Nicole did not want her husband to go to jail, but that she was concerned about his inability to control his temper and its consequent effect on their children. In fact, Nicole told the prosecutors that her husband had returned home "coked up" and beat her up while she lay in their bed. When the city attorneys asked how they could help her, she replied that she wanted her husband to receive counseling to help him manage his temper.

Later, Simpson had written two letters to his wife, apologizing in one for getting "so crazy" that night. In the other letter, Simpson wrote: "The detective that spoke to me made it clear I'll have to deal with the law for my action of the other nite and its know [sic] on my record, so if it ever happens again I would face a matatory [sic] jail term."

Pingel tells Lange and Vannatter that Simpson appeared openly contemptuous after pleading "no contest" to one count of misdemeanor spousal battery. He was sentenced to 120 days of community-service work—which consisted of throwing a fund-raiser for Camp Ronald McDonald—but he received little, if any, therapy, even though it had been required as part of his sentence. Somehow, this part of his rehabilitation had been overlooked.

After speaking with Clare, Pingel, and St. George, the two detectives interview LAPD Officer Spencer Marks, one of the two responding officers to Nicole Brown's Greta Green Way home at 10:05 P.M. after her 911 call to the police on October 25, 1993.[113]

Upon his arrival, Marks observed Simpson's white Bronco parked illegally in the middle of the street. The lights were on, his engine off. Nicole Brown met Marks and his partner at the door, saying, "O.J.'s in the back. I want him out!" After seeing the French doors in the rear of Brown's home smashed and splintered, Marks talked to Simpson—who admitted kicking in the doors after Brown refused to let him in the house. Kato Kaelin was also present, but he was trying to keep a low profile, remaining neutral in the dispute between Simpson and his ex-wife.

After Lange and Vannatter talk to Officer Marks, he sends Vannatter a follow-up report, providing additional details about the prior dispute.

> Both O.J. and Nicole dated other people. Nicole saw evidence of O.J.'s ex-girlfriend and asked him to remove all pictures, etc. of his time spent [with] the other woman. . . . Earlier [in the day], when he had been invited, he saw a picture of Nicole [with] her ex-boyfriend and asked her to reciprocate by removing this and any other pictures, etc. of her relationship. According to O.J., Nicole refused to remove these photos, and that created the tension and anger later the same night.
>
> O.J. was angry and upset and was talking with us loudly (at first), until we calmed him down. And we spent approximately one hour talking to him. Nicole refused [to press charges] for trespass, etc., and wanted to make sure that O.J. was going to pay for the damage. O.J. insisted he would pay for the repairs, and we convinced him to leave. After he left, we spent some time [with] Nicole. . . . [A]nd during that time, she voiced her concerns about his temper. . . .
>
> Lastly, Nicole stated that although they had attempted to

get back together several times since their divorce, she was not sure it would work due to his violent acts and common [their] differences.

Also on September 9, LAPD Sergeant Craig Lally, who was Marks's supervisor on the night of the 1993 incident, calls Lange and Vannatter. During his conversation with the detectives, he informs them that he had tape-recorded an interview with Brown that night. During this conversation, Brown said, "When [O.J.] gets this crazed, I get scared. . . . He gets a very animalistic look in him. . . . His eyes are black. I mean, cold, like an animal.".[114]

Endnotes

113. Officer Robert Lerner was Marks's partner that night.

114. Sergeant Lally was upset with the prosecution because he was not called to testify at the Simpson trial to reveal this important information. Lange and Vannatter supported him on this matter. However, Lally later became the subject of a LAPD internal review after he gave the tape to a tabloid televison show. The result of the probe was not made public.

20

The LAPD on the Defensive

September 21–October 5, 1994

During a September 21 pretrial challenge to the original search warrant Phil Vannatter obtained for Simpson's estate on June 13, Simpson's defense attorneys claim that the detective had made several mistakes. In their attempt to discredit this warrant, defense attorneys apparently hope that all of the evidence recovered on the basis of that warrant—which included all the blood evidence found at North Rockingham, as well as in the Bronco and on the right-hand glove—will be ruled inadmissible.

In his search warrant, Vannatter had made one assumption that was incorrect, two others that were true but unconfirmed at the time, and one omission of fact:

Vannatter had written that Simpson's trip to Chicago was "unexpected." In fact, it had been scheduled for some time. However, Vannatter had based his conclusion on Kato Kaelin deferring to Arnelle Simpson when they first contacted him during the early-morning hours of June 13, asking for Simpson's whereabouts. Arnelle initially said that she believed her father was in his house. As a result of the statements of both Kaelin and Simpson's daughter, Vannatter believed that Simpson's trip to Chicago was "unexpected."

Also in his warrant, Vannatter omitted that Simpson had voluntarily agreed to return to Los Angeles. However, unlike Lange and

Phillips, he had not been a party to the phone calls with Simpson at North Rockingham when the notification of his ex-wife's death was made. In the midst of everything that was going on during those early-morning hours on June 13, neither Lange nor Phillips had explained to him that Simpson had volunteered to leave Chicago, as opposed to being ordered by the detectives to return to Los Angeles.

The other mistake Vannatter had made was his premature identification of red spots on the driveway and the red substance on the right-hand glove as blood. Even though Dennis Fung later confirmed this as blood evidence, Vannatter had made these claims in his search warrant without that confirmation, relying instead on his observations from years of experience dealing with blood at crime scenes.

Commenting from the bench—even though there was no evidence of malice on Vannatter's part or that he had deliberately lied—Judge Ito charges, "I cannot make a finding that this was merely negligent. I have to make a finding that this was reckless."

Sitting in the courtroom watching this unfold before him, Vannatter waits for Marcia Clark to get up and defend him. She does not. While a judge has just harshly slapped down Vannatter for the first time since he graduated from the LAPD Academy in 1969, prosecutor Clark—who had heard and approved the draft of Vannatter's search warrant *before* he took it to Judge Linda Lefkowitz for authorization on June 13—listens quietly as Ito overreacts to her colleague's innocent mistakes. She never comes to Vannatter's defense, even though she was involved with Vannatter in the preparation of the warrant. Vannatter is furious with her. It is a blatant betrayal.

But, despite Vannatter's anger and disappointment, he makes a conscious decision not to say anything to Clark. He simply does not want to do anything that might jeopardize their case, and a major falling out between the lead detective and the lead prosecutor could do just that. However, their once friendly relationship will clearly never be the same again.

Even though Lange doesn't give him an "I-told-you-so" speech, Vannatter tells his partner, "Tom, you've been right about Marcia. She has no loyalty to us at all."

Nevertheless, Judge Ito upholds the search that was based on

Vannatter's supposedly "reckless" warrant and admits the challenged evidence.

On Sunday, September 25, a secret source who knows someone on the defense team tells Vannatter that Simpson's attorneys are planning to mount another major offensive against him, challenging the manner in which he had handled the blood evidence. Although it is just another bogus ploy, Vannatter knows that an important but obscure issue like the handling of blood could be played deviously by the defense to confuse the members of a jury.

By this time, Lange and Vannatter, as well as the LAPD and the prosecution, fully expect the defense to charge that the lead detectives involved in the investigation, not just Detective Fuhrman, have framed O.J. Simpson. In fact, Commander John White tells both detectives that a contact at *Time* magazine has informed him that Simpson's defense attorneys have told the magazine that the police had planted evidence at *both* crime scenes—and that the magazine is planning to publish the allegation.

The detectives believe that this is *Time*'s effort to atone for the widespread criticism it had received for darkening its June 27, 1994, cover photograph of Simpson, provoking charges that the magazine was anti-Simpson and "racist." Now, after hearing the news Commander White received, the detectives begin to view *Time* as an anticop, public-relations arm for the Simpson defense team. It is a harsh opinion, but the detectives make no secret of their belief, telling friends and colleagues of their suspicions about *Time*.[115]

The detectives' worst fears begin to be realized on Monday, September 26, when they are notified that the defense wants their hair samples—especially Fuhrman's—as well as a search of the clothing they wore at the time of the investigation and the vehicles they drove. Simpson's attorneys even want photographs of the bottoms of their shoes—to determine whether one of them had left the bloody shoe prints.

Lange and Vannatter view all of these requests as nothing short of harassment, especially since the bloody shoe prints were discovered at the crime scene hours before the detectives had ever arrived.

To Lange and Vannatter's dismay, Clark and the district attorney's office agree to this request without a murmur of protest.

Suddenly, the cops begin to feel that they are being placed on trial by the defense attorneys—and the prosecution is letting them get away with it.

The two detectives meet with Clark in her office and voice their angry opinion that she is capitulating to Simpson's defense team on these and other matters. "Just do it, Tom," she says to Lange. "You have nothing to hide."

"That's not the point, Marcia," Lange protests. "Simpson's supposed to be on trial, not us."

Clark refuses to budge, seemingly prepared to humiliate the members of her own team to facilitate yet another wild-goose chase by the defense.

Consequently, that same night, the four detectives—Lange, Vannatter, Phillips, and Fuhrman—hold a group meeting, trying to decide what to do. Fuhrman has vehemently denied to his colleagues the extreme racist views attributed to him by the media, and Lange and Vannatter have still yet to see anything other than Jeffrey Toobin's article in *The New Yorker* linking Fuhrman to those views. Because Fuhrman feels that he is being unjustly isolated by the LAPD, the prosecution, and the media, the three other detectives decide to stand together *with* Fuhrman.[116]

The four detectives talk to attorney Darryl Mounger, a former LAPD officer on retainer by the Los Angeles Police Protective League and a close friend of Phillips. Based on Mounger's advice, the detectives decide that they will provide the defense team with their hair samples—which, in and of itself, is virtually unprecedented.

Despite this act of goodwill, Simpson defense attorney Gerald Uelmen plays off the "reckless" disregard label placed on Vannatter by Judge Ito, and accuses the detective during a pretrial hearing on Wednesday, October 5, of a "well-orchestrated ticket of lies" and false testimony. Suddenly, Fuhrman is not the only detective being singled out for the wrath of the defense. Vannatter is now sharing the spotlight right alongside him.

Immediately, other police officers, seeing how those with a badge are now being bludgeoned, begin to shy away from the Simpson case. One LAPD detective—from a division other than RHD—is so intimidated by what's going on that he balks at any suggestion of testifying, even though he has already gathered some general background information for the case. In fact, he fears the potential consequences, real or imagined, that might result if anyone even knows that he has been involved in the Simpson investigation.

Endnotes

115. Perhaps in retaliation for this opinion, *Time* published an article on October 16, 1995—after Simpson's criminal trial—with, perhaps, the cheapest shot of all against the detectives. Staff writers Howard Chua-Eoan and Elizabeth Gleick, who never even approached Lange and Vannatter for comment, wrote an error-filled portion of their story about the detectives, which included the following statement: "[Vannatter] and his partner Tom Lange were popular, old-time cops who worked hard and enjoyed a drink or two, spending nights at the Central Cafe in a grimy section of downtown. But Lange and Vannatter were also known as 'Mutts' or 'Dumb and Dumber'—by the D.A.s who had to work around their sloppiness in court."

Lange immediately responded with a letter to *Time*'s editors, writing, in part: "Your article . . . gets an 'A' for your attempts to insult my reputation and that of my partner, Philip Vannatter. It gets an 'F' for accuracy and integrity." Having some fun with this, Lange also throws back the "dumb and dumber" tag at *Time*, calling it "an obvious reference to the two authors of your article." Not surprisingly, *Time* refused to publish his letter.

116. It should be noted that at the time of this group meeting among the four detectives, all of them had already testified under oath before the grand jury and during the preliminary hearing. In subsequent testimony at the criminal trial, the detectives—with the exception of Fuhrman—were consistent with their previous sworn statements.

In other words, nothing said during this group meeting or any other meeting altered or influenced what they would later say under oath at the criminal trial.

21

Pretrial Complications

October 17, 1994–January 21, 1995

On October 17, Faye Resnick, a close friend of Nicole Brown, publishes her book, *Nicole Brown Simpson: Private Diary of a Life Interrupted*, with great media fanfare. Although Resnick's gossipy but popular work primarily chronicles the drug use and sexual exploits by her, Nicole, and their friends, she also details Simpson's spousal abuse and threats against Nicole Brown—both during and after their marriage. Resnick also discusses the short period of time that she stayed with Brown at the South Bundy address, ending on June 3 when she left. Resnick immediately becomes the darling of the talk-show circuit, as her book heads for the coveted number one spot on *The New York Times* best-seller list.

Because of the immediate impact of Resnick's book, Judge Ito suspends jury selection temporarily. Both Lange and Vannatter read what she has to say, and Vannatter interviews her on October 20. For the most part, both the book and Resnick provide further confirmation of what the detectives already know about the turbulent Simpson-Brown relationship. But her testimony is not critical. Resnick—who will not be called to the stand at the trial because of her personal history with drugs—is adamant that Simpson killed his ex-wife.

The defense team asks that the trial be suspended for a year and that Simpson be released on bail while the publicity generated from Resnick's book subsides. With a straight face, defense attorney Robert Shapiro suggests that Simpson should be considered for bail "and be placed under house arrest."

Later, Simpson's defense team finds a role for Resnick, who has been in and out of drug rehabs, in their own case. The defense attorneys claim in court that drug dealers had targeted Resnick for murder and killed Brown and Goldman instead.

Despite the problems caused by Resnick's book, an eight-woman, four-man jury, which is soon sequestered, takes the oath on Thursday, November 3. The twelve-member jury is composed of eight African Americans, two of mixed descent, one Hispanic, and one Caucasian. Nine women and three men are selected as alternates, composed of seven African Americans, four Caucasians, and one Hispanic.

Clark is satisfied with the composition of the jury, believing that politically aware African American women will be sensitive to issues of domestic violence. Both Lange and Vannatter, as well as the LAPD and the prosecution, feel confident that this jury will weigh the evidence carefully and, ultimately, convict Simpson. After all, they have their smoking gun: the fact that Simpson's blood has been found at the South Bundy crime scene and the victims' blood is in Simpson's car and on his estate. It all will come down to the blood evidence, or so they think.

On Wednesday, January 4, 1995, the prosecution believes that they have won a huge victory when the defense team waives a formal hearing that could have challenged the prosecution's DNA evidence. However, nine days later, after Cochran and Darden have a heated exchange over Detective Fuhrman's then alleged use of the "N-word," it becomes clear why the defense did not earlier challenge the DNA evidence: because they are really going to claim that a handful of police officers, including the alleged racist Fuhrman, had planted all of the evidence in a diabolical attempt to frame Simpson for murder.

On Tuesday, January 17, the prosecution counters with more evidence of Simpson's spousal abuse. However, this time it concerns Simpson's relationship with his first wife, Marguerite, whom he had allegedly repeatedly beaten while they were married.

A week earlier, on Tuesday, January 10, Lange and Vannatter had received a call from Officer Terry Schauer of the West Los Angeles Division. Nearly twenty years earlier, Schauer had responded to a "screaming-woman call" on Mulholland Drive. The screaming woman was Marquerite Simpson, who refused to press charges— even though she had allegedly been beaten by her husband. At that time, a batterer could not be arrested unless the victim filed a formal complaint.

Another retired LAPD officer, Richard Deanda, also contacted Lange and Vannatter, telling them about a situation in 1969. While working as a patrol officer in the West Los Angeles Division, he received a radio call, ordering him to report to a residence on Beverly Glen and Mulholland. When Deanda arrived, he saw a woman, dressed in a nightgown and obviously in distress, run into the street. Deanda climbed out of his car and saw her holding the side of her face, as if she had been struck there. The woman, who identified herself as Marguerite Simpson, kept repeating, "I don't want to ruin his career. I don't want to ruin his career."[117]

On Wednesday, January 18, Judge Ito rules that the prosecution could present evidence of Simpson's domestic abuse. And two days later, the judge also permits the defense team to introduce evidence of Fuhrman's racism, leading to the alleged police conspiracy to frame Simpson. The battlelines have clearly been drawn.

On Thursday, January 19, Lange and Vannatter meet with Detective Ron Phillips at the West Los Angeles Division. During their conversation, Phillips, who is still Fuhrman's supervisor and friend, tells them that prior to the earlier preliminary hearing, Fuhrman had been working with a woman screenwriter, who had been interviewing him about general police work. Fuhrman expected some sort of a consultant's fee if she sold her story to Hollywood. Concerned about this relationship, Phillips tells Lange and Vannatter that he had given his detective direct orders to cease his business relationship with her after Fuhrman's testimony at the preliminary hearing. Phillips had no idea of the specifics of what Fuhrman had discussed with her; he also had no idea whether their interviews had even been taped.

Since the Toobin article in *The New Yorker*, Fuhrman had received an avalanche of press attention, ranging on everything from his alleged racist past to tabloid claims of an alleged affair with Nicole Brown. Fuhrman continued to deny all of this to his colleagues—Phillips, Lange, and Vannatter.

The latter rumor about the affair began after Fuhrman was identified as the LAPD officer who had responded to a 1985 call to the police from Nicole, then pregnant with her first child. (Phillips had mentioned this radio call to Lange and Vannatter on the morning after the murders before the detectives first went to Simpson's estate.) At the time, Nicole had complained that her husband was in the midst of a violent rampage. When Fuhrman arrived at Simpson's home, he noticed that Simpson had shattered Nicole's car window with a baseball bat. No charges were filed against Simpson by either his wife or Fuhrman.

This story, in particular, fuels much of the gossip that Brown had somehow turned to Fuhrman for protection and loving support as early as 1985.[118] The situation becomes so bad for Fuhrman that LAPD Chief Willie Williams authorizes a squad of Metro officers to protect him around the clock.

Endnotes

117. Marguerite Simpson Thomas refused to cooperate with the prosecution about her ex-husband's alleged spousal abuse.

118. In his book, *Journey to Justice*, Johnnie Cochran wrote on page 308 about the talk going around about Fuhrman and comments he had allegedly made to several people during the mid-1980s, adding: "Many of these stories centered around Fuhrman's frequent mention of Nicole Brown in conversations they had had with him. . . .

"One such officer, Detective Mark Arneson of the 77th Division, had told [district attorney filing deputy Lucienne] Coleman and another deputy D.A., Jeanette Bernstein, that he had personally spoken with two officers there who told him that Fuhrman had bragged to them of having an affair with Nicole Brown after meeting her when he responded to a call to the Simpsons' Rockingham estate during one of their domestic disputes. According to Arneson, Fuhrman had even made a point of describing to these officers what he called Nicole's 'boob job.'"

In 1995, the LAPD Internal Affairs Division conducted an investigation of Fuhrman's alleged affair with Brown, as well as his alleged comments about her breast implants. The IA probe cleared Fuhrman, finding no credible basis for any of the charges.

22

The Trial Begins

January 24–February 12, 1995

On Tuesday, January 24, 1995, the murder trial of O.J. Simpson officially begins, again before a national television audience. Lange and Vannatter attend the jam-packed opening day but cannot find a place to sit. As a result, they leave the courtroom and watch the prosecution's opening statement on a television in Patti Jo Fairbank's office.

Although Vannatter is optimistic about a conviction, Lange is already starting to backtrack. To Lange, even though this trial will be a battle between two talented legal teams, too many other factors have already complicated the process. Lange believes that the media has become a wild card in this drama and will cover the trial as they would an election campaign—like a horse race. He foresees that in order to maintain commercial interest in a trial for a man most people believe is guilty, the media will give more exposure to the defense team's wild theories about police misconduct. And once that news is created, the media will more than likely feature numerous "talking heads," with no investigative or crime-scene experience, to debate these theories. Lange believes that all of this outside publicity is sure to have an impact inside the courtroom, as attorneys from both sides begin to play for the camera.

Once decorated in Vietnam in 1966 for saving a soldier's life by

236

going into a minefield, Lange now feels that he and Vannatter are about to walk into another one.

In their opening statements, prosecutors Marcia Clark and Chris Darden summarize their case, telling the jury that "jealousy" was Simpson's motive for killing his ex-wife. After years of being physically and mentally abused, stalked, and spied upon, Nicole Brown had resisted her ex-husband's recent attempts to reconcile. She had moved on with her life and had formed new relationships with other men. Seeing that he could no longer control her and then being rejected by her and her family at his daughter's dance recital on June 12, a bitter and sullen Simpson decided to kill his ex-wife. Then, in a classic case of bad timing, Good Samaritan Ronald Goldman, simply returning Juditha Brown's eyeglasses, walked into a deadly scene on the walkway in front of Brown's home and lost his life as well.

Although the evidence clearly indicates that Simpson's weapon for the murder was a knife, the prosecution has been unable to find it and has only circumstantial evidence of how and where this weapon had been obtained. Consistent with the coroner's report, the prosecution claims that Simpson had attacked both victims from behind—minimizing the amount of blood splattered on him.

Opportunity is a key argument in the prosecution's case. Simpson could not reasonably account for the period between the time he and Kato Kaelin returned from McDonald's at about 9:40 P.M. and when he responded to limousine driver Allan Park's calls on Simpson's intercom at about 10:55. The prosecution argues that the murders occurred at about 10:15 P.M., which was when neighbors first heard Brown's white Akita barking. The prosecution claims that this gave Simpson plenty of time to commit the murders and return home in his white Bronco after a five-minute drive from the crime scene.

At the end of the day, an upbeat Clark and Darden ask Lange and Vannatter to join them in Clark's office. She wants to go over details of evidence and witnesses. She's also fishing for compliments on her performance during her opening statement. The detectives oblige. They tell her, "You did a great job today, Marcia." The four of them end the evening by cracking open a bottle of scotch and a box of chocolates to celebrate. For this brief moment, Vannatter thinks, it seems like old times.

The following day, Wednesday, January 25, Lange and Vannatter, with the help of Patti Jo Fairbanks, arrange for ringside seats to watch Johnnie Cochran perform his opening statement.

The defense team claims that Simpson had accepted the dissolution of his marriage to Brown. At the time of the murders, Paula Barbieri, not Nicole Brown, was the most important woman in his life.[119] At his daughter's dance recital, Cochran claims, Simpson was upbeat and friendly. The defense will introduce a videotape of a smiling Simpson to illustrate their point. Cochran insists that Simpson remained in this positive mood for the rest of the day, even while on his trip to Chicago, where he had shaken hands and even signed autographs on the plane.

The defense claims that the murders occurred *after* 10:15 P.M., giving Simpson no opportunity to commit the killings, return home, rid himself of his weapon and bloody clothing, shower, dress, and respond to Allan Park by 10:55 P.M.

In Cochran's statement, the defense provides an accounting of Simpson's activities at the time of the murders—chipping golf balls in his front yard, napping, showering, dressing, and packing for Chicago.

Regarding the cuts on the middle finger of his left hand, the defense claims that he had injured himself after angrily shattering a glass into the sink in his Chicago hotel room in the wake of hearing that his ex-wife had been killed.

Both the detectives and the prosecution had expected the defense team to make these claims and alibis. But, as Cochran continues his presentation, neither Lange nor Vannatter know for sure what case he's talking about. For instance, he discusses having a witness who saw four Hispanic and Caucasian men, wearing knit caps, running from the crime scene "carrying something." Then, they entered an "unmarked vehicle" and sped away into the night.[120] In other words, Brown and Goldman's killers are supposedly still at large.

For the rest of the day, Cochran, a wonderful showman and speaker, continues his voyage through *Alice in Wonderland*—where dreams seem to be reality and truth is fiction. With his "house of cards" defense, Cochran challenges the prosecution's emphasis on the connection between Simpson's domestic abuse and the murder of Nicole Brown. "This is a murder case," Cochran insists, pretending that one could not possibly have anything to do with the other.

Cochran's presentation culminates with Simpson, who stands up and slowly hobbles over to the jury box, showing the jurors his scarred knee, supposedly indicating that the former football star is physically unable to commit the double murder for which he has been accused.

Later that same day, after Judge Ito excuses the jury, Simpson attorney Carl Douglas stuns the court by admitting that the defense has failed to reveal to the prosecution the names of numerous defense witnesses—in violation of the state's reciprocal discovery laws. When he reviews the list of witnesses, Darden identifies many of them as "heroin addicts, thieves, felons . . . and a court-certified pathological liar."

Caught before a national television audience, Douglas replies in open court, "Your Honor, I will fall on my sword. . . . I acknowledge when I am wrong, but there has not been any malice. . . . This is a mistake."

Prosecutor Bill Hodgman is furious over the defense team's continuing unscrupulous tactics and, later that night, is admitted to a local hospital after complaining of chest pains. He will remain there for two days and then retreat to a supervisory role in the case both in court and at the office. To Lange and Vannatter, who have total respect for Hodgman's legal and diplomatic skills, this is a staggering blow to the prosecution's case.

On Thursday, January 26, during arguments outside the jury's presence, Cochran continues his remarkable fairy-tale defense, claiming that Brown and Goldman might have been killed by Colombian drug dealers who had actually targeted Faye Resnick. However, Judge Ito later bars this theory because the defense has absolutely no evidence that can support it.

The defense team's behavior, tactics, and withholding of information also seems to infuriate Judge Ito, who permits Marcia Clark and the prosecution to amend their opening statement and to rebut the defense team's fantasy alibi witnesses. Judge Ito also advises the jury of the defense team's misconduct.

Simultaneously, Lange, who is actively involved with five other murder cases at the moment, prepares to testify in one of them. The case revolves around a 1982 murder for hire in which a Hollywood character actor—Frank Christi, who appeared in *The Godfather*, among other films—was found gunned down in his driveway. Lange's key witness in this long-running investigation is a Los Angeles Mafia figure turned government witness, Craig Anthony Fiato, also known as "Tony the Animal."

As Lange walks down the hall toward the courtroom, he sees Cochran talking to Barry Levin, the defense attorney who is about to cross-examine Lange in the murder-for-hire trial. After being called over to them, Lange shakes hands with the two lawyers. Cochran slaps Lange on the back and tells Levin, "Hey, do me a favor and soften this guy up while you have him on the stand."

The three men have a good laugh as Cochran goes about his business. Lange and Levin walk into the courtroom. Then, doing as Cochran asked, Levin snipes at Lange from every conceivable angle, trying to embarrass him in front of the jury by gratuitously accusing him of sloppy police work. Lange is furious at this treatment—but receives some solace after Levin's client is found guilty.

A few weeks earlier, while preparing for the Christi trial, Lange had asked Vannatter to accompany him to a meeting with Craig Fiato and his brother, Larry, who was also a government witness. (The Christi investigation had begun before Lange and Vannatter became partners in 1989.) The meeting had taken place at the Doubletree Hotel in Marina del Rey.

During their conversation about general police work, Tony Fiato asked Vannatter in general terms about homicide investigations, "What do you do when you have a case?" Both of them recognized Vannatter and knew of his role in the Simpson case.

Vannatter answered, "Well, you always investigate the immediate family members and you investigate anyone who had personal contact with the victim."

Fiato then asked Vannatter whether Simpson had been a suspect when he first heard about the murder of Nicole Brown, Vannatter replied, "Of course, we would have investigated Simpson at some point. He was a potential suspect. Everybody who had contact with the victim is a potential suspect until you investigate the case."

The following month, during a second meeting with the Fiatos at the district attorney's office, Vannatter and Larry Fiato had another exchange about the Simpson case—in which Vannatter repeated what he had said at the Doubletree Hotel.

Vannatter had no idea that his conversations with the Fiatos would later come back to haunt him.

The prosecution's first witnesses concentrate on Simpson's physical and mental abuse of Nicole Brown, followed by a presentation of witnesses who can establish the prosecution's timeline of events, leading up to the discovery of the two bodies on South Bundy.

Then, LAPD Officer Robert Riske, the first police officer on the scene, takes the stand and explains how he found Brown and Goldman's bodies and what he did in response. On Sunday, February 12, in the midst of Riske's testimony, the judge, jury, and both legal teams take a widely publicized, heavily secured field trip from the downtown courthouse to the South Bundy and North Rockingham crime scenes.[121] A large contingent of officers from the LAPD Metro Division—its SWAT team and air patrol in helicopters, as well as the California Highway Patrol—provide the escort for this motorcade. Of course, the media follows in its own onslaught of vehicles and choppers. Portions of the highways, including on and off ramps, are shut down along the route. For the second time in less than a year, O.J. Simpson has taken over Los Angeles's freeways.

Lange rides in a van with the prosecutors; everyone in the vehicle is struck by the carnival-like atmosphere. None of them have ever seen anything like this before—as well-wishers and naysayers along the parade route both cheer and taunt O.J. Simpson. Both detectives wonder why this couldn't have been scheduled after dark when there would be fewer people and less traffic—and especially since the murders occurred at night. Apparently, Judge Ito wants it this way.

The procession stops first at Ron Goldman's apartment building on Gorham Avenue. Then it moves about two blocks away to the Mezzaluna restaurant. These are quick stops, in which no one leaves their vehicles. Everyone does get out and walk around at both the South Bundy and North Rockingham crime scenes.

Obvious changes have been made to these two locations. The foliage around the walkway at Brown's home, which had nearly concealed the bodies from street view, has been thinned out considerably, especially looking toward the area where Goldman fell. Lange fears that jurors might now find it harder to believe that several pedestrians walking by Brown's home at about the time of the murders didn't see anything. A neighbor later alleges to Lange that representatives from the defense team had earlier appeared at Brown's home with a gardener.[122]

At North Rockingham, the detectives, who have conducted two searches of Simpson's property, can't help but notice immediately that photographs of his favorite scantily clad women and his white golfing buddies have now been replaced with pictures of Simpson's mother and Dr. Martin Luther King. But when Lange and Vannatter see the Holy Bible on Simpson's nightstand by his bed, they think that he has overplayed his hand and that the jury will recognize the con.

While the jury moves through Simpson's residence, Robert Shapiro teases Lange about the night of the murders, saying in a whisper, "Did you hear what O.J. said in the van on the way over? . . . 'Hey, this isn't the route I took!' "

Endnotes

119. During the Brown and Goldman families' wrongful-death suit against Simpson, Barbieri said in her sworn deposition that she had left a "Dear John" message on Simpson's answering machine, ending their relationship at 7:00 A.M. on June 12, 1994, the day of the murders. (This matter did not come up at Simpson's criminal trial because the detectives didn't know about it. Barbieri had simply refused to talk and continued to visit Simpson in prison. Lange persisted, even calling a police officer who lived in her Florida community and had gone to high school with her, hoping that he could arrange a meeting. But he didn't succeed. Nevertheless, Marcia Clark asked Lange to keep trying. Finally, Barbieri's attorneys complained to Judge Ito, who ordered Lange to cease his attempts to question her.)

Simpson, during his testimony at the civil trial, insisted that he had not received her June 12 message. However, during Lange and Vannatter's interview with him on June 13, Simpson said that he *did* receive a message from Barbieri on June 12, the day of the murders. Specifically, Simpson told the detectives, "I checked my messages, and [Barbieri] had left a message that she wasn't there, and that she may have to leave town."

Cellular phone records showed that Simpson called her at 2:12, 2:13, 2:22 (twice), 2:23, and 2:24 P.M.; eight times during the course of the day of the murders, not including the times he may have called her from the phones inside his home. (The telephone company does not keep records of local calls, other than those made with a cellular phone.)

Those same records showed that he called her twice on June 12 at 10:03 P.M. Simpson indicated to Lange and Vannatter on June 13 that he had made the 10:03 P.M. call to "as I was going to her house." However, during the civil trial, he appeared to change his story. Simpson would claim he removed his cellular phone from his Bronco and made the call to Barbieri from his front yard.

If Simpson had stuck with the version he told the detectives, he would have placed himself in his Bronco within fifteen minutes to a half hour of the murders.

Contrary to Simpson's claim not to have received Barbieri's message, he allegedly telephoned models Traci Adell and Gretchen Stockdale after receiving Barbieri's message, notifying both women that he was looking for a new girlfriend.

At the civil trial, the plaintiff's attorneys claimed that Simpson's loss of Brown *and* Barbieri had taken him over the edge on June 12, causing him to commit the murders.

120. The witness was Mary Anne Gerchas, a local businesswoman. Almost immediately after she was named as a defense witness, the prosecution branded her a "liar," who had a history of writing bad checks and committing fraud. She never testified at the trial.

121. During the trip, one of the jurors wore on his clothing the logo of the San Francisco 49ers, the last team on which Simpson played. The juror was later dismissed for an unrelated incident.

122. This issue was later raised during a sidebar conference among the attorneys for the prosecution and the defense, but Judge Ito refused to examine the matter further. The allegation of a defense-inspired scheme to thin out the foliage at Brown's condominium in order to influence the jury has never been confirmed.

23

Lange Testifies

February 16–March 8, 1995

On the evening of Thursday, February 16, Lange sits at his desk in the den of his home and prepares for his trial testimony the following day. The other members of his family are in another part of the house, leaving him alone to work.

Lange knows the defense team cannot compare their evidence of their client's innocence with his evidence of Simpson's guilt, because the defense has no such evidence. Consequently, Lange believes the defense will instead attempt to come after him personally, trying to embarrass him and to get him to explode on the witness stand. But he isn't too worried. He's been through this drill too many times to be caught in a trap.

Lange bones up on the facts of the investigation, knowing that Johnnie Cochran, his cross-examiner, will literally test his memory, as well as his actual investigation. Lange wants to ensure that he can clearly explain what his job as a homicide detective is and how he handled this particular case. He will think about each question after it is asked, try to put everything else out of his mind, and answer it as though it is the only question he is there to answer.

On Friday, February 17, Lange takes the stand for the first of his eight days of testimony. Vannatter is not present in the courtroom; the courts prohibit police partners from attending each other's testimony. The prosecution has selected Lange to walk the court through the crime-scene evidence. Questioned on direct examination by Marcia Clark, Lange performs well, speaking in his usual slow, deliberate, and authoritative cadence.

On cross-examination, Cochran tries to impeach Lange, throwing him a variety of challenges. As Lange predicted, the purpose of Cochran's attack is to question his competence and integrity. Although Cochran has the right to phrase his questions in any manner acceptable to the court, Lange has no choice but to answer whatever question Cochran asks and nothing more.

Lange credits Marcia Clark for being a perfectionist when prepping a witness for trial and drawing out the witness's story on direct examination. However, Lange adds that Clark was one of the worst prosecutors he had ever seen on redirect examination. After cross-examination, a trial attorney must rehabilitate the witness on redirect so that the witness's story remains complete and credible. Clark rarely accomplishes this during the trial and certainly doesn't during Lange's testimony.

Consequently, a number of serious issues Cochran raises but distorts throughout his questioning have been left publicly unanswered in the wake of Lange's testimony. They include:

* *Did Lange's decision to place a blanket over Brown's body at the crime scene compromise or contaminate the crime scene?*
Response: The LAPD/SID's analysis of Brown's clothing showed no foreign hair or fibers. In short, the blanket caused no contamination.
* *Was the crime scene compromised after the coroner's investigator moved the blue knit cap and the white envelope containing Juditha Brown's eyeglasses at the crime scene?*
Response: There was nothing to suggest that the slight movement of the envelope and the knit cap altered the composition of the hair and fiber evidence discovered on the knit cap by the LAPD/SID. Thus, the only issue remaining was the original position of this evidence—which was mooted because it was documented by the orientation photographs taken before this minor accident occurred.
* *Why weren't the hands of Brown and Goldman bagged for further examination?*
Response: In fact, Lange had their entire bodies packaged in plastic bags before they left the crime scene.

• *Why didn't the police conduct a tire track study on Brown's driveway?*

Response: Lange determined that there were so many tracks superimposed over one another that isolating any of them for testing was an impossibility.

• *Why were the bloodstains on Brown's back gate found on June 13 not collected until July 3?*

Response: When Lange had left the South Bundy crime scene to go downtown and to interview Simpson at about 12:30 on June 13, he ordered all of the investigators and criminalists to finish the work he had assigned and then break down the crime scene. They were all professionals and did not need someone hovering over them while they did their work.

Because of his presence at Parker Center, Lange, as the lead detective, was not available to conduct his usual final walk-through of the crime scene—in which he makes sure that everything that needed to be done has been done. By the time Lange left Parker Center at 4:30 P.M., the South Bundy crime scene had already been broken down forty-five minutes earlier, at 3:45 P.M. Unknown to Lange, one task he had assigned was left undone: the collection of the blood on the rear gate.

During a walk-through of the South Bundy crime scene with detectives on July 3, Bill Hodgman noticed the blood spot on the rear gate and told Lange, who replied that he had caught it on June 13 and asked Dennis Fung to collect it. Hodgman and Lange called Fung, who did not remember this assignment. Later on July 3, the bloodstains on the rear gate were finally collected.

Lange tried to find out what had happened but could not get a straight answer. Greg Matheson of the SID Serology Unit insisted that he was "out of the loop." SID trainee Andrea Mazzola said that she did not remember seeing the blood on the gate.

After the Simpson defense began to charge that the blood on the rear gate had been planted by police, the LAPD conducted an administrative inquiry into the circumstances revolving around the failure of its investigators to collect this blood evidence. But there was no final resolution as to what had specifically gone wrong—other than the criminalist had simply overlooked it.

Later, the LAPD Internal Affairs Division launched its own probe of this matter. This investigation was based on a written statement from an employee of the LAPD/SID crime lab, who alleged that the blood on the rear gate had not been collected *intentionally*. According to the employee, the Simpson case came in the midst of a budgetary war among various departments within the LAPD. After Lange had left the South Bundy crime scene to interview Simpson, the employee claimed, a supervisor for the crime lab had specifically instructed Fung *not* to collect the blood on the rear gate. Playing politics with this evidence, the supervisor allegedly wanted to use this debacle to argue that the crime lab was understaffed and needed a bigger budget.

The findings of the LAPD Internal Affairs Division in this matter have never been publicly released.

• *Why didn't Lange and the other investigators wear booties over their shoes during the crime-scene search?*

Response: During his investigations of no fewer than 250 murders, Lange had never worn booties over his shoes at a crime scene—although he always wore gloves. There was no state law or LAPD regulation requiring homicide detectives to wear booties at a crime scene.

• *Why did an* Inside Edition *videotape show police officers trampling through the South Bundy crime scene indiscriminately?*

Response: The videotape was taken *after* the crime scene had been broken down at 3:45 P.M. on June 13. Earlier in the videotape, officers were filmed removing the yellow police tape surrounding the perimeter, indicating that the police had ended their search.[123]

• *Why did Lange and Vannatter find only two cuts on Simpson's left hand, when Dr. Robert Huizenga, during his examination of Simpson on June 14, found seven injuries—including a jagged cut on the ring finger on his left hand?*

Response: Lange and Vannatter had Simpson's hands examined on June 13—the day *before* Huizenga looked at them. The detectives insisted that they did not see any other apparent injuries to Simpson's hands—nor did LAPD registered nurse Thano Peratis, who had also examined them. Clearly, if Simpson had any other injuries, the detectives would have documented them, knowing that such evidence would only strengthen their case.

In short, the injuries discovered on Simpson's hands by Dr. Huizenga on June 14 probably occurred *after* the LAPD's examination on June 13.[124]

• *What happened to the "wad of money"—nearly $8,000 in cash and checks—that Simpson implied was stolen by the police from his closet during the June 13 search?*

Response: Unknown to Lange during his testimony, Simpson had already acknowledged to his defense team that he had simply misplaced this money. Nevertheless, the defense team decided to use Simpson's missing money as another smear on the LAPD—and, in particular, on Lange, who had searched Simpson's closet. This matter was not cleared up during Simpson's criminal trial.

• *Why didn't the coroner save the victims' stomach contents, which could have established a more precise estimated time of death?*

Response: Normally, crime labs do not maintain stomach contents—unless they are somehow involved in the cause of death. The stomach takes two to three hours to begin to empty. When the heart stops, the digestive process ceases. However, the digestive process can be impaired by stress, which might be brought on, for instance, if the victim participated in an argument, or if the victim has been stalked for a half-hour or longer and is aware of it.[125] If Brown had been killed quickly and without warning, the stress she suffered probably lasted less than a minute.

Generally speaking, no pathologist can accurately fix a time of death beyond a two-and-a-half-hour window. In this case, Dr. Golden fixed the time of death for both victims from between 9:00 P.M. to midnight.

• *Why didn't the coroner use a rape kit to determine whether or not Brown had been sexually assaulted?*

Response: Because there was no indication of sexual assault, Dr. Golden only visually examined her vagina. The rape kit provides the tools for an internal examination, which neither Golden nor the detectives felt was necessary. Specifically, Lange said under cross-examination, "In my observations and my experience, sex was the last thing on the mind of this attacker. It was an overkill, a brutal overkill. There was no evidence of rape, no evidence of sexual assault."

• *What was the basis for the conclusion that only one person had been responsible for the murders?*

Response: There are four reasons. The first was that there was only one set of bloody shoe prints leading away from the scene. The second was the commonality of the wounds, as to severity, amount, dimensions, and locations. Also, both victims had been hit in the back of the head. In other words, both were victims of similar rage killings. The third was that the blood found on the bottom of Goldman's boot was a mixture of blood from both victims, indicating that it was "castoff" blood from the same

knife. And, fourth, blood evidence linked only three people to
the crime scene: Brown, Goldman, and Simpson.

• *Why didn't the LAPD investigate the possibility that the
murders were drug related, aimed at Faye Resnick? Did this
indicate the LAPD's "rush to judgment"?*

Response: The LAPD received 518 leads in this case, 50 of which
concerned suspects other than Simpson. In fact, any lead that
came to the Robbery/Homicide Division, regardless of merit,
received follow-up investigation. The records of these inquiries
were on file at the LAPD in its "clue books"; and *all* of them were
turned over to the defense team, as required under the state's
discovery laws.

But Lange and Vannatter received absolutely *no* evidence from
anyone—including the defense team—that Colombian drug
dealers had murdered Brown and Goldman, as defense attorneys
repeatedly theorized. Lange, who had investigated nearly 125
drug-related homicides, knew from experience, as well as by the
specific evidence, that these were not drug killings. For one
thing, in most drug-related murders there are drugs and/or
drug-related paraphernalia somewhere on the scene. Also, ran-
sacking is commonplace as killers usually search for either
drugs, weapons, or money. But, in this case, the killer had not
entered Brown's home.

In fact, the evidence collected by Lange and Vannatter only
pointed in one direction: O.J. Simpson.

While Lange is on the stand, Cochran tries another low blow by
pointing out to the predominantly black jury that Lange lives in
Simi Valley, a much maligned community in the wake of the 1991
Rodney King beating. The town had been the site of the first trial of
the police officers who assaulted King. The jury from Simi Valley
acquitted the officers, leading to the Los Angeles riots, the worst in
urban American history. Cochran knows that Simi Valley has
become a code name for a white-racist community. His message to
the jury is simple: Tom Lange lives in Simi Valley; therefore, like
Mark Fuhrman, he, too, is a racist. Lange winces every time
Cochran brings this up, knowing exactly where Cochran is leading.

However, Lange remains calm during cross-examination, speaking in a Jack Webb–like monotone and refusing to be rattled by
Cochran's provocative, almost evangelical questioning. During his

time on the stand, Lange rarely looks directly at Simpson, fearing that if he does, some of the jurors might feel that he has a vendetta.

During a break in his testimony on Wednesday, February 22, Lange, along with Vannatter, meets with Marcia Clark and Chris Darden. The prosecutors are critical of his manner of testifying. Essentially, Darden complains that Lange is not being "contentious" enough.[126]

Lange explains to the prosecutors that it's simply not his style, adding that the defense team wants nothing more than for him to become contentious and blow up in front of the jury. Lange knows that if he tries to dish out as much as he's taking, Cochran, who has all the power in this situation, will eat him alive on the stand.

Vannatter stands by his partner. He understands how effective Lange is when just answering questions, calmly and authoritatively.

The following day, Lange and Vannatter learn from another detective in the office that Darden, apparently on a whim, had decided to call Geraldo Rivera on his CNBC program, *Rivera Live*. Darden wanted to complain that Lange was not being "aggressive" enough on the stand.

"I would like the officers to be a bit more aggressive," Darden said to Rivera. "They are answering the questions being put to them by the defense; and some of the questions, I think, are a bit ridiculous. And I just wish they would point that out to the jury sometimes."

Both Lange and Vannatter have always admired Darden. After hearing this news, they are more baffled than angry. They wonder why Darden, in view of his important role in this trial, would go out of his way to criticize a colleague and one of his key witnesses on a nationally televised program. But, once again, just as Vannatter refused to confront Marcia Clark after she hung him out to dry over the issue of the search warrant, Lange refuses to confront Darden.

Endnotes

123. The LAPD does not provide security at crime scenes after investigative work has been completed. Although pedestrians could look into the area, the gates in front and in back of the condominium were closed and locked. The blood on the walkway and the surrounding area was hosed away by one of Brown's neighbors on June 14.

124. In his sworn deposition in the Brown and Goldman's wrongful death suit against Simpson, Simpson stated that he had received other injuries to his hands after he returned to Los Angeles on June 13.

125. Lange has always been troubled by the kitchen knife the police found on her stovetop counter. Did Brown receive some warning that she was being stalked and then took out the knife as a means of self-protection? Did she not go outside with the knife, because Goldman had called in on her intercom—and she thought he was the only person out there?

Whatever happened that night, she never had the chance to use the knife. The SID found no trace evidence, blood or fingerprints, on the knife.

126. On page 246 of his book, *In Contempt*, Darden added: "I thought Lange should react with outrage to the allegations of planting evidence, that he should point out how impossible it would have been to plant blood and a glove. When Cochran suggested the [victims'] hands should have been individually bagged by the coroner, I hoped he would have let the jury know how ridiculous that was. But he didn't. Like the cops who had gone before him, Lange answered in that monotone that lent credence to the ridiculous line of questioning."

24

Vannatter and Fuhrman
Under Siege

March 9–March 21, 1995

The already controversial Mark Fuhrman follows Lange to the stand on March 9. Knowing that Fuhrman will be under intense fire during his testimony, Lange volunteers to be a "friendly face" in the courtroom for the younger detective. Lange, who basically respects Fuhrman as a detective, sits in during his testimony. Fuhrman has continued to assure Lange and the other detectives that he is innocent of the racist charge.

As expected, defense attorney F. Lee Bailey, who did not appear to have taken a single note during Clark's direct examination, ferociously attacks Fuhrman on cross-examination, portraying him as a racist who had planted evidence against Simpson. For several days, Fuhrman sits in the witness chair and heatedly denies the charges.

Bailey suggests that Fuhrman had found the bloody right-hand glove at the South Bundy crime scene, placed it in a bag, stuffed it in his sock, and then planted it at Simpson's home. Lange doesn't worry about these inquiries, knowing that Fuhrman could not possibly have planted evidence.

Lange is pleased with Fuhrman's performance on the stand. He believes that he is doing well, defending himself and their investigation. Then, on March 15, Bailey methodically walks Fuhrman through a series of charges that he has used the "N-word" to describe African Americans. When Bailey climaxes his line of questioning by asking Fuhrman whether he has used the "N-word" during the last ten years, Lange takes a deep breath when Fuhrman replies that he has not.

At that moment, Lange realizes that Fuhrman has been brilliantly set up by Bailey. Clearly, the defense knows something that neither the detectives nor the prosecution know. Lange knows instinctively that it will be bad news for the case when it's finally disclosed—whatever it is.

Immediately reacting to Fuhrman's testimony in the media, defense counsel Alan Dershowitz claims that police officers are routinely trained to lie on the witness stand.[127] In fact, Dershowitz later writes, "We charged a handful of Los Angeles police officers with conspiring to lie about why they went to Simpson's house and entered his property without a warrant. . . . Having established its likelihood, we then raised questions about the actions of an even smaller number of bad cops—Vannatter and Fuhrman—who could easily have sprinkled Simpson's blood, which Vannatter had been carrying around for three hours, on the socks, the glove, and the back gate. That was the conspiracy."[128]

Taking all of this in stride, Lange and Vannatter recognize that Dershowitz's irresponsible charges—especially that Vannatter "sprinkled Simpson's blood" on existing evidence—indicates that either he is completely unfamiliar with the evidence or simply fabricating lies.

Dershowitz knows that Lange and Vannatter's interview with Simpson at Parker Center on June 13 began at 1:35 and ended at 2:07 P.M. After the interview, Simpson was taken to be fingerprinted. Then, his left middle finger was photographed in the SID Photo Unit. After that, Simpson agreed to have his blood drawn at the dispensary of the city jail in back of Parker Center.

When Lange, Vannatter, and Simpson returned to the Robbery/Homicide Division at 3:30 P.M., Vannatter had Simpson's blood with him. Simpson and his attorneys, who had returned from lunch, then left. Up to that time, Vannatter had never even been alone with Simpson's blood. In fact, up to 3:30 P.M., Simpson is Vannatter's best witness that the detective never left the building with his blood.

After Simpson and his attorneys left the office, Lange and Vannatter discussed the situation between them, as well as with Captain Gartland, a man known and respected for his impeccable integrity, until about 4:30 P.M. At that time, Lange and Vannatter drove through rush-hour traffic on the Santa Monica Freeway in their separate cars to Simpson's estate. Vannatter arrived at 5:17 and gave the vial of Simpson's blood to Dennis Fung at 5:20 P.M.—which was documented by a media videotape.

Where was this three-hour period of time Dershowitz refers to that Vannatter was in possession of Simpson's blood—and anywhere near Simpson's estate where this blood had been supposedly planted? When did Vannatter even have the opportunity to have "sprinkled Simpson's blood" around Simpson's home?

Most importantly, the record is clear that all of the blood evidence, including the blood evidence at the South Bundy crime scene—with the exception of the stains on Brown's rear gate—was collected and cataloged by Fung *long before* Vannatter had returned to Simpson's estate with the vial of blood.

Further, Dershowitz places all police officers under a catch-22 with his theory of "the blue wall of silence, . . . a code that forbids one policeman from testifying against another and requires policemen to 'back up' a fellow officer, even if they know he is lying."[129]

Thus, the inference is, according to Dershowitz, if a cop doesn't plant evidence, then he is probably covering up for those who do.

Lange and Vannatter have never been aware of any written or unwritten code of silence within the LAPD. Neither detective is willing to perjure himself for a bad cop or for any other reason. And their spotless records as police officers confirm that. During the O.J. Simpson trial, the only code of silence is the gag order issued to the police by Chief Willie Williams; and that declaration was made to help protect Simpson's rights as a defendant.

In the same vein, throughout the trial, Cochran repeatedly and dishonestly characterizes Vannatter as a bad cop who was prepared to frame an innocent man of a double murder. He also charges that Lange had simply stood by and allowed this to happen.

Specifically, Cochran later charges that Lange and Vannatter "fixed immediately on O.J. Simpson as their suspect and simply ignored anything that might have deflected them in another—perhaps more arduous—direction. Having rushed to that judgment, Vannatter decided to 'improve the case,' to make sure things came out the way he thought they should. . . . Lange, his partner, well schooled in the department's traditional code of silence, simply looked away, as he doubtlessly had many times before."[130]

In a few well-chosen words of opinion—carefully disguised as fact and protected under the First Amendment—Cochran, like Dershowitz, falsely and irresponsibly characterizes Lange and Vannatter's combined fifty-four years of police experience, charging them with a career-long pattern of criminal misconduct. Needless to say, Lange and Vannatter, both in and out of court, vehemently deny all of these claims, which simply have no foundation. Significantly, a police officer found guilty of framing an innocent person for first-degree murder or covering up such a crime would face severe legal retribution, even possibly the death penalty.

On Wednesday night, March 15, Vannatter is at home with his wife, getting his mind organized for his testimony the following day. He feels completely prepared and confident. He knows exactly what he has done in the case and is ready to tell the court. He and Chris Darden, who will examine him on direct testimony, have met at least three times to review Vannatter's testimony. He realizes that Robert Shapiro, who had cross-examined him at the preliminary hearing, will, once again, attack his credibility.

On Thursday, Vannatter takes the stand for his first of four days as a prosecution witness on direct testimony. He recounts the events at Simpson's estate during the early-morning hours of June 13—leading up to the discovery of the right-hand glove and the trail of blood on the driveway.

Confirming Lange and Fuhrman's version of events at North Rockingham, Vannatter awaits cross-examination by Shapiro, who is wearing a blue-ribbon pin, a citywide exhibition of support for the LAPD. When he saw it, Vannatter almost started laughing at him in disbelief on the stand.

In court, Shapiro goes after Vannatter for his handling of the blood evidence—just as Dershowitz had in the media. In fact, Vannatter's handling of all the blood evidence—including Simpson's blood on June 13 and the victims' blood from the coroner's office on June 15—was consistent with LAPD guidelines and regulations.

Shapiro even criticizes Vannatter for not collecting the Ben & Jerry's ice cream at the South Bundy crime scene—which was actually under Lange's authority. Shapiro asks, "If you had to do it all over again, you still wouldn't take that ice cream cup?"

To the delight of Marcia Clark and Chris Darden, Vannatter, who knows how to be sarcastic when called for, replies sharply, "Monday morning quarterbacking is wonderful. I still to this day don't believe that the ice cream is connected to the crime scene."

And, of course, Shapiro returns to the subject of the detectives' decision to go to Simpson's home on the morning of the murders.

"When you said you were going to check on the welfare of someone," Shapiro asks, "whose welfare were you going to check on, sir?"

"Mr. Simpson's," Vannatter responds.

"Because you were concerned about him, weren't you?"

"I wasn't so much concerned about him," answers Vannatter. "I had concerns for the children. . . . I was informed that a commander of the police department had ordered an in-person notification. I knew it was going to be a very newsworthy case, and I thought it best that we make a notification before the press did."

Regarding the question of *when* Simpson became a suspect, Vannatter replies, "He became a suspect as soon as I saw the glove at the side of the house. After coming out into the driveway and finding the blood trail, he became a very strong suspect."

Endnotes

127. LAPD Chief Willie Williams openly criticized Dershowitz for his comments. The California Organization of Police and Sheriffs issued a statement, saying: "A civilized, law-abiding society should no longer accept the unprofessional, counterproductive conduct of individuals such as Alan Dershowitz. One has to wonder why any credible university would allow Mr. Dershowitz the opportunity to spew his anti-law enforcement venom under the guise of freedom of speech. Speech lacking responsibility is nothing more than the ranting and ravings of a hate-filled, anti-social fool."

The *Los Angeles Times*, on March 21, 1995, quoted Dershowitz as saying, "Of course, I will not apologize for telling the truth. Nor will I be coerced by the threatening and intimidating language used by certain police officers. . . . Until and unless the police of this country begin to understand that their job of protecting citizens does not include perjury, the liberty of all Americans will be placed in danger."

128. Dershowitz, *Reasonable Doubts*, page 137.

129. Dershowitz, *Reasonable Doubts*, page 54.

130. Cochran, *Journey to Justice*, pages 274–275.

25

Simpson at LAX and the Blood Witnesses

March 21–May 10, 1995

Following Vannatter on the stand are to be a series of witnesses who will establish Simpson's opportunity to commit the murders, including Kato Kaelin and Allan Park. But first, through its next witness, the prosecution demonstrates what may have happened to Simpson's bloody clothing and, possibly, the murder weapon:

On Wednesday, March 29, James Williams, the skycap who handled Simpson's luggage at LAX on June 12, testifies that he had seen Simpson near a large trash can on the sidewalk by the skycap's stand. The inference is that Simpson had dumped the clothing in the container.

That same day, after Williams's testimony, Lange receives a call from another eyewitness—who also was at LAX waiting for his wife at 11:25 P.M., the same time as Simpson arrived. After hearing his story, both Lange and Vannatter immediately interview him in person at his office in Los Angeles.

The eyewitness, an architect with a solid reputation, tells the detectives that he saw Simpson get out of the limousine and watched as Simpson's driver loaded his bags on a skycap's cart. Looking away momentarily to find his wife, the eyewitness's eyes returned to Simpson, who, at that moment, was removing his arm from inside a large trash can. On top of the container was a small travel bag, shaped like a half-moon, which Simpson then zipped up.

That half-moon-shaped bag, which Simpson had earlier refused to allow Kato Kaelin to touch, has never been found.

The detectives take the eyewitness back out to LAX—where he gives them a walk-through of what had happened that night. A police photographer accompanies them.

Incredibly, Simpson's attorneys have known about this witness at LAX for months before he called Lange and Vannatter. Soon after the murders, when little was known about the case, the witness had contacted a defense investigator, because he believed himself to be an alibi witness for Simpson. He saw Simpson at the airport during a period of time when everyone seemed to be questioning his whereabouts.

The defense investigator took his story but must have quickly realized that this witness would be no help to the defense and was potentially a very damaging witness against Simpson. The prosecution was never informed of this witness—even though, under California's discovery laws, the defense was required to identify him if they had planned to use him.

Now, after returning from the LAX walk-through, Lange and Vannatter call for an appointment with Marcia Clark, giving her the opportunity to question their new witness. But after talking to him for about a half hour, she turns to Lange and gives him the thumbs-down sign. She refuses to use him, leaving the detectives shaking their heads in complete disbelief. Lange and Vannatter continue to believe that this witness and his story are solid. They are never told why Clark doesn't want him.

Back in the courtroom, the prosecution begins its technical phase of the trial, calling to the stand SID crime lab staffers Greg Matheson, Dennis Fung, and Andrea Mazzola.

The Simpson defense team engages Fung, in particular, in a series of grueling exchanges over a handful of minor errors he made at the crime scene. Nevertheless, by blowing all of this out of proportion, the defense attorneys contend that the collection of blood evidence in this case had been sloppy and that the LAPD crime lab is a cesspool of contamination.

Perhaps the best example of this tactic occurs during defense attorney Barry Scheck's cross-examination of Fung. Scheck manages to elicit testimony from the criminalist that Lange, while at the South Bundy crime scene on June 13, had told Fung he wanted to see the right-hand glove found at North Rockingham, where Fung had just collected it. The glove, now cataloged as evidence, was in Fung's truck. Lange had wanted to see for himself that the two gloves matched.

Through a skilled and deceptive line of questioning, Scheck is able to create the illusion that Lange had actually asked Fung to take the glove out of his truck and to bring it to the detective right in the middle of the South Bundy crime scene. Adding to this subterfuge, Scheck dramatically shows the court a videotape, depicting Fung carrying a paper bag, commonly used by the SID to collect evidence, onto the South Bundy crime scene. Scheck suggests that the glove was in the bag—which, of course, it was not. With Fung confused and on the ropes, Scheck has made his point and then moves on to something else.

In fact, Fung had shown Lange the right-hand glove *in his truck*. The glove never left Fung's truck and certainly was never brought into the middle of the crime scene.

Such questioning, seemingly peripheral to issues dealing with Simpson's guilt or innocence, causes the Simpson case to shift from a straight murder case to a jury referendum on the competence of the LAPD.

After nine days of serving as Scheck's straight man, Fung finally leaves the stand. He immediately walks over to the defense table to shake hands with Scheck, his tormentor, and the defense team. Watching this scene on television, Lange and Vannatter feel they have never seen a witness so thrilled to be finished with his testimony.

After Fung, testimony in the prosecution's DNA case begins on Wednesday, May 10. The evidence appears overwhelmingly technical but mind-numbingly convincing. Four different laboratories, used by the prosecutors, have placed blood consistent with that of both Brown and Goldman in Simpson's Bronco, as well as on the right-hand glove found on North Rockingham. Blood consistent with Brown's has been discovered on the socks found on Simpson's bedroom floor. And the five blood drops found at the South Bundy crime scene, according to the DNA/RFLP analysis, are consistent with Simpson's blood—to the exclusion of nearly every other person on earth. What evidence could be more solid?

26

Highs and Lows

May 16–June 15, 1995

On Tuesday, May 16, four hundred people attend a dinner in the gymnasium at the LAPD Academy, celebrating Captain William Gartland's fortieth year with the LAPD. Prior to the dinner, the district attorney's office had issued a search warrant for Brown's safe-deposit box, which contained the three photographs of her beaten face and body after the 1989 spousal-abuse incident, as well as her will, three letters from Simpson, and a journal that detailed the physical abuse Simpson had allegedly inflicted on her. However, Clark and Darden, who introduced this material at trial, obtained the warrant without notifying Lange and Vannatter, who heard about it later from a newspaper reporter. Their cool relationship continues.

Although the detectives are seated at the same table with the two prosecutors for Gartland's dinner, few words are exchanged between them. In fact, Clark and Darden—who remain together at the bar, apparently to minimize their contact with the detectives—have to be summoned to supper after the dinner salads have already been served.

Clark leaves early, missing Lange and Vannatter's presentation of a new clock to Gartland, with the inscription: THANKS FOR BEING THERE—O.J. '94—TOM AND PHIL. Gartland deadpans, "With all the overtime they're making, you'd think they could afford a bigger clock!"

Even though their problems with Clark appear irreconcilable, Lange and Vannatter continue to have enormous respect for Darden, as well as Bill Hodgman, who appears to remain loyal to the detectives in his supervisory role in the case. In fact, Hodgman has become so intent on helping the detectives place Simpson's Bronco at the crime scene that he sends $600 to a Texas company, which claims to enhance pictures of objects taken by satellites orbiting the earth. There have been rumors that the company has identified a getaway car, helping to solve a murder in Mississippi. But those hopes are dashed after Hodgman discovers that the company is under investigation by the Federal Communications Commission for fraud.

Despite all the trouble the Simpson case has caused them, Lange and Vannatter are uncomfortably amazed by their own newfound celebrity status. They have become accustomed to high-profile cases in Los Angeles, but few cops find themselves in the middle of such a well-publicized national firestorm. During an earlier trip to Washington, D.C., to transport their blood evidence for DNA evaluation, they were mobbed by tourists at the Capitol rotunda who wanted their autographs and to have their pictures taken with the detectives. Pedestrians on the street were treating the detectives like movie stars. Women they had never met before were throwing themselves at them.

In the midst of the trial, Lange, Vannatter, and Phillips had gone to the Bicycle Club bar and restaurant in West Los Angeles for dinner. As they walked in and passed the bar on the way to their table, they heard a loud cheer. When they turned around, everyone seated at the bar was now on their feet, giving them a standing ovation. The detectives were embarrassed but appreciated the gesture of support.

Perhaps no one loved the detectives more than the street hawkers who worked in the area around the courthouse, selling O.J. Simpson trial memorabilia. Lange and Vannatter had become acquainted with several of them, who also cheered when they walked by. When Lange once asked one of these salesmen—who was selling "Free O.J.!" T-shirts—why he was always so happy to see them, the vendor replied, pointing to the courthouse, "The longer you have Simpson in there, the more money I make out here."

And, then, there were the death threats. Earlier in the year, Darden and deputy district attorney Cheri Lewis felt their lives in peril after receiving threatening telephone calls and asked Lange and Vannatter to help them obtain gun permits, which they did. But a more serious death threat had already been leveled against Lange, Vannatter, and Fuhrman. The suspect mailed a tape to the police department, making his slow and deliberate pledge to kill all three of them. Of all the threats made against the detectives or anyone else involved in the case, this was the one taken most seriously.

Although Lange ignores all of this, Vannatter has become extremely ill at ease. He doesn't like the fact that everyone on the street seems to know him. Now, more than at any other time in his career, Vannatter feels that his safety—and more importantly his family's—are in constant jeopardy. He becomes more cautious and suspicious of strangers and spends almost all of his down time at home.

In late May, Lange and Vannatter receive information that investigators for the defense team have been conducting background probes of several jurors, including Francine Florio-Bunten, who has recently been dismissed from the jury. Allegedly, she had been planning to write a book about her experience as a juror, which had been described in a letter allegedly written to a literary agent. Florio-Bunten, who was viewed as a pro-prosecution juror, vehemently denies the charges, claiming that the letter was a forgery and that she had been sabotaged. To the delight of the defense team, she is replaced on the jury by a seventy-one-year-old woman, a racetrack enthusiast, who had claimed that she had never heard of O.J. Simpson.

After two more jurors, the ninth and tenth, are dismissed on Monday, June 5, the final jury is set.

Lange and Vannatter are mortified when they hear the postdismissal comments to the media from one of these dismissed jurors, Willie Cravin. He tells reporters that the police could not violate "a man's rights and go over his wall." During the trial, the police had repeatedly explained their justification for this action. Also, discussing the blood evidence while dismissing the DNA testing, Cravin claims, "Just because there's blood, it doesn't mean much. A lot of people have the same kind of blood." And regarding the gloves found at the two crime scenes, Cravin insists, "No one would be stupid enough to leave a glove on their front porch for everyone to see."

The detectives wonder how anyone could have so misunderstood the trial testimony. Lange believes it's an omen. He starts to think that they just might lose this case.

On June 15, after the lengthy testimony of Los Angeles Coroner Lakshmanan Sathyavagiswaran—who again insists that one person could have committed both murders—the prosecution presents testimony from witnesses who can link Simpson to the two matching gloves found at the South Bundy and North Rockingham crime scenes. These witnesses include Brenda Vemich of Bloomingdale's and Richard Rubin of Aris Isotoner.

To demonstrate the fit of the gloves, Christopher Darden, during a sidebar meeting among the attorneys, asks that Simpson be required to try on a *new* set of gloves, the exact same make, model, and size as the two recovered gloves. However, when Cochran objects, Judge Ito rules that Simpson try on the actual extra-large-size gloves found at the two crime scenes.

Clark hesitates but then assents. She knows that Vannatter, who, she figures, has hands as big as Simpson, had already tried on the new gloves the day before—at Clark's request. They fit perfectly. But in addition to the possible shrinkage of the actual crime-scene gloves, Clark fears that the defense's insistence that Simpson wear latex gloves under the crime-scene gloves might alter the fit.

Initially, Clark wanted Vannatter and Mike Stevens, an investigator for the district attorney's office who also has big hands, to try on two new pairs of gloves in the courtroom. Then, she wanted to call Richard Rubin, the Aris Isotoner glove executive Vannatter had found, to take the stand and have him testify that since the gloves fit Vannatter and Stevens, they would, most likely, fit Simpson.

Darden boldly persists. He wants the drama of Simpson trying on the actual crime-scene gloves in front of the jury.

But, like it or not, Simpson will ultimately be in control of whether or not the gloves fit. Even if they do, he can contort his fingers and thumbs to give the appearance that they don't. Darden asks Simpson to stand in front of the jury and to place the leather gloves on his hands. With the latex gloves underneath, Simpson appears to struggle to get the leather gloves on, saying out loud, "They're too tight!"

Lange and Vannatter watch this scene in the courtroom while rolling their eyes. They are incensed that Judge Ito has given Simpson the opportunity to exhibit his acting abilities in front of the jurors, two of whom are now laughing openly. During a recess after this debacle has ended, Lange runs into F. Lee Bailey on the way out of the courtroom. Bailey laughs, "Why did you let him do that?"

Although Richard Rubin testifies that moisture has caused the extra-large gloves to shrink nearly a full size, and even though a new pair of the exact same gloves *do* fit Simpson during another exhibition in the midst of Rubin's testimony, the damage to the prosecution's case has clearly been done.

27

Cops vs. Prosecutors

June 21–July 6, 1995

In an effort to goad Simpson, perhaps in retaliation for Simpson's behavior during the initial glove demonstration, the prosecution decides to explore other personal areas. On June 21, Lange learns that the prosecution team is making inquiries in Las Vegas to obtain specific records at the Mirage Hotel for the night of the murders. Lange knows what's going on: Simpson's girlfriend, Paula Barbieri, has been rumored to have spent time that evening at the hotel with singer Michael Bolton.[131]

Already knowing that Barbieri and Bolton were supposedly together that night, Lange asks deputy district attorney Alan Yochelson, "Why do we want this?" Yochelson, who is standing next to Dana Escobar, another deputy district attorney, asks, "Dana, why do we want this?" Escobar spreads his arms in some frustration and asks the two men, "I don't know. Why *do* we want this?"

Laughing almost in unison, the three of them say out loud, "Marcia wants it!" But Lange will never find out why.

Lange and Vannatter also have an ongoing dispute with Clark and Darden over the time of the murders—which the detectives believe is one of the most critical parts of the case. The two detectives believe that the killings occurred closer to 10:35 than to

10:15 P.M., which is the time the prosecutors believe the murders happened.

The focus of this most recent argument on Monday, June 26, revolves around Brown's neighbor, Robert Heidstra, who had been walking his dogs near the Bundy location on the night of the murders. During their interviews with him, Lange and Vannatter had gained some additional information about his story.

At about 10:35 to 10:40 P.M.—twenty to twenty-five minutes *after* the prosecution's 10:15 time of the murders—Heidstra claimed to have heard a white man yell, "Hey! Hey! Hey!" Then, he heard the voice of a black man—which he had actually recognized as O.J. Simpson's voice—and the sound of a gate slam. Also, he saw a car that resembled a white Bronco, speeding away from the crime scene.

To the detectives, Heidstra's story perfectly complements that of limousine driver Allan Park, who had presumably seen Simpson walking into the front of his residence at 10:55. Both Lange and Vannatter believe that Heidstra is the closest thing to an actual eyewitness to the murders. Assuming that both Heidstra and Park are correct, Simpson had plenty of time for the five-minute drive from the South Bundy crime scene back to his home on North Rockingham.

But both Clark and Darden refuse to budge. They are stubbornly determined to stick with their estimated 10:15 P.M. time of the murders—which is pegged instead to the wailing of Brown's white Akita. As a result, Heidstra becomes an unlikely witness for the defense.

Because of the prosecution's insistence on the 10:15 time, the defense is able to use several witnesses on its witness list whose stories fit with that of Heidstra. Three witnesses called by the defense passed by Brown's condominium just after the time the prosecution claimed that Simpson had committed the murders: Francesca Harmon, a hotel executive, at 10:25 P.M.; and Ellen Aaronson and Danny Mandel, who passed by the South Bundy address on their way back from the Mezzaluna restaurant between 10:15 and 10:25 P.M. None of them saw or heard anything.

On Wednesday, June 28, as the prosecution begins to complete its case, Lange has a telephone conversation with Bill Hodgman—

in which Hodgman gives the detective the bad news. The prosecution has decided *not* to present much of Lange and Vannatter's best evidence, deciding instead to risk everything on the DNA blood analysis and the evidence of Simpson's spousal abuse.

The detectives now see the pattern clearly: The prosecution does not want to use anything initiated by the LAPD unless absolutely necessary. Any such evidence brought in will have to be accompanied by the testimony of a police officer and the legacy of a now tarnished police department. By this time, it is clear to both the prosecution and the defense team that the LAPD is on trial, as well as O.J. Simpson. In short, this is no longer a case about evidence. It has become a political drama, and the police are being portrayed as the villains.

Among those items on the detectives' evidence list which have been dismissed by the prosecution are:

- Officer Craig Lally's tape-recorded interview with Nicole Brown, who feared Simpson was going to kill her, after the October 1993 abuse incident on Greta Green Way.
- Testimony from the limousine driver in Connecticut who had seen and heard Simpson fantasizing about killing someone with a knife just three days before the murders and who had passed a polygraph about his story.
- Dominique Brown's identification of a style of Bruno Magli shoes she saw Simpson wearing around Easter 1994.
- Lange's discovery of the light bulb removed from the ceiling of Simpson's Bronco.
- Earshot-witness Robert Heidstra's estimate that the murders occurred between 10:35 and 10:40 P.M. when he was out walking his dog.
- Testimony from the eyewitness who had seen Simpson withdrawing his arm from a large trash container and then zip up his travel bag that he had placed on top of the container—at LAX on the night of the murders.
- The Hertz employee in Chicago who saw "how empty" Simpson's travel bag was.
- Lange and Vannatter's June 13 tape-recorded interview with Simpson with all of his contradictions and inconsistencies, as well as his lack of a remotely solid alibi.
- Simpson's June 17 "suicide note," which had been recovered from Kardashian's house.

- The events, involving the LAPD, leading up to Simpson's attempt to flee followed by the slow-speed Bronco chase on June 17.
- Lange's tape-recorded telephone conversations with Simpson during the chase.
- All of the evidence found in Simpson and Cowlings's possession after the Bronco chase, including Simpson's passport, disguise, gun, and money.
- The two keys found in Simpson's large leather travel bag that fit Brown's front gate and front door.

Although both Lange and Vannatter are upset about the decision *not* to use any of this evidence, only Lange believes that this decision will be fatal to the prosecution's case.

On Thursday, July 6, the prosecution completes its hair and fiber evidence, showing, among other things, that fibers found on the knit cap and the right-hand glove are consistent with the carpet in Simpson's Bronco. Also, multiple hairs found in the cap and a single hair found on Goldman's shirt are consistent with Simpson's. Hair consistent with Brown and Goldman's hair has also been found on the right-hand glove.

After this phase of its case is concluded, the prosecution rests. The defense will begin its case four days later.

Endnote

131. In another investigation involving Paula Barbieri, RHD Detectives Bert Luper and Cliff LeFall had gone to San Diego on August 23, 1994, to interview an inmate who had stolen Barbieri's car. When the car was found, a diary was discovered. In cryptic language, the author of the diary described his surveillance activities on Nicole Brown several months before her murder.

The inmate admitted that the diary was his, claiming that he had been hired by a person or persons unknown to follow Brown. However, he feared that if he told what he knew, he would "get a shiv" in the back while in prison.

The LAPD continued its investigation of this matter. But, in the end, the suspect retained an attorney. At that point, the suspect, upon the advice of counsel, refused to cooperate with any further investigation.

28

Fuhrman Self-destructs

August 8–September 6, 1995

As the dog days of summer hit Los Angeles, Lange and Vannatter cannot help but feel additional heat from some members of the jury. Two jurors, in particular, appear to look at them with piercing stares of contempt and disdain that could drill a hole through steel. Increasingly, the detectives are uncomfortable just being there.

They even begin to discover that their friends are turning against them. On Tuesday, August 8, Vannatter is outside the courthouse, smoking a cigarette with Peter Bozanich, a top official with the district attorney's office and a longtime acquaintance. During their conversation, Bozanich tells Vannatter that he now has "reasonable doubt" about whether Fuhrman had planted the right-hand glove at Simpson's home.

Upon hearing that, Vannatter is extremely upset and shouts at him, "Peter, what the hell are you talking about! Are you saying that you think I'm involved in some kind of a frame-up against O.J.? You're saying you think I'm part of a goddamn conspiracy?"

Surprised that Vannatter has taken his comment about Fuhrman so personally, Bozanich replies, "No, no, no, Phil. I'm not saying that."

"Well, that's what you said, and I resent it deeply. That's the implication you're giving, and I don't like it."[132]

The fact is that both Lange and Vannatter have been getting hit so hard that they are becoming raw nerves, reacting against anyone who rubs them the wrong way.

On Thursday, August 10, to crown its bogus police-conspiracy claims against the LAPD, Simpson's defense team throws a box of dynamite into the trial by turning over to Judge Ito the tapes of Detective Fuhrman's thirteen hours of interviews with screenwriter Laura Hart McKinny. In the midst of the preliminary hearing in early July 1994, Detective Phillips had ordered Fuhrman to cease his professional relationship with her.

By Tuesday, August 15, 1995, it becomes clear that the tapes will be absolutely devastating, and everyone involved in the trial seems to know it. Judge Ito sums it up best, saying in open court: "Just when you thought we couldn't have anything crazier happen . . ."

But the judge is also a victim of the tapes. Fuhrman describes Ito's police captain wife as a "fat slob" who "sucked her way to the top."[133] Judge Ito, now almost in tears, painfully says in open court, "I love my wife dearly, and I am wounded by criticism of her." When Marcia Clark makes an issue about his obvious conflict of interest with this evidence, Ito considers recusing himself from the trial.

Lange and Vannatter are in complete shock over all of this. They have known about the existence of the tapes for over a week, but they had no idea what they contained. They had received only bits and pieces of information from the prosecutors. The tapes still haven't been released—although portions of the tapes' transcripts have been circulating.

Once allowed into evidence, Fuhrman's rough talk on the tapes becomes common knowledge, as well as his unabashed use of the "N-word." His attorney, who has not heard the tapes, tells reporters, "These comments were made as part of a story conference for a fictional screenplay. They're not Mark speaking as himself."

"Go to Wilshire Division," Fuhrman reportedly says on one tape. "Wilshire Division is all [n———s]. All [n———s]. [N———s] training officers." Vannatter—who, as a young detective, had worked at the Wilshire Division for nearly three years—is disgusted. Lange, who has stood by Fuhrman and believed his denial of the charges, feels double-crossed.

Adding insult to injury, Fuhrman, who reportedly used the "N-word" over forty times, also told McKinny on July 28, 1994, "I am the key witness in the biggest case of the century. And if I go down, they lose the case. The glove is everything. Without the glove—bye-bye."[134]

When they hear that remark, Lange and Vannatter know that Fuhrman has disobeyed Detective Phillip's July 1994 direct order by continuing his professional relationship with McKinny. Also, the detectives now know that Fuhrman lied to them and concealed his clear-cut history of fanatical racism.

They further realize that Fuhrman has completely exaggerated his importance to the investigation. Lange and Vannatter know the Simpson case better than anyone, and they have a full appreciation for the strength of their evidence. They recognize that Fuhrman had played an important role during the first few hours of the investigation—but then he was gone from the case. The evidence he discovered—the red speck on the Bronco and the right-hand glove—could have been eliminated from the investigation, and the detectives still would have easily made their case.

As Lange and Vannatter watch the proceedings on television, Cochran reacts to the Fuhrman tapes by saying in open court, without the jury present, "This is a blockbuster! This is a bombshell! This is perhaps the biggest thing that's happened in any case in this country in this decade, and they [the prosecutors] know it. They've got to face up to it!"

As difficult as it is to hear, Lange knows Cochran's exclamation is true and believes that the case is really over. However, Vannatter still holds out hope that the jury will disregard the Fuhrman sideshow and vote to convict Simpson based on the evidence against him.[135]

The morality of the tapes' contents aside, both detectives are particularly upset because Fuhrman, whom they had liked and supported, did not tell anyone in the LAPD or on the prosecution team about the tapes. Apparently hoping that the tapes would not be revealed, Fuhrman has instead allowed everyone to be blindsided by the defense team's revelation of their existence.

As one of those hit hardest, Chris Darden appears weary and depressed in the wake of the Fuhrman debacle. While talking to Lange and Vannatter in Clark's office, Darden jots something down on a piece of paper. Holding up the paper toward the detectives, Darden says, "This is going to be the title of my book." The paper reads: "Another Black Guy Caught Up In White Man's Shit." "Chris," Vannatter laughs bitterly, "wait until you see how that white man's shit catches up with us—the two white cops."

Outside the courtroom, during an impromptu press conference, Cochran suggests that Fuhrman couldn't have planted all of this evidence alone. Insisting that Fuhrman had help, the defense attorney appeals to the media to look at the "other three detectives in this case," namely Lange, Vannatter, and Phillips.[136]

While the court considers which of the Fuhrman tapes the jury can hear, Simpson's defense attorneys continue to pound away at the collection of evidence by the LAPD/SID's crime lab. On Monday, August 21, criminalist Larry Ragle, the former head of the Orange County police crime lab, testifies as an expert for the defense—even though he has not "worked" a crime scene in the past nineteen years. However, he still feels comfortable trashing the work done by the LAPD/SID criminalists in the Simpson case. Ragle tells the court, "What I see are lots of blunders on top of blunders." Lange and Vannatter later learn that Ragle has received $35,000 from the defense team to participate in the defense case, as well as $50 an hour to look at some pictures and watch the testimony of other criminalists on television.

As Ragle is leaving the courtroom, he runs into Vannatter. Ragle smiles and says, "Hi, I've wanted to meet you." Ragle then extends his hand. Incensed by the testimony Ragle has just given, Vannatter replies, "I don't want to shake your hand."

"I'm sorry you feel that way," Ragle responds, recoiling from the detective.

"Well," Vannatter shoots back, "you are a sorry individual. You are a *very* sorry individual. I don't ever want to shake your hand!"

Ragle backs off and then walks over to Cochran at the defense table. As he storms away, Vannatter knows exactly what Ragle is telling Cochran.

The following morning, the defense team protests in open court, claiming that big, bad Phil Vannatter has attempted to intimidate a defense witness. They want to hold a hearing, calling both men to testify. Recognizing that this is kid's stuff, Judge Ito refuses the defense request.

* * *

On Tuesday, August 29, screenwriter Laura McKinny testifies, setting the stage for the playing in open court of sixty-one excerpts from her taped interviews with Fuhrman—without the jury present:

After actually hearing all of the tapes now, Lange and Vannatter know for sure that Fuhrman is a confirmed racist who has lied in court, impeached a portion of his testimony, and struck a major blow against the prosecution's case. Further, Fuhrman has not only crippled himself, but he has cast a long shadow over the other three detectives who have been defending him—Lange, Vannatter, and Phillips.

Earlier, with all of the momentum now behind the defense team, Cochran asks Judge Ito for permission to speak with Lange, who is back at Parker Center. The judge grants the request after consulting with Darden. When Lange appears in the courtroom, Cochran and his associate, Carl Douglas, corner the detective. Douglas says to Lange informally, "No bullshit now. I'm trusting you. I believe you are honest and honorable. Was Fuhrman at the autopsy?" It is their only question to the detective. Clearly, the defense wants to use Fuhrman to taint every aspect of the case—even those parts he had nothing to do with, like the autopsy.

Lange replies simply, "You have some bad information. Fuhrman was nowhere near the autopsy. I keep telling you guys, after the first few hours, Fuhrman was out of this case. He had nothing more to do with it."

The following day, Shapiro, equally serious, comes up to Lange. After a brief discussion about the Fuhrman tapes, Shapiro says, "I think we really need to do something about this. I'm really concerned about reputations—yours and a lot of police officers." Shapiro then calls Hodgman over and repeats what he has just said to Lange, adding, "Some of the lawyers on my own team belong in jail." Shapiro even suggests that they issue a joint press release addressing their concerns.

Lange simply laughs when he hears Shapiro make this statement. Ever since the pre-Bronco-chase negotiations for Simpson's arrest on June 17, 1994, Bob Shapiro has become notorious for stroking the right hand of the detectives and then slapping the left. They have learned from experience to distrust everything he says and does. In fact, they refer to him in casual conversation only by his initials; "B.S."

On Thursday, August 31, Judge Ito, who does not want to inflame the jurors, permits the defense to play only two excerpts from the Fuhrman-McKinny tapes to the jury. Cochran immediately accuses the judge of being part of the police conspiracy against Simpson. Specifically, Cochran, again overstating his case, claims that Judge Ito's decision proves, "The cover-up continues. . . . This inexplicable, indefensible ruling lends credence to all those who say the criminal justice system is corrupt."

On Tuesday, September 5, for the first time, the jury hears the two excerpts, as well as Fuhrman's flagrant use of the "N-word," which appears in both. On one of the tapes, Fuhrman has been discussing the role of policewomen in the LAPD. Fuhrman explains to McKinny, "They don't do anything. They don't go out there and initiate a contact with some six-foot-five-inch [n———r] that's been in prison for seven years, pumping weights."

The devastating tapes are followed by several other defense witnesses who have also heard Fuhrman use the N-word.

In other testimony, LAPD photographer Rolf Rokahr confounds the situation further by claiming to have photographed Fuhrman at 4:00 A.M. on the morning after the murders—before Lange and Vannatter arrived—pointing to the left-hand glove found at the South Bundy crime scene.

In fact, Rokahr had taken this photograph at about 7:00 A.M.— after Fuhrman returned from Simpson's estate on Vannatter's orders. No close-up photographs of the evidence were taken until Lange returned to the South Bundy crime scene from North Rockingham at about 6:50 A.M.

At the time of his testimony, Rokahr is on off-duty status because of his poor health and is under heavy medication. Like Thano Peratis, he has acute heart problems. Consequently, he is a visibly sick and confused witness of whom the defense team takes full advantage. One defense counsel even manages to get Rokahr to state falsely that he was present when the four detectives decided to go over Simpson's wall. Anyone who had followed the case knew that was simply not true.

In addition, during his earlier official interview with Detective

Cliff LeFall on November 22, 1994, Rokahr claimed that he arrived at the South Bundy crime scene at "about midnight." However, the official log had him signing in at 3:25 A.M. During his interview with LeFall, Rokahr also claimed to have arrived before Detectives Phillips and Fuhrman, who, in fact, had signed in an hour earlier at 2:30. Later, he cleared up this confusion.

On Wednesday, September 6, Detective Fuhrman, now completely isolated and a pariah throughout the country, is recalled to the witness chair—without the jury present. Defense attorney Gerald Uelmen asks, "Detective Fuhrman, was the testimony that you gave at the preliminary hearing in this case completely truthful?"

Conferring briefly with his attorney, Darryl Mounger, Fuhrman replies, "I wish to assert my Fifth Amendment privilege."

"Have you ever falsified a police report?"

Once again, Fuhrman takes the Fifth.

"Is it your intention to assert your Fifth Amendment privilege with respect to all questions that I ask you?"

"Yes."

As Uelmen pauses momentarily, Mounger tells the judge that further questioning will serve no purpose.

Before Judge Ito can respond, Uelman adds, "I have only one other question, Your Honor."

After the judge gives his permission, Uelmen, playing for the television audience and swinging for the fence, asks, "Detective Fuhrman, did you plant or manufacture any evidence in this case?"

Even though that question is just for show, Fuhrman again takes the Fifth before being excused.

Watching this on television in Patti Jo Fairbank's office, Lange is aghast. Saying nothing, he pounds the table in front of him. Vannatter, sitting in the courtroom when Fuhrman takes the Fifth, immediately feels like vomiting.

By taking the Fifth—even without the jury present—Fuhrman is essentially saying to everyone watching on television that he has something to hide. Consequently, all of the other detectives—by pure association—are marked with the same stigma. That "white man's shit" that Darden had earlier joked about has just landed squarely on Lange, Vannatter, Phillips, and the LAPD. And everyone knows it.

Neither Lange nor Vannatter has ever seen or heard of a LAPD officer taking the Fifth. To them, this is an unforgivable sin. Even though they realize that Fuhrman had been advised to take the Fifth by Mounger to avoid a flat-out charge of perjury, the detectives hoped that Fuhrman would at least defend his role in the Simpson case. Clearly, Fuhrman has lied under oath about his use of the N-word and is now going to take the Simpson case down with him.[137]

Endnotes.

132. Bozanich later served as a key source in Joseph Bosco's book, *A Problem of Evidence,* which embraced the theory of a police conspiracy against Simpson.

133. York, who headed the LAPD Internal Affairs Division, had earlier executed a sworn statement indicating that she had never previously ordered or conducted an investigation of Detective Fuhrman. During the mid-1980s, she had served as a watch commander at the West Los Angeles Division where Fuhrman worked. York said she didn't remember him.

134. Also on the tapes, Fuhrman had boasted to McKinny that, after the shooting of two police officers, he and other officers had cornered a couple of Hispanic suspects and then beat their faces to "mush." Fuhrman added that they had to wash the blood off their uniforms. The LAPD's Internal Affairs Division conducted a lengthy investigation of this incident and concluded that Fuhrman had fictionalized the entire matter.

RHD Detective Bert Luper had been among those officers present with Fuhrman at the alleged beating incident, which occurred in 1978 in the LAPD's Hollenbeck Division. In fact, Luper had helped to transport the suspects to jail. The supervisor of the arrest was a friend of Tom Lange, Sergeant Mike Middleton, who, like Luper, stated that Fuhrman's version of events had simply not occurred.

None of the suspects had been injured or filed any complaints against any of the detectives, including Fuhrman—until the Fuhrman tapes were made public. The two suspects, after seventeen years, suddenly claimed they had been the victims of police brutality. This complaint led to an Internal Affairs investigation, which cleared the police officers. There was no evidence that the incident Fuhrman had described on the McKinny tapes had ever occurred.

135. Lange has been skeptical of the prosecution's case for some time. On Thursday, June 29, 1995, Lange and Vannatter were stopped at Parker Center by a film crew from CBS's *48 Hours* program. During the quick interview, Lange told a reporter that he "wouldn't be in shock" if the jury acquitted Simpson. Vannatter replied that he *would* be "shocked" by an acquittal.

136. Actually, the LAPD later conducted two separate internal audits regarding allegations of a possible police conspiracy. The first concentrated on whether blood had been planted in the LAPD/SID's crime lab in an effort to incriminate Simpson. This probe yielded no evidence that anyone had even attempted to commit this crime.

A second audit, concentrating specifically on Lange and Vannatter, addressed whether they had used any improper tactics during the course of their investigation. This probe of their work concluded that they had performed in a responsible manner. Commander John White, the LAPD's chief of detectives, called Lange, personally, to give him the results of the investigation. White had been concerned that Lange, in particular, appeared particularly "defensive" during recent discussions about evidence and procedure in the Simpson case. Lange replied that his defensive posture had been caused by "all of the unfounded allegations of planting, tampering, contaminating and out-and-out manufacturing of evidence."

137. Fuhrman, who had already retired from the LAPD, pleaded "no contest" to one count of perjury on October 2, 1996. He was sentenced to three-years' probation and fined $300.

29

Legacy

The worst fears of many black Americans—that cops hate them and target them with fabricated evidence—now appear to be confirmed for those who want to believe it. Perhaps that is the most tragic of all the consequences resulting from Mark Fuhrman's perjury, as well as the entire Simpson trial.

On September 6, Lange talks to Fuhrman's supervisor, Ron Phillips, who feels as though he must, somehow, share the blame for Fuhrman's behavior. Lange tells Phillips to put those thoughts out of his mind; Fuhrman's destruction has been self-inflicted.

Phillips adds that earlier in the day, Los Angeles mayor Richard Riordan and his staff were at the West Los Angeles Division, looking for some smiling police officers with whom to shake hands for a photo opportunity. As Phillips was shaking the mayor's hand, a mayor's aide introduced him as one of the original Simpson investigators and Fuhrman's immediate supervisor. Riordan dropped Phillips's hand as if it were on fire and quickly walked away.

In discussing the fallout from the Fuhrman tapes, *Los Angeles Times* reporter Jim Newton, who has been covering the Simpson case, would later write: "Citizens have come to believe that anything is possible at the LAPD. Black men may be beaten because of their race; communities may be abandoned during riots for political purposes; officers may lie—indeed, even the chief may lie—if it suits them.

"In that environment, circumstantial evidence is woven into a fabric of presumed perjury and accepted mistrust. It is a cynicism for which the LAPD has no one but itself to blame. And it is a public crisis that the Simpson case only has deepened. . . . [D]etectives and prosecutors have noted a new willingness by juries to accept at face value the most unsubstantiated claims of LAPD evidence tampering.

"That legacy will haunt Lange and Vannatter, two good, honest police detectives who did their jobs well only to find themselves victimized by their department's reputation."

Not surprisingly, the day after playing the excerpts from the Fuhrman tapes for the jury, Cochran announces that Simpson will *not* be taking the stand to testify in his own defense. Neither Lange nor Vannatter expected him to take the stand unless his case was in big trouble—which was why the detectives had wanted the prosecution to use their June 13 taped interview with him.

In the wake of Fuhrmangate, the defense wants Judge Ito, in a statement to the jury, to explain that Fuhrman has taken the Fifth, and, in doing so, allow the jurors to use this as a factor in determining the detective's overall credibility.

Judge Ito agrees. Of course the prosecution objects, forcing the California State Court of Appeals to decide the issue. Simpson's defense team refuses to rest until the matter is decided. So, while the appellate court weighs the issue, Judge Ito permits the prosecution to present its rebuttal witnesses.

On Monday, September 18—four days after the court of appeals rejects the defense motion on the Fuhrman matter—the prosecution rests its case on the condition that the defense team doesn't pull any more surprises. In her rebuttal phase, Marcia Clark does virtually nothing to rehabilitate the testimonies of her police witnesses.

In its rebuttal commencing on September 19, Simpson's defense team again launches a direct attack against Phil Vannatter, trying to challenge the LAPD's contention that Simpson was *not* a suspect when Vannatter—along with Lange, Phillips, and Fuhrman—first went to Simpson's estate on the morning after the murders.[138]

Having failed to convince the judge to throw out all of the evidence after making an issue out of the minor errors in Vannatter's search warrant, the defense attempts a last-ditch effort to challenge Vannatter's version of when Simpson became a suspect. If they are successful, the prosecution stands to lose much if not all of the evidence found at North Rockingham. In other words, Simpson's lawyers are attempting a "fruit of the poison tree" defense.

Rejecting the defense theory again under oath, Vannatter tells Shapiro, "I didn't know who the suspect was. Anyone could have been a suspect at that time. Mr. Simpson was no more of a suspect at that point than you were, Mr. Shapiro."

When Shapiro asks him about his two conversations with the Fiato brothers the previous January and February, Vannatter replies, "There was just general conversation going on. If something was said in jest or taken out of context, I can't answer to that."

In fact, when Larry Fiato had asked Vannatter if Simpson was a suspect early on, Vannatter told him, "Of course, we would have investigated Simpson at some point. He was a potential suspect. Everybody who had contact with the victim is a potential suspect until you investigate the case."

When asked on cross-examination by deputy district attorney Brian Kelberg whether he feels that his integrity has been unfairly questioned throughout the trial by the defense team, Vannatter says sternly, "You bet I do. I have dedicated over twenty-five years of hard service to this city, and I've done a lot of work. And I've seen a lot of people murdered, innocently murdered. And I have attempted to do the best I can to come to successful conclusions."

Responding to this latest attack with its final witness, the prosecution calls to the stand Commander Keith Bushey of the LAPD West Bureau, who had given the orders for Vannatter and the other three detectives to go to Simpson's house and notify him of his ex-wife's death on the morning after the murders. Consistent with what Lange, Vannatter, Phillips, and Fuhrman have testified, Bushey says that he directed the detectives to make the notification in order to make arrangements for Simpson's children, who had been taken to the West Los Angeles Division in the aftermath of their mother's murder.

That was simple truth, but with Fuhrman as part of this mix, it was anyone's guess how much credence the jury would give to Bushey's testimony. With their creative means of presenting evidence, by twisting Vannatter's words and deeds, Simpson's defense team hopes that they have created confusion in the minds of jurors. For out of that confusion can come reasonable doubt.

Endnote

138. On page 397 of his book, *American Tragedy*, Lawrence Schiller takes on Lange rather than Vannatter: "By the time Johnnie was finished, Lange had admitted that Mark Fuhrman had mentioned Simpson's past history of wife-beating to him. So at the time Fuhrman climbed the Rockingham wall, O.J. must already have been a suspect."

Schiller is incorrect on this point. Lange *never* had a conversation with Fuhrman about domestic abuse in the Simpson household. As stated earlier in this book, Lange learned from Detective Ron Phillips that Fuhrman had once responded to a radio call at Simpson's home, but he did not know why.

Lange has repeatedly said, under oath, that Simpson was not an *actual* suspect when the detectives first went to North Rockingham and at the time they decided to go over his wall to enter his property.

30

The Verdict

September 22–October 3, 1995

On Friday, September 22, both the prosecution and defense rest their cases. While working on their other investigations, Lange and Vannatter continue to monitor the Simpson trial, watching events as they unfold on television.

That same day, because Simpson has not testified on his own behalf, the court needs his waiver of that right on the record. Judge Ito, over the strenuous objection of the prosecution, gives Simpson the opportunity to say something in open court—without the jury present. In his brief statement in front of the court and the national television audience, Simpson insists, "I did not, could not, and would not have committed this crime."

Simpson then officially waives his right to testify.

On Tuesday, September 26, Marcia Clark and Chris Darden sum up the prosecution's case in their closing arguments. Darden speaks to the issues of motive; Clark argues the material evidence. Clark and Darden hinge nearly their entire case on Simpson's physical abuse of Nicole Brown, the overwhelming but complicated DNA evidence, and their stubborn timeline on June 12.

Even though they disagree with the manner in which the prosecution has presented its case during the trial, Lange and Vannatter believe that both Clark and Darden perform extraordinarily well during the early portions of their closing arguments. The attorneys, especially Darden, speak with sincerity, conviction, and passion. Although Lange believes it is all for naught, Vannatter insists that it is a shoestring catch. He still believes that the jury will convict after Clark and Darden finish summarizing their case.

In listening to the latter parts of Clark's summary, however, Lange and Vannatter sense that she appears willing to sacrifice much, including the detectives, the criminalists, and the coroner's office. Speaking of the defense team's case, Clark states to the jury, "So they took you through all this tortured and twisted road, one moment saying that the police are all a bunch of bumbling idiots. The next moment they are clever conspirators." That is the closest Clark comes to a defense of the police. It is destructive to the LAPD and her own case.

Both Lange and Vannatter know that they have been "framed" by the defense team through its misleading allegations of police ineptness during the investigation and police dishonesty in its wake. Their small and insignificant mistakes have been unjustifiably magnified into major crimes and dishonorable acts. During the trial, Marcia Clark appeared, at first, to fight this trend. But as the case rolled on, she sat back and allowed it to develop, probably realizing that she had been outgunned by her opponents. Then, in her closing arguments, she uses her former friends in the LAPD— the real target of the defense—as her foil.

The prosecution's summary is followed on Wednesday, September 27, by Johnnie Cochran's statement. From beginning to end, Cochran appears to stretch for pure jury nullification. He wants the jurors to ignore the evidence and to send a message to society. Cochran takes the preacher path: "One of the things that has made this country so great is people's willingness to stand up and say, 'That is wrong. I'm not going to be part of it. I'm not going to be part of the cover-up.' That is what I'm asking you to do."

Cochran appeals to the jury to deny that all of the evidence against his client is real. In an odd way, his arguments seem to mirror Clark's, appealing to the jurors to blame the LAPD, blame Fuhrman, blame the criminalists, and blame the coroner. Cochran wants the jury to blame everybody but Simpson.

Speaking of the knit cap found at the South Bundy crime scene, Cochran pleads, "It's no disguise. It makes no sense. It doesn't fit. If it doesn't fit, you must acquit."

Then, quoting from a wide variety of authorities, ranging from the Bible to Frederick Douglass, Cochran begins his tirade on Fuhrman—which is justified—and Vannatter—on whom it is not. Based on Vannatter's innocent mistakes in the search warrant, the continuing debate over *when* the detective viewed Simpson as an actual suspect, and Vannatter's handling of the vials of Simpson's and the victims' blood, Cochran displays a large chart in the courtroom, entitled, "Vannatter's Big Lies."

On the morning of Thursday, September 28, as Cochran continues his relentless assault, Vannatter has just returned home from a trip to South Dakota where he had attended a police conference. When he walks into his living room, he turns on the television and sits down.

Still playing on Vannatter's alleged lies about when Simpson became a suspect, Cochran passionately tells the jury, "The Book of Luke talks about that. If you are untruthful in small things, you should be disbelieved in big things. . . .

"This man with his big lies—and then we have Fuhrman coming right on the heels—the twins of deception." Later, Cochran adds to his description, calling Vannatter and Fuhrman "twin demons of deception" and then "the twin devils of deception."[139]

Upon hearing all this, Vannatter, who is now on his feet again, almost feels like grabbing his service revolver to shoot out the television set. Instead, he just switches it off, knowing that everyone in America has heard or soon will hear what Cochran has just said.

Just moments later, his wife, Rita, calls him from work in tears. She had just seen and heard Cochran make his charge against her husband on a television in her office. Then Vannatter's son, a cadet at the LAPD Academy, telephones, solemnly asking his father whether he should quit. Vannatter's married daughter also calls from her own home, crying uncontrollably.

In the course of his previously unblemished career as a police officer, he has never heard such charges leveled at him. Alone at his home and as angry and as humiliated as he has ever felt, he runs out the back door and into his backyard, gets down on his hands and knees, and furiously begins to pull weeds from his beloved rose garden. For the next hour, he wants to work hard physically—grabbing, pulling, and sweating out his anger.

* * *

Inside the courtroom during Cochran's closing arguments, the usually cool and collected Lange sits behind the prosecutor's table, seething, as Cochran unjustifiably assaults his partner. Lange, who already believes this case is over, moves his eyes between the defense attorney and the sitting jurors, who appear to be lapping up his fantasies.

During the morning break—after hearing more of Cochran's misrepresentations and embellishments—Lange walks outside and is immediately besieged by reporters, who know that Lange rarely says anything to them. But this time, Lange, defying Chief Williams's gag order, does have something to say. "Connecting Vannatter with Fuhrman is bullshit," he declares angrily. "And you can quote me. . . . Johnnie Cochran is a preacher who has turned into a snake-oil salesman."

Later in the day, Lange and Vannatter talk on the telephone.

"I want you there in that courtroom tomorrow," Lange says to his partner, adding that Cochran had pointed out Vannatter's absence to the jury—without noting that Vannatter had been out of state on police business.

"Are you kidding me?" Vannatter asks, as angry as Lange has ever heard him. "I'll be there if I have to crawl in from the valley! I'll be sitting in the goddamn first row! I want Cochran, that lying motherfucker, to look straight at me!"

After his conversation with Vannatter, Lange returns alone to the district attorney's office to meet with Hodgman, Clark, and Darden in Clark's office. During the meeting, Lange, still fuming over Cochran's comments about his partner, tells the prosecutors that Vannatter will be present in the courtroom the following day, sitting in the front row.

Surprisingly, Hodgman responds to Lange's anger by saying that he doesn't normally like his investigators in the courtroom during final arguments. Not surprisingly, Clark says that she doesn't want them there either. Darden—who from the outset has appeared torn between his loyalty to Clark and his respect for Lange and Vannatter—remains silent on the matter.

"Listen," Lange tells them slowly and deliberately as if he is still testifying in court, "this has not been a normal case for any of us. When was the last time you prosecuted a case in which your investigating officers were accused of any number of felonies by the defense? This has now gotten personal, and this must be addressed."

Seeing how serious Lange is, both Hodgman and Clark relent.

"I'll see you in court tomorrow," Lange says, leaving the DA's office still in a huff.

On the morning of Friday, September 29, Vannatter, accompanied by Lange and Detective Bert Luper, walks tall into the jam-packed courtroom. Perhaps by coincidence but maybe not, Clark has asked everyone on her prosecution team to attend as well. Those members not sitting at the prosecution's table have already taken the seats where Lange and Vannatter usually sit.

Lange and Luper immediately go to the crowd of attorneys in the front row and sternly tell them, "Make room for Phil."

A couple of the prosecutors scoot over, allowing Vannatter to squeeze in while Lange and Luper return to the rear of the courtroom to sit on a bench.

Through the remainder of Cochran's closing argument, Vannatter glares at the defense lawyer. There will be none of that "twin devils of deception" talk on this day, as Cochran refuses to make eye contact with Vannatter. However, several members of the jury do look at Vannatter during Cochran's oratory, and some of them even appear to smile and nod.

That afternoon, Judge Ito wraps up his instructions to the jury and gives the case to its members. In less than five minutes, the jurors have selected their forewoman.

Judge Ito orders the jurors back to their hotel, telling them *not* to begin their actual deliberations until Monday, October 2.

On Friday afternoon, after the jury returns to their quarters, Lange and Vannatter, for the first time, agree to participate in a press conference in the lobby of the Criminal Courts Building. But their appearance is quite brief. When asked how he felt about Cochran's description of him, Vannatter replies, "It's nonsense. It's lies. It's ridiculous." With smiles on their faces, Lange and Vannatter remind the reporters that there is still an internal LAPD gag order, restricting them from making further comment.

The media, for the most part, appear supportive of the detectives—especially the *Los Angeles Times*, whose reporting on this case has been daily must-reading for the detectives from the outset.

One reporter teases Vannatter on his way out, asking, "Hey, Phil, are you really one of those 'twin devils of deception'?" Vannatter, who has lightened up considerably since the previous day, replies in good humor, "No, no. You must be talking about Johnnie and Bob Shapiro."

At 9:16 A.M. on Monday, October 2, the jurors begin their deliberations on the Simpson case. At 2:28 P.M., the jury notifies Judge Ito that a verdict has been reached. Earlier, in the midst of their brief discussions, the jurors had asked to review only one piece of evidence: the trial testimony of Simpson's limousine driver on the night of the murders, Allan Park, who is a critical prosecution witness.

Just before 3:00, Judge Ito tells the courtroom and the national television audience that the jury will return and the verdict will be announced the following morning at 10:00.

Lange and Vannatter are working separately that afternoon. Vannatter is in the office at the Robbery/Homicide Division; Lange is out on a mandatory tactical training day in Long Beach. When they independently hear the news, they are floored, refusing, at first, to believe that the jury has come in so quickly.

But when someone tells Vannatter that Park's testimony is the only piece of evidence the jurors asked to review, he is sure that he has been right all along: Simpson will be convicted.

Following this same logic, the talking heads on television—who have been providing endless color commentary throughout the trial—appear to agree with this analysis. With few exceptions, they seem to believe that the jury's review of Park's testimony indicates a probable conviction.

Lange sloughs all of this off, insisting that the jury will acquit Simpson. Lange predicts that Simpson will be back at his North Rockingham estate by the end of the following day.

At 8:30 A.M. on Tuesday, October 3, ninety minutes before the verdict is scheduled to be read, Lange and Vannatter are in the district attorney's office, along with the prosecution team, the Brown and Goldman families, and friends of the families. The small crowd appears extremely nervous but optimistic. Nevertheless, no postverdict party has been scheduled in the DA's office; there is no champagne on ice.

At about 9:45 A.M., the large group goes downstairs into Judge Ito's courtroom. The laughter and the precelebration have ceased. Everyone in the room becomes still and quiet as the jury files in. Lange and Vannatter are sitting with Mike Stevens, an investigator for the district attorney's office, who is sandwiched between them.

As they take their seats, the members of the jury hardly make eye contact with the families, let alone the detectives.

Then, everything seems to happen very quickly. Judge Ito rules the court in session and asks the forewoman to give the court clerk, Deirdre Robertson, the jury's verdict.

Robertson nervously reads: "Superior Court of California, County of Los Angeles, in the matter of the State of California versus Orenthal James Simpson, case number BA097211. We the jury, in the above-entitled action, find the defendant, Orenthal James Simpson, *not guilty* of the crime of murder."

The courtroom erupts in complete bedlam, even before the second not-guilty verdict is announced.

Lange immediately turns to comfort Kim Goldman, Ron Goldman's sister, who is sitting in back of him and crying uncontrollably with her father. Lange reaches out and holds her hand. Shaking his head in disbelief, Vannatter appears to be in shock.

After a few moments, Lange and Vannatter get up from their chairs and stand next to each other. They both look over at Simpson, who is laughing and shaking hands with his attorneys, knowing that he is about to walk away a free man.

With his eyes now fixed on Simpson, Lange says solemnly to Vannatter, "Phil, a guilty man has just gotten away with murder."

Endnote

139. Cochran was not using religious rhetoric here as an interpretation of facts; in fact, he was blatantly playing the race card for this jury. As Lawrence Schiller noted on page 660 of his book, *American Tragedy*, which chronicled the inside story of the Simpson defense team: "The term 'twins of deception' was intended to invoke the devil. In the jargon of the Nation of Islam, 'devil' meant white. Vannatter and Fuhrman were twin *devils* of deception. White devils."

Interestingly, Cochran did not repeat this comparison of Vannatter and Fuhrman in his book, *Journey to Justice*, even though he reprinted much of his closing argument on pages 338–351.

Epilogue

A new day, a new year.

Tom Lange and Phil Vannatter are on a conference call with their writer, making last-minute changes in the manuscript for this book. Their deadline is less than forty-eight hours away, and they have some final thoughts about their experiences.

Within the past year, both Lange and Vannatter have retired from the Los Angeles Police Department—Vannatter in February 1996, Lange last August. Phil and Rita are finally living back on a farm in the Midwest, raising a couple of quarterhorses and seeing their three grandchildren during their frequent trips back to Los Angeles. Their daughter, Donna, who is raising two of those grandchildren, tries to forget the pain caused by the false accusations made against her father.

The Vannatters' son, Matthew, graduated from the LAPD Academy the month before Phil retired. The torch has now been passed—a Vannatter remains at the LAPD. Rita tells her friends, "I don't know what's worse: being the *wife* of a police officer or being the *mother* of a police officer."

Tom and Linda Lange are still in Ventura County with their two teenage daughters, Melissa and Megan, and staying active. Upon retiring, Lange became a licensed private investigator and a recognized expert in homicide investigations and blood-splatter examinations. He now carefully picks and chooses the cases he wants to work on and the attorneys with whom he wants to work. Linda Lange no longer worries about her husband running out to some job in the middle of the night. Tom now works at home and has supper every night with his family.

The O.J. Simpson case made the thought of retirement easier for both detectives. They don't miss their jobs, just the people with whom they worked for so many years. On October 3, 1995, the day of the jury's verdict, Lange and Vannatter, accompanied by Captain Will Gartland and Detective Ron Phillips, were invited to the private office of LAPD Chief Willie Williams. This was their first meeting with Williams, who had kept his distance from the detectives throughout the investigation and trial. The detectives vividly remember Williams's controversial predecessor, Daryl Gates, who would have demanded daily in-person reports from his detectives in such a major case, wanting to know everything they knew. However, Williams maintained a different management style. He preferred reports from his deputy chiefs and commanders, not the grunts on the street. Even at this first and only meeting about the Simpson case, Williams, perhaps preoccupied with all of his other responsibilities, could only muster small talk about the fickleness of juries.

Lange and Vannatter, wanting to use this rare opportunity with their chief, tried to take the conversation up a few notches, saying that the message sent by the verdict was that the public doesn't want police officers doing their jobs. When officers make bold decisions, they open themselves up for annihilation by well-dressed defense attorneys who drive Rolls-Royces and have sharp tongues. In the privileged sanctuary of a courtroom, defense attorneys may use embellished testimony, distort and omit relevant evidence, flat-out lie about what police officers did and didn't do, and then frame a police conspiracy around them.

Specifically, Lange wanted to know how the chief felt this case would affect the younger detectives coming up through the ranks. "Will *they* go over the wall if they believe someone needs help?" the detective asked Williams, "or will they just go to breakfast after remembering what happened here, fearing that they, too, will be placed on trial?" Vannatter added, "Of all the people who attacked us as detectives, would they feel the same way if one of their loved ones had been the victim of such a brutal murder?" Williams nodded but left these questions hanging. A busy man, he had been glancing at his watch throughout the meeting. He had other things to attend to.

Still reminiscing with their writer on New Year's Day, Lange and Vannatter remind him that next week, in a Santa Monica courtroom, O.J. Simpson's defense team is expected to resume direct testimony in the wrongful-death civil lawsuit filed by the families of Nicole Brown and Ronald Goldman.

Simpson doesn't stand to lose his freedom in this case, just his money. The legal threshold for liability is much lower in this matter: Only a preponderance of the evidence is required, versus evidence beyond a reasonable doubt. The jury doesn't have to be unanimous in its verdict; the winner will only need nine of twelve votes.

But this time around, the detectives make no predictions. Less than two weeks ago, Simpson won another huge legal battle, regaining custody of his two children, Sydney and Justin, from the Brown family. Who could have predicted that two years ago?

Both detectives were subpoenaed to testify as friendly witnesses for the plaintiffs and hostile witnesses for the defense. After Detective Mark Fuhrman pled "no contest" to perjury in early October, his attorney announced that he would take the Fifth again if called at the civil trial. In fact, he will not appear at all. Simpson's defense team badly needed a whipping boy to depict their police-conspiracy theory in this case.

Reenter Lange and Vannatter.

In the midst of a flurry of publicity, Lange and Vannatter took the stand one right after the other. Once again, they went through the same evidence they had testified to during the grand jury hearing in 1994 and the criminal trial in 1995. They explained the conditions of the murdered victims, the bloody shoe prints, the drops of blood, the left-hand glove at South Bundy, the right-hand glove at North Rockingham, the knit cap, the bloodstained envelope with the eyeglasses inside, the speck of blood on the Bronco, and the melt-down rate of Ben & Jerry's ice cream. They could now recite the facts of this case in their sleep, even those revolving around the only two real mistakes they had made: Vannatter's minor misstatements in the June 13 search warrant and Lange's inability to make his final walk-through at the South Bundy crime scene, which would have caught the failure of the criminalist to collect the blood on Nicole Brown's rear gate. Nevertheless, through all of this, neither detective strayed from his previous sworn statements.

When cross-examined, Lange and Vannatter found the atmosphere in the courtroom during the civil trial remarkably different than during the criminal trial. Cochran, Shapiro, Bailey, and company had played to the television camera while trying to con the jury with their elegance and style. In the wrongful-death suit with no television coverage, Simpson's lead defense attorney, Robert Baker, acted like he was in a dogfight. Baker growled and barked, like a pit bull. While on the stand, Lange and Vannatter each caught themselves protecting their hands and fingers, fearing that Baker might bite. Dripping with sarcasm, nearly every question was rife with unadulterated confrontation and accusation. He made the members of The Dream Team look like Phil Donahue.

But this time, the plaintiffs' attorneys were on the cops' side. With the benefit of hindsight and a detailed analysis of the prosecution's earlier mistakes, they planned a surgical strike against Simpson. They listened when Lange and Vannatter encouraged them to change their minds about the time of the murders. They shifted their timeline from 10:15 P.M.—which Marcia Clark and the prosecution team had stubbornly adhered to during the criminal case—to 10:35 P.M. In Lange and Vannatter's minds, that's when the murders of Nicole Brown and Ron Goldman occurred. With that change, several witnesses who had hurt the prosecution during the criminal trial, like Robert Heidstra, suddenly became witnesses against Simpson.

Also, evidence brought to the prosecution by Lange and Vannatter and then dismissed by them was evidence embraced by the plaintiff's attorneys, including the detectives' June 13 tape-recorded interview with Simpson, which included all of his contradictions and inconsistencies, as well as his lack of a remotely credible alibi. Among other evidence, the plaintiffs also brought in Lange's tape-recorded conversations with Simpson during the Bronco chase through which the world could hear one of the cops Simpson would later accuse of framing him begging for Simpson to throw his gun out of the car and to give up peacefully. Had Lange and

Vannatter planted evidence against this man, their move would have been to send in the SWAT team right there on the 405 freeway and force Simpson to shoot himself or be shot by the police. Instead, Lange, with Vannatter's assistance, spared and probably helped save Simpson's life.

From the outset of the Simpson case, too many in the media had not been balanced or fair in their coverage of the detectives' work. The roles of Lange and Vannatter were judged by extraordinary standards to which no other police investigators had ever before been publicly subjected. Their work and decisions were placed under a microscope and evaluated not by their huge successes but by the smallest of errors, which were then magnified and blown out of proportion.

While playing amateur sleuths in front of the camera, the talking heads attempted to speak with authority on such issues as the reasons why Lange and Vannatter decided to go over Simpson's wall and their handling of the blood evidence, as well as the metaphysics of when Simpson became a "suspect" and the substance of Vannatter's search warrant. After reviewing the detectives' interview with Simpson, they criticized their technique, conveniently forgetting that Lange and Vannatter, who had nothing to nail Simpson with at that point, had kept the suspect's goodwill long enough to get his fingerprints, photographs of the fresh wounds on his left hand, and a vial of his blood without the need for a court order.

The uninformed media criticism of Lange and Vannatter precipitated and even legitimized the environment in which Simpson's defense attorneys could lie and fabricate evidence against two honest detectives, as well as an entire police department. Cops out in the field doing their jobs well is rarely news; cops who *maybe* planted evidence and framed a celebrity defendant is big news, regardless of whether there is any evidence to support the claim.

Wrapping up their conference call on New Year's Day, the detectives tell their writer that they don't expect to be recalled by either side during the final weeks of the civil case. Soon, the O.J. Simpson case will be behind them. As they say: It's all over but the shouting . . . on the talk-show circuit with the talking heads. Now unbridled like Vannatter's horses, the cops are finally able to defend themselves and their investigation. No gag orders from this point on, they both finally feel free.

The obvious question is put to Phil Vannatter: "So tell me, if you had to do it all again, would you have made the decision to go over O.J. Simpson's wall?"

"You bet we would," Vannatter replies firmly with no hesitation. "That was our job."

Afterword

On Tuesday, February 4, 1997, the jury in the wrongful-death suit against O.J. Simpson found the football legend responsible for the murders of Nicole Brown and Ronald Goldman—in a unanimous verdict. On paper, at least, the decision would cost Simpson millions of dollars in compensatory and punitive damages. Simpson, who immediately appealed the decision, claimed to be broke and unable to pay.

The specter of Mark Fuhrman had hung over the trial like rush-hour smog over the city of Los Angeles. But, in the end, he, along with the revelations of his racism and perjury during the criminal trial, had no effect on the final outcome of the civil case. The defense team's claim of a police conspiracy prior to Simpson's arrest was blown away by the release of the contents of Tom Lange's conversations with Simpson during the Bronco chase, as well as by thirty newly discovered photographs of Simpson wearing a pair of Bruno Magli shoes, which Simpson had denied, under oath, ever owning.

Also, as referred to in the Epilogue, much of the evidence dismissed by the prosecution during the criminal trial was evidence introduced during the civil case. Clearly, the star of the second trial was Daniel Petrocelli, the lead attorney for the Goldman family, who, along with the other plaintiffs' attorneys, stood by the LAPD and the work of Tom Lange and Phil Vannatter.

At the exact moment that the verdict was being read, Lange and Vannatter were in the backseat of a chauffeur-driven limousine. They were speeding along on the Ronald Reagan Freeway in Ventura County, en route to an appearance on ABC's *Nightline*, which had just booked them an hour earlier. Program executives had sent the limo to guarantee on-time delivery. As President Clinton's State of the Union Address was about to begin, the two detectives watched the report of the jury's decision on a color television with a three-inch screen and a fuzzy picture, held in the front seat by their coauthor, who had just flown into Los Angeles earlier that day.

After hearing the verdict against Simpson, neither Lange nor Vannatter cheered or gloated. There were no high fives, no gleeful back-slapping. They simply looked at each other with considerable relief, smiled, and shook hands.

Moments later at the ABC studio, Lange, dressed casually in a golf shirt and windbreaker, and Vannatter, wearing a West Virginia Mountaineers sweatshirt, appeared on *Nightline*. When asked how he felt in the wake of the verdict, Vannatter, praising the jury and the LAPD, told the national television audience, "I am really, really overjoyed for the Goldmans and the Browns. . . . It will give them some closure in the deaths of their children."

It also promised to give some closure for Lange and Vannatter, especially along with the release of the hardcover edition of this book, which had occurred on January 28, the same day that the case went to the jury.

During the past week, as the panel deliberated, the two detectives had appeared on *Dateline NBC*, *Good Morning America*, *Larry King Live*, *Rivera Live*, and even Howard Stern's morning radio show, among many other programs—as the network news on ABC, CBS, CNN, Fox, and NBC played and replayed the audiotape of Lange's conversation with Simpson during the Bronco chase.

With the verdict now in, the two detectives were invited to appear or reappear on nearly every talk show on the circuit. Predictably, the interviews with Lange and Vannatter focused on the decision in the civil trial. The most commonly asked question of them was, "Do you feel vindicated?"

Lange replied on one program, "I don't know that we have to say we have been vindicated. We didn't do anything wrong. What we did was our job." Then, reflecting for a moment, Lange added,

"Our only real mistake was not sending Mark Fuhrman home that night."

Finally, Lange and Vannatter had begun receiving some acknowledgment for their work on the case. They were—and continue to be—embraced by the law-enforcement community, which invited them to speak at police conventions from coast to coast. Lange's private investigation firm was prospering, and he had become a certified instructor for the State of California's Department of Justice, specializing in crime-scene management and high-profile murder investigations. Vannatter became the national spokesperson for Stop Stick, a tire-deflating device used by police departments to stop high-speed getaways. He also became a public-relations representative, specializing in police-emergency communications, for GTE, the California-based telephone company.

Although the television and radio media were unbridled in their coverage of this latest episode in the Simpson drama, the major print media were apparently weary of the Simpson case. With the exception of *The Los Angeles Times*, newspapers and magazines, failed to report any of the new revelations contained in Lange and Vannatter's book. In addition, not one single major newspaper or magazine reviewed this book—with the exception of Laura Mansnerus's short-shrift analysis in a March 19, 1997, "Books in Brief" review in *The New York Times*, which did, at least, praise the book's documentation. In spite of this nearly complete blackout by the print media, *Evidence Dismissed* immediately leaped onto all of the national best-seller lists, including that of the *New York Times*.

If two books about the same controversial murder case ever cried out for tandem reviews, they were *Evidence Dismissed* and Mark Fuhrman's *Murder in Brentwood*, which was released just a couple of weeks later, in mid-February. But no newspaper, with the exception of the *Philadelphia Inquirer*, seized the opportunity.

Meantime, Lange and Vannatter were stunned by the outrageous charges made by Fuhrman in his book. At first, both detectives merely brushed off Fuhrman's claims to have discovered evidence at the South Bundy and North Rockingham crime scenes that Lange and Vannatter had allegedly missed.

But neither man was prepared for what followed.

The television media that had, for a while, made Lange and

Vannatter the beneficiaries of its awesome market power suddenly put the two detectives back on the defensive.

During the week of February 10, Lange and Vannatter learned of Fuhrman's impressive upcoming book tour. The key to his publicity campaign was ABC's *Prime Time Live*. Lange and Vannatter's publisher, Pocket Books, had earlier rejected *Prime Time Live*'s bids to be the first program to interview the two detectives after the publication of their book. Instead, Pocket Books opted for the more highly rated *Dateline NBC*, which assigned Katie Couric to conduct the interview with Lange and Vannatter. That interview with Couric was broadcast on the evening of January 29, 1997. *Prime Time Live* refused to go second, which is a common practice in the television industry.

Moving quickly in the wake of this decision, Diane Sawyer, one of the anchors of *Prime Time Live*, pushed her scheduled February 19 segment on Fuhrman with considerable zeal. Earlier that day, Sawyer made her first appearance ever on the *Oprah Winfrey* show, for the primary purpose of promoting Fuhrman's exclusive appearance that night on her program.

Actually, Sawyer had also interviewed Fuhrman four months earlier, on October 8—six days after Fuhrman pleaded "no contest" to the charge of perjury during his 1995 sworn testimony at O.J. Simpson's criminal trial. Fuhrman had been sentenced to three years' probation, which he was in the midst of during his book tour.

On her own program, Sawyer asked the well-prepared Fuhrman ostensibly tough but predictable questions about his racism and perjury—for which he had already given pat answers in his book. But then she rolled over for him regarding his claims about crime-scene evidence supposedly missed by Lange and Vannatter, who were permitted to respond during the show—but only in brief and heavily edited film clips. Even though Fuhrman had little experience as a homicide detective, Sawyer depicted him as a seasoned investigator. As subjectively portrayed by Sawyer, Fuhrman was the clear winner in what would soon become a war of words among the detectives involved in the Simpson case.

Remarkably, Sawyer seemed hell-bent on rehabilitating the reputation of this admitted perjurer on national television—at the expense of Lange and Vannatter. (Not surprisingly, considering the preshow hype, the Fuhrman program yielded *Prime Time Live*'s highest rating of the season.)

Neither Sawyer nor the *Prime Time Live* staff included or even mentioned Lange and Vannatter's fifteen-page, single-spaced response to Fuhrman and his book, which had been faxed to a top *Prime Time Live* executive the day *before* the broadcast—at his request. (See the Appendix for the text of this February 18 statement, which has been edited for this edition of their book.)

The day after Diane Sawyer's piece on Fuhrman aired, Oprah Winfrey followed suit, accepting Fuhrman's claims about Lange's and Vannatter's alleged mistakes—without challenge. That same night, Fuhrman was interviewed on CNN's *Larry King Live*, where the disgraced detective's rehabilitation continued.

On Friday, February 21, Fuhrman appeared on ABC's *Good Morning America* while Lange and Vannatter were simultaneously being interviewed on NBC's *Today* show—to defend themselves and to refute Fuhrman for the first time. That night—in the midst of Fuhrman's media blitz—Geraldo Rivera became the first and only journalist to take on Fuhrman, during his *Rivera Live* program on CNBC, specifically challenging Fuhrman about his crime-scene claims and quoting extensively from Lange and Vannatter's fifteen-page statement. Later, Larry King, always a considerate host, featured Lange and then Vannatter on separate nights to respond to Fuhrman, who had nearly become a regular on King's show since the release of his book.

Although both Lange and Vannatter were invited to appear with Fuhrman in a debate forum, the two detectives, trying to take the high road, rejected such offers, believing that Fuhrman was beneath contempt and not worthy of a face-to-face response. (This decision was not made without stirring dissent; but the dissenters, who included their coauthor and some executives at Pocket Books, respected and supported the detectives' position.)

Consequently, the television media looked for others to go up against Fuhrman. On CNN's *Crossfire*, Fuhrman, a one-time high-school dropout, debated Harvard professor Alan Dershowitz and, amazingly, ate the prominent attorney alive, managing to move the discussion away from Fuhrman's racism and toward the crime-scene issues in the Simpson case. On these matters, Dershowitz seemed poorly informed and impotent in his responses.

After Fuhrman annihilated Dershowitz on *Crossfire*, the former detective seemed to come into his own. Even though he continued to base his presentation on false charges against Lange and

Vannatter and misleading assumptions about the case, Fuhrman, attractive and articulate, was relentless, seemingly willing to appear on any television or radio program that wanted him. It seemed unlikely that Fuhrman, an electrician's apprentice in Idaho prior to the publication of his book, would be returning to that job in the wake of his media tour.

Apparently Fuhrman was viewed, by those like Diane Sawyer and Oprah Winfrey, as not unlike Richard Jewell, a man wrongly accused. And, as with Jewell, the rehabilitation of Mark Fuhrman was somehow thought to be somewhat of a humane act. Fuhrman was now apologizing, with moist eyes and a boyish look, for his use of the N-word and then lying about it. What white person could not accept his apology, especially when he was being pampered by television media goddesses Sawyer and Winfrey?

After Fuhrman allowed himself to be humiliated with questions about his sordid past and then seemed to atone for his racism and perjury, the validity of his alleged discovery of "new evidence" at the crime scenes was, inexplicably, accepted without question. Consequently, Fuhrman was deemed credible by dint of what appeared to be his good intentions—even though he was a proven liar who was in the midst of three years' probation for perjury. "Yes," the television talking heads seemed to be saying, "Fuhrman is a racist and a perjurer, but he was also a good detective." No one who interviewed him, with the exception of Geraldo Rivera, voiced any disagreement—even though there was plenty of information available to discredit him.

On March 19, as Fuhrman's book quickly climbed to number one on the national best-seller lists, Diane Sawyer and her producer, Shelley Ross, struck again, allowing *Prime Time Live* to trumpet the claim that Fuhrman had passed a polygraph test. But Sawyer and Ross used the vagueness of the questions posed to Fuhrman to attack Lange's and Vannatter's credibility once again. (Fuhrman later admitted to personally wording the questions for the test.)

According to the results of the exam, Fuhrman had shown no obvious deception in response to such questions as "Did you plant evidence in the Simpson case?" Of course, as they have made clear in this book, Lange and Vannatter were second to none in their support of Fuhrman against the charge of evidence-planting.

However, Fuhrman also passed the lie-detector test in regard to such questions as whether or not he believed that he had seen evidence at the two crime scenes that Lange and Vannatter had missed. The most heralded of these alleged discoveries was a bloody fingerprint on the knob area of the rear gate at Nicole Brown's home. (See page 49, endnote 17.)

On Sunday, March 23, *The New York Times Book Review* weighed in with a full-length review of Fuhrman's book, written by Craig Wolff, a professor at the Columbia University Graduate School of Journalism.

Along with nearly everyone else in the media, Wolff made much of former LAPD junior detective Fuhrman's alleged discovery of this bloody fingerprint at the scene of the murders of Brown and Goldman. As Wolff pointed out, Fuhrman referred to this supposed evidence in his crime-scene notes.

However, the issue wasn't whether Fuhrman simply *believed* he saw a bloody fingerprint. The real question was whether this bloody fingerprint ever existed.

In his review, Wolff never mentioned that Fuhrman made several major mistakes in his crime-scene notes. In fact, the claim of a bloody fingerprint was just one of the errors Fuhrman made.

For instance, Fuhrman wrongly speculated in his official notes that the two stabbed and slashed victims might have died from gunshot wounds, and that their killer had possibly been bitten by a dog. Fuhrman also erroneously reported that a menu from a nearby Thai restaurant found under Brown's leg had come from a local pizzeria, and that a simple knit cap next to Goldman's body was a ski mask. (The mistake concerning the menu could have been particularly catastrophic if the detectives had later linked a suspect to the Thai restaurant.)

Including the claim of a bloody fingerprint, these five independent observations were the only new contributions Fuhrman had made to what was already known about this crime scene—and, incredibly, all five were wrong. Everything else in Fuhrman's notes had earlier been reported by other police officers who had logged in during the two-hour period before Fuhrman arrived.

As a professor of journalism, Wolff should at least have voiced some skepticism about Fuhrman's identification of a bloody fingerprint, considering the other mistakes in the detective's official crime-scene notes. Instead, Wolff embraced Fuhrman's far-fetched story, ignoring Fuhrman's errors while touting "Mr. Fuhrman's allegiance to an unemotional step-by-step chronology . . . [that] returns the case to ground zero."

Assuming for a moment that Fuhrman did discover an actual bloody fingerprint, he would have been required, even as a junior investigator on the case, to protect such crucial evidence. But, by his own admission, he did nothing to secure it. He just walked away without even assigning a police officer to guard the area where he had supposedly made this discovery.

More important, Fuhrman had a responsibility to call attention to this alleged evidence, verbally, to a superior. While Fuhrman claims otherwise neither Fuhrman nor his partner, Brad Roberts—who suddenly corroborated his old friend's discovery in the midst of Fuhrman's book-promotion tour—said anything to their supervisor, Detective Ronald Phillips, about finding a bloody fingerprint. (Lange and Vannatter believe that this "bloody fingerprint" may have been nothing more than some sort of blood smudge, which was all that Phillips remembered seeing.)

Fuhrman and Roberts certainly did not discuss either a bloody fingerprint or a blood smudge with the lead detectives, Lange and Vannatter, who arrived at the crime scene two hours after Fuhrman, Roberts, and Phillips. If this evidence ever did exist, both Fuhrman and Roberts were, at best, negligent for not immediately telling the senior detectives what they had found.

In the predawn hours of the morning after the murders, Phillips guided both Lange and Vannatter through their separate and routine "walk-throughs" of the crime scene—during which all of the known evidence was pointed out and described. But Phillips said nothing about an alleged bloody fingerprint—because he was unaware of one. (Significantly, Phillips didn't mention a blood smudge either.) Instead, Fuhrman—who spent the next two hours with Lange and Vannatter but never said a word about a bloody fingerprint—chose to hide his alleged discovery in his error-filled crime-scene notes, which senior detectives found laced with inappropriate suppositions.

Regardless, to *New York Times* reviewer Wolff, the culprit was not Fuhrman. Instead, he blamed Lange and Vannatter, two honest detectives with a combined fifty-six years of spotless service to the LAPD. "Thus," Wolff wrote, "the bloody fingerprint . . . was never pursued, and was ultimately lost."

Yet, according to the official report of the LAPD's Latent Print

Section, *none* of the four fingerprint technicians at the Brown-Goldman crime scene, who made seventeen fingerprint and palm-print lifts, found a bloody fingerprint on or near the dead-bolt knob area of the rear gate—where Fuhrman claimed to have discovered it.

As everyone who followed the Simpson case knew, the killer wore gloves, one of which came off his left hand, which was injured in the midst of a struggle with Goldman. Would the killer, who was known to be right-handed, have handled the knob on the rear gate with his injured and ungloved left hand, or with his gloved right hand?

Readers of *The New York Times Book Review* wouldn't know about any of these discrepancies from reading Wolff's review, because Wolff failed to mention them. Like Diane Sawyer and Oprah Winfrey, Wolff did express some skepticism about Fuhrman's repeated denials of his racist past; but he accepted Fuhrman's accounts of crime-scene matters without question.

In short, the evidence remains overwhelming that Fuhrman and Roberts were simply mistaken in their identification of a bloody fingerprint—which came in the dead of night, at about 2:30 A.M., approximately four hours after the murders. It simply defies belief that these two junior detectives spotted evidence that no one else saw—particularly in view of the other mistakes in Fuhrman's crime-scene notes and the junior detectives' failure to notify Lange and Vannatter of this evidence.

In his book, Fuhrman made other claims about evidence—for which he took no notes. In fact, he took no notes at the Rocking-ham scene, but he later insisted that he found blood streaks on the lower outside door panel of Simpson's Bronco, black sweat clothes in Simpson's washing machine, smudges of blood on a light switch near the washing machine, and an empty Swiss Army knife box on Simpson's bathtub.

But, once again, Fuhrman told no one in authority about these discoveries—assuming that they were any more real than his bloody fingerprint or his wild speculation that Brown and Goldman might have been shot to death.

Fuhrman had a decision-making role in the Simpson case only for about a half hour, when he was replaced by Lange and Vannatter of the LAPD's elite Robbery/Homicide Division, who, together and individually, had investigated over five hundred homicides. After being taken off the case, Fuhrman did little more than stand in the street outside the perimeter of the crime scene, waiting for the detectives from Robbery/Homicide to arrive.

Fuhrman remained under Lange and Vannatter's direct supervision for a two-hour period, between 5:00 and 7:00 A.M. During that time, Fuhrman performed well, finding a speck of blood above the outside door handle of Simpson's Bronco, as well as the famous bloody right-hand glove on a walkway on Simpson's estate.

But, unlike in the case of his discovery of the alleged bloody fingerprint, Fuhrman, with considerable excitement, gave separate tours to Lange, Vannatter, and Phillips to show them the glove and to explain how he found it. Why didn't he do the same when he supposedly found the bloody fingerprint?

After 7:00 on the morning following the murders, Fuhrman's role was reduced to general detail work, far from the investigative and decision-making processes. In his book, though, Fuhrman completely exaggerated his importance to the Brown-Goldman murder investigation after that. Nevertheless, Wolff accepted without challenge and even praised Fuhrman's statements—many of which were wholly inaccurate (see Appendix)—about details of the Simpson case in which he was not involved.

Demonstrating how truly uninformed this reviewer was about the overall Simpson investigation, Wolff concluded "that something was lost when Mr. Fuhrman fell out of the case."

Significantly, Fuhrman had earlier applied for a transfer to the Robbery/Homicide Division—as mentioned in Chapter One—but his request was rejected by the LAPD's high command just before the Brown-Goldman murders. Fuhrman—who was destined to remain a junior detective for the remainder of his twenty-year career—was angry and bitter after his transfer was denied. If he was aware of that, Wolff didn't bother to mention it.

However, this rejection best explains the motive behind the unfounded attacks on detectives from the LAPD's Robbery/Homicide Division by Mark Fuhrman, an admitted perjurer who chose to take the Fifth Amendment rather than defend his brief role in this investigation.

Dan Moldea, Lange and Vannatter's collaborator, responded, in writing, to the Wolff review, defending his partners in a lengthy letter to the editor. However, *The New York Times* refused to publish Moldea's defense of the two detectives, allowing Fuhrman's false and misleading account to stand unchallenged—thus, giving legitimacy to Fuhrman and the charges contained in his book. The success of Fuhrman's book—as well as his own remarkable rehabilitation with the help of an uncritical media—was a classic victory of style over substance. But his newfound public acceptance—now with the help of *The New York Times*, which prides itself as the newspaper of record—did nothing more than add to the confusion, disinformation, and circus atmosphere revolving around this bizarre murder case.

In his book, Mark Fuhrman wrote about his first meeting with Marcia Clark on the day after the Brown-Goldman murders. Fuhrman claimed:

> Around noontime, Marcia Clark from the district attorney's office arrived. She was another person I had never met before. Clark asked to be shown what I had seen, what I did, and where I had found any evidence. So I walked her through the crime scene and explained my discoveries and observations. . . .
> Clark asked me if I could describe everything that had taken place at Bundy and Rockingham that concerned me. . . .
> As I described everything that I observed, noted, and found, she sat smiling and nodding.

However, in her book, *Without a Doubt*—which was released on May 9, 1997—Clark stated: "Fuhrman would later claim to have found a bloody fingerprint on the back gate at Bundy, as well as an empty Swiss army [*sic*] knife box on the edge of the tub in O.J. Simpson's master bathroom. It's worth noting here that during our tour of Rockingham, he did not *once* mention either the print or knife box to me."

In short, Fuhrman was a rookie homicide cop who made rookie-homicide-cop mistakes. He did not protect, preserve, or properly document those items he believed to be evidence—if those items ever existed. His crime-scene notes contained inappropriate and off-base speculation and supposition, and he allowed his ego to cloud his judgment then and now.

Clark also absolved Lange and Vannatter from other charges made by Fuhrman and others. For instance, Clark addressed the question of the blood found on the back gate at Brown's home, saying: "On his first pass at Bundy on June 13, [Dennis] Fung hadn't picked up the bloodstains on the rear gate. *This, after Tom Lange had specifically instructed him to do so* [emphasis added]." She also gave Fung full responsibility for failing to collect *all* of the blood in Simpson's Bronco. In addition, Clark described her confrontation with Fung, who admitted seeing dark sweat clothes in Simpson's hamper—but never collected them and didn't tell anyone, including Lange and Vannatter, about his discovery.

Speaking of Lange's investigation of the crime scene, Clark wrote: "Tom came out squeaky clean. His only *possible* error in judgment at the crime scene was the blanket he'd use to cover Nicole on the scene. Nicole had lain uncovered in full public view for more than three hours. In a gesture of decency, Tom had found a blanket in a closet to spread over her. Now, of course, the defense was going to argue that the incriminating trace evidence found on Ron's body and the knit cap—hair and fibers that matched Simpson's—had somehow come from that blanket."

Just to be clear, respect for Nicole Brown's body, which lay in plain view, was only a secondary reason for placing the blanket over her. Prior to the criminal trial, Lange had sent a memorandum to Clark entitled "Why Cover the Body?" In this memo, Lange listed his reasons:

A. To protect the body, which is still evidence, from the prying eye of the video cameras and still cameras, and to protect any evidence (i.e., blood splatters) on the body.
  1. The body position itself is evidence.
  2. The way the decedent is attired may be evidence.
  3. Any jewelry or lack thereof on the decedent may be evidence.
  4. Any blood patterns on the decedent are evidence.
*This evidence may be corroborative of or may eliminate any potential suspect or witness.

B. Secondary purposes:
  1. Respect for the decedent in public view.
  2. Regard for family and friends of decedent who may potentially view the crime scene.

As stated elsewhere in this book, in Chapter 23 and the Appendix, *no* contamination of the crime scene resulted from Lange's decision to place the blanket over Brown's body.

However, this is not to say that Clark remained as kind to Lange and Vannatter throughout her book. This was underscored, once again on ABC, during Clark's first interview on her book tour, with Barbara Walters of *20/20*. Walters, who during the show, portrayed Lange and Vannatter as obstacles in the investigation, laid the groundwork for Clark to attack the two detectives for their June 13, 1994, interview with Simpson. Both Clark and Walters slapped down Lange and Vannatter for not being rough enough with Simpson—a criticism that had already become the most common and unfair rap against the detectives.

In fact, Clark was much tougher on Lange and Vannatter in her book, saying:

> In defense of Phil and Tom, I do know there's something to be said for developing rapport with your suspect to get him talking. It's just that at some point, push has to come to shove. And during this interview the shove came way too late and way too gently. . . .
>
> That interview was one of the worst bits of police work I'd ever seen—but I kept my thoughts to myself. I couldn't afford to alienate my chief investigators. Besides, it was spilt milk. Complaining about their ineptitude would not help me get through this case.

But, like so many others, Clark wouldn't concede that the results of that interview gave the prosecuting attorneys—and, later, the plaintiffs' attorneys in the civil case—the evidence that served as the basis for their entire case against Simpson: his blood.

It is important to remember that Lange and Vannatter's interview with Simpson was conducted just hours after the murders and minutes after Simpson returned from Chicago. Although Simpson was clearly the top suspect, little was known about the case at that time and none of the evidence had been analyzed. In short, as stated in Chapter Seven, Lange and Vannatter had nothing with which to nail Simpson, who was not required to cooperate and could have walked out of the interview at will.

Nevertheless, this interview that Clark called "one of the worst bits of police work I'd ever seen" yielded:

- inconsistencies in Simpson's alibi;
- inconsistencies about his account of where and when Simpson parked his Bronco;
- evidence that he was in his Bronco the evening of the murders;
- Simpson's admission that he parked his Bronco *behind* Brown's condominium when visiting her home;
- Simpson's denial that he had ever bled at the South Bundy crime scene, where blood consistent with his was later determined to have been on the walkway;
- conflicting statements on how Simpson cut the middle finger of his left hand;
- Simpson's admission that he dripped blood at his North Rockingham estate on the night of the murders;
- Simpson's lie that he had worn a pair of Reeboks on the night of the murders; and
- inconsistencies regarding Simpson's account of his activities both at Rockingham and in Chicago.

Most important, Lange and Vannatter kept Simpson's goodwill throughout the interview, which led to his giving his permission for the detectives to:

- fingerprint him;
- photograph the fresh wounds on his left hand, which explained the trail of blood leading away from the South Bundy crime scene; and
- obtain a sample of his blood, which served as the basis for all of the DNA testing done in preparation for the trial. Essentially, Clark based her entire case on the blood Lange and Vannatter obtained from Simpson that day.

Significantly, the plaintiffs' attorneys in the civil case used Lange and Vannatter's interview with Simpson during their presentation. In the end, jurors cited that interview as one of the major reasons for finding Simpson liable for the murders of Brown and Goldman.

Clark, on the other hand, decided against introducing the interview as evidence during the criminal trial.

Who was right?

In another complaint against Lange and Vannatter—which they had never even heard before the publication of her book—Clark described the detectives' decision to release Simpson after the interview as a "blunder." She continued: "Why had they let Simpson walk? It was true that once the police formally arrest someone, they must be prepared to charge him within forty-eight hours. If they're not sure of their evidence, they can cut him loose, then pick him up later when they have something more solid. But why in this case, where the evidence seemed so strong?"

Lange and Vannatter's reasons for not arresting Simpson were expressed in Chapter Six:

> Vannatter has no intention of arresting Simpson right now. The detective recognizes that he has a mandatory forty-eight-hour filing deadline with the district attorney's office after an arrest is made. If he takes Simpson into custody and doesn't file his paperwork within that period of time, he must, under law, release him. With the whole world already watching this case, Vannatter knows that Deputy District Attorney Marcia Clark, as well as the LAPD, will want the blood-analysis work completed before the case is formally cleared and filed with the DA's office. Vannatter knows that they are several days away from receiving the critical blood reports from the LAPD/SID crime lab.

Clark ignored this explanation in her book, claiming that the detectives "worshiped O.J. Simpson." She continued, "I believe in my heart that they were actually resisting the idea that the Juice could have caused this horror."

Understandably, Clark probably didn't appreciate the revelations about the ineptness of her handling of the Simpson case that appeared in *Evidence Dismissed*, which she clearly *did* read before the publication of her own book. Her absurd charge of "hero worship" was one of several gratuitous and baseless attacks against Lange and Vannatter.

In a particularly galling assault on Lange and Vannatter, Clark claimed in her book that they had rejected her support after the Simpson defense team demanded hair samples from the detectives and officers at the South Bundy crime scene. Although it was Clark who had hung the LAPD out to dry and made herself unavailable to the detectives—even Vannatter, her old friend—Clark had the audacity to write: "The thing that annoyed me was that I'd really gone to bat for those guys, and still they went around grousing that I was disloyal. I could already see the police distancing themselves from this case. By late September [1994], Tom and Phil were 'too busy' to do anything I asked. Finally, I just quit calling them and used our D.A. investigators instead."

Nothing could be further from the truth.

The facts contained in *Evidence Dismissed*, especially about the activities of Lange and Vannatter after September 1994, clearly refute this ludicrous claim by Clark. Both detectives logged in hundreds of hours for the Simpson prosecution team, producing numerous documents and evidence that strengthened the case against Simpson—much of which Clark never used. Lange and Vannatter remained faithful to this case—even though they were being undercut by Clark—while actively involved in no fewer than five other murder investigations. All of these cases were older and more complex than the "turkey on a platter" Lange and Vannatter presented to Clark, who wound up distancing herself from the LAPD and its investigation.

Like Mark Fuhrman, Clark has attempted to rewrite history in an effort to minimize the long-term impact of her own mistakes in preparing for and during the criminal trial.

As the bloodletting among the principals in the Simpson drama continues, Lange and Vannatter continue to stand by their investigation, as well as their account of this case in *Evidence Dismissed*.

Tom Lange and Philip Vannatter
with Dan Moldea
May 14, 1997

Appendix

Statement of Tom Lange and Philip Vannatter in Response to Mark Fuhrman's Book, *Murder in Brentwood* February 18, 1997

"Psychiatrist Dr. John Hochman filed a report, quoting Fuhrman as saying: 'I have this urge to kill people that upset me.' Hochman speculated that this and Fuhrman's similar statements were a 'conscious attempt to look bad and an exaggeration of problems which could be a cry for help and/or overdramatization by a narcissistic, self-indulgent, emotionally unstable person who expects immediate attention and pity.'"

Mark Fuhrman's book, *Murder in Brentwood,* about the O.J. Simpson case is a desperate, cynical, and cowardly attempt to redeem himself at our expense. If it were a sworn affidavit, he would be risking another indictment for perjury. Fuhrman's expressed opinions of our work as the lead investigators in the case—as well as the work of other detectives in the LAPD's Robbery/Homicide Division—are built on nothing more than a series of false and misleading "facts." We will detail many of them in the following statement.

The true motive behind Fuhrman's malicious attack on the

Robbery/Homicide Division and us, in particular, cannot be completely understood from simply reading his book. We believe that the motive has much to do with Fuhrman's failed request for a transfer to the Officer-Involved Shooting Section of the Robbery/Homicide Division. Fuhrman's request was rejected by the LAPD's high command just prior to the June 12, 1994, murders of Nicole Brown and Ronald Goldman. We wrote about this on pages 10 and 15 (endnote 4) in our book. Fuhrman doesn't address this matter in his book.

It is important to note that former prosecutor Vincent Bugliosi, who inexplicably lent his considerable credibility to Fuhrman by writing the introduction to his book, wrote on page xx: "I don't agree with [Fuhrman's] particularly harsh assessment of the investigative job done in the Simpson case by lead detectives Tom Lange and Philip Vannatter."

Consequently, those in the media who seek to rehabilitate Fuhrman's image during his public-relations blitz for his book should note that every charge this admitted liar has made against us is addressed in our book, *Evidence Dismissed*, which Fuhrman obviously did not read prior to publication of his book.

Fuhrman's Specific Charges

Fuhrman levels eight specific charges against us on page 57 of his book. These charges and our responses, partially drawn from *Evidence Dismissed*, are as follows:

1. Fuhrman's charge: "The bloody fingerprint was never recovered."

Our response: No one else reported this "fingerprint," including the LAPD print technicians who made seventeen lifts during their own crime-scene search. Also, neither Fuhrman nor his supervisor ever mentioned this alleged "fingerprint" during or after our June 13 walk-throughs of the crime scene. (See page 49, endnote 17.)

2. Fuhrman's charge: "Lange never made a thorough inspection of the walkway gate at Bundy."

Our response: Lange, who had already completed his work, had to leave the scene to interview Simpson. He left the crime scene in the hands of numerous professionals, who were told about the evidence on the rear gate. Lange's full explanation for this is in our book. (See pages 59–60; 94; 100, endnote 39; and 247–248.)

3. Fuhrman's charge: "My return to the Bundy scene to compare the glove there with the one found at Rockingham was unnecessary."

Our response: Vannatter primarily sent Fuhrman back to the Bundy crime scene to have the left-hand glove photographed, and he was then to return to Rockingham with the photographer, who could take pictures of the right-hand glove, among other items of evidence. (See pages 30 and 32–33.)

4. Fuhrman's charge: "Vannatter's search warrant was brief, and lacked sufficient detailed information about the investigation, opening up our legal search at Rockingham to legal challenge."

Our response: Vannatter's search warrant, which did not need to be any more detailed, was approved by a municipal court judge. The actual problems with the search warrant are fully detailed in our book. (See pages 40–47 and 225–227.)

5. Fuhrman's charge: "The Bronco was not impounded early on and taken to Parker Center. Instead the exterior and interior were needlessly contaminated."

Our response: As soon as Vannatter declared Simpson's Rockingham estate a crime scene, he ordered the Bronco impounded. Police officers on the scene did not comply with this order until Vannatter returned to Rockingham after noon on June 13. Nevertheless, the issues of interior contamination did not result from the delay in impounding the Bronco; the issue of exterior contamination was mooted by the fact that there was no proven contamination of any evidence on the Bronco. The full details of the alleged contamination of the Bronco are explained in our book. (See pages 34, 56, and 63, endnote 26.)

6. Fuhrman's charge: "Lange had a blanket from inside the townhouse placed over Nicole's body, furthering the defense's claim of crime scene contamination."

Our response: Lange makes no apology for this decision for the reasons cited in our book. This was done to prevent compromise of this evidence. There has never been any indication that his decision caused *any* contamination of the Bundy crime scene. (See pages 37–38; 49, endnote 14; and 246.)

7. Fuhrman's charge: "Vannatter carried a vial of Simpson's blood sample to the Rockingham scene instead of booking it as evidence."

Our response: This was the proper procedure under the circumstances. Vannatter makes no apology for this decision for the reasons cited in our book. (See pages 90–92; 93–95; 100, endnote 37; and 101, endnote 41.)

8. Fuhrman's charge: "Lange ordered Dennis Fung to test and recover blood on the back gate on June 13, but did not confirm that Fung had done so. As a result, the blood was not recovered until weeks later."

Our response: This charge essentially repeats Fuhrman's charge #2. (See pages 59–60; 94; 100, endnote 39; and 247–248.)

Fuhrman's Contributions and Delusions

In *Evidence Dismissed* and in our previous sworn statements, we have defended Fuhrman's performance between 5:00 and 7:00 A.M. on June 13. We credit him with discovering the blood speck above the outside door handle on Simpson's Bronco (pages 19–20), as well as his discovery of the bloody right-hand glove in back of Kato Kaelin's bungalow (pages 29–30). We also credit his partner, Brad Roberts, with discovering the drops of blood inside the foyer of Simpson's home (page 33).

Fuhrman's primary role in this investigation ended at 7:00 A.M. on the morning after the murders. (See page 34.) After that time, he performed in a backup role on general police details. Any facts or opinions he states in his book about the events that occurred after 7:00 A.M. on June 13 are speculation by a junior detective who was out of the loop and not part of the decision-making process.

Fuhrman is absolutely delusional about the importance of his role in this investigation after 7:00 A.M. on June 13. He claims to have seen and done things that have no basis in reality.

He also wrongly leaves the impression that he unilaterally discovered evidence that all of the detectives at Rockingham— Lange, Vannatter, and Phillips—found together, including:

- Kato Kaelin's Nissan 300ZX (page 25; see *Evidence Dismissed*, page 18);
- a splintered piece of wood near the rear tire of Simpson's Bronco (page 27; see *Evidence Dismissed*, pages 19–20); and
- the odd position of Simpson's Bronco as it sat parked in the street (page 28; see *Evidence Dismissed*, page 18).

On pages 35–36 and 39 of his book, Fuhrman claims that his partner, Brad Roberts, discovered blood in Simpson's Bronco, as well as the blood drops that led from the Bronco to the front door of Simpson's home. These claims are clearly refuted by sworn testimony during the 1994 preliminary hearing and at the 1995 criminal trial, as well as on pages 32–33 of our book. In short, Vannatter found the blood evidence in both the Bronco and on the driveway and then pointed out this evidence to Fuhrman when he returned to Rockingham from Bundy with Roberts and the LAPD photographer shortly after 7:00 A.M. on June 13.

As a further indication of how Fuhrman exaggerates the facts of this case in his book, Fuhrman alleges on page 17 of his book that the bloody fingerprint he supposedly found on the locking mechanism of the rear gate, "was *identifiable, comparable, and high in quality* [emphasis added]." On page 218, he continues: "The print was no doubt Simpson's, and it would have *irrefutably* [emphasis added] connected him to the scene with his own blood, and possibly that of the two victims."

Yet, during his sworn trial testimony, Fuhrman was nowhere near as sure, claiming: "I saw a *partial, possible* fingerprint that was on that knob area."

Somehow, between Fuhrman's sworn testimony and the writing of his book, a "partial, possible fingerprint" has become one that is "identifiable, comparable, and high in quality," "which would have irrefutably connected" Simpson to the crime scene.

Fuhrman's Other Claims and Errors

In his book, Fuhrman lies, misleads, distorts reality, and makes numerous errors. The following is a partial list of Fuhrman's claims, with the pages they appear on in his book, and our response, with the corresponding pages from our book:

• **Fuhrman's claim (page 29):** Fuhrman writes that he talked to a Westec patrolman who informed him that a live-in maid should be in Simpson's home, which, Fuhrman adds, "I relayed to the other detectives."

Our response (pages 18–19): This is not true. Lange, Vannatter, Phillips, and Fuhrman all talked to the Westec patrolman and received this information.

• **Fuhrman's claim (page 37):** "Vannatter said he was going to the station himself to write a search warrant and asked Brad [Roberts] to write a description of the property for the warrant.

Placing his hand on my shoulder, and with confidence in his voice, Vannater [*sic*] said, 'You're in charge of this crime scene.'"

Our response (page 34): "Then, turning to Fuhrman and Roberts, Vannatter says, 'I want you to secure and control this crime scene, because I have to go write out the search warrant. I'll be back later when I've finished.'" Vannatter never relinquished authority over the Rockingham crime scene to anyone but Detective Bert Luper, just after 12:00 noon on June 13. (See page 57.) Vannatter only gave Fuhrman and Roberts an assignment to stand guard and protect this crime scene. He relinquished no other authority to them—especially since at that point he had not yet obtained the search warrant.

• **Fuhrman's claim (pages 37 and 48–49):** Fuhrman claims that he and Roberts found Simpson's socks on the floor in the bedroom at 8:00 A.M. on June 13. Fuhrman continues: "I found Vannatter in the kitchen and told him about the socks."

Our response (pages 94–95): This is not true. Vannatter, who had left Simpson's residence by 7:30 A.M. on June 13, was not notified that the socks had been found until he returned to the Rockingham crime scene at 5:17 P.M. on June 13—in the midst of the search directed by Detective Bert Luper. Fuhrman's alleged search at 8:00 A.M., when there was no search warrant, could have jeopardized this crucial evidence.

• **Fuhrman's claim (page 38):** Fuhrman, who had earlier claimed to have found red streaks on the outside door panel of Simpson's Bronco, writes: "I showed [Dennis Fung] the blood spot on the door and the streaks on the sill. Although he tested the spot, which did prove to be blood, he apparently never tested the streaks. And strangely enough, Rokahr never photographed them."

Our response (page 27, endnote 9): "Fuhrman later testified that he also saw red stains on the bottom panel of the driver's door. Yet, at no time did he communicate this information to either Lange or Vannatter. The first time they heard about this was during his courtroom testimony." It is also unlikely that Fuhrman told Fung, Rokahr, or anyone else.

• **Fuhrman's claim (page 41):** "Moments later, Vannatter approached Simpson and engaged him in conversation. Simpson asked to have the handcuffs taken off, saying it was really embarrassing with all the media cameras on him. Vannatter took the cuffs off. It has been previously reported elsewhere that Howard Weitzman, Simpson's attorney, asked to have the cuffs removed, but the truth of the matter is that Simpson himself asked."

Our response (pages 57–58): This is not true. Weitzman asked Vannatter to remove the handcuffs, and Vannatter complied. Vannatter had no intention, at that time, of arresting Simpson.

• **Fuhrman's claim (pages 41–42):** "Vannatter approached Brad and asked if we could take Simpson down to Parker Center. Then he asked if just Brad could assist him with the transport. Brad went back inside to give me his car keys. By the time he came out, Vannatter was driving off with Simpson and Weitzman."

Our response (page 58): This is not true. Vannatter drove Simpson to the station with Detective Cliff LeFall in the car, not Howard Weitzman, who drove to Parker Center in his own car, along with Simpson attorney Skip Taft.

• **Fuhrman's claim (page 42):** "As Vannatter and Simpson were driving away from the estate, Brad related to me the conversation he had had with Simpson. We both realized the importance, not only of the statement, but the involuntary bodily reaction that Brad had observed. I suggested Brad put this to paper immediately, which he did. His written statement was then given to Vannatter and Lange. Brad's statement could have been very helpful when they interrogated Simpson, but they did not use it."

Our response (pages 58–59): This is a flat-out lie, which Fuhrman's own words prove. As Fuhrman states, he only learned about Roberts's information "as Vannatter and Simpson were driving away" from Simpson's Rockingham estate. How could Roberts, at Fuhrman's request, have drafted a "written statement [that] was then given to Vannatter and Lange"? Vannatter had already left to interview Simpson at Parker Center; Lange, who would soon join Vannatter and Simpson for the interview, was nowhere near the Rockingham crime scene at the time.

• **Fuhrman's claim (page 42):** "Then we all returned to searching the residence and premises. Brad alerted Robbery/Homicide to freshly washed clothes in the washing machine. Brad described the clothes as black sweats, then and now. Also, in the half bath next to the maid's quarters, Brad found blood smears on the light switch and various other locations. Up in the master bedroom, at the edge of the tub, we found an open knife box with the Swiss Army logo. It was empty, but meant to package one of the larger knives. I also pointed this out to the detectives."

Our response: This is not true. Neither Lange nor Vannatter nor any other detective involved in the search, including Bert Luper, either saw or received any information about these alleged discoveries.

• **Fuhrman's claim (page 49):** "Vannatter cancelled the impound and simply had two officers guard the vehicle. Because of Vannatter's decision, the Bronco sat outside for several hours with countless people around it."

Our response (pages 34, 56, and 63, endnote 26): This is not true. Vannatter *did* order the Bronco impounded and was furious when he returned to the Rockingham scene at noon on June 13 and discovered that his order had not been followed.

• **Fuhrman's claim (page 50):** "When I read the autopsy reports during the trial, I was surprised to learn that Lange and Vannatter didn't have Nicole checked for semen."

Our response (page 107): "As a matter of routine [Nicole's] vagina and rectum are visually inspected for possible rape; there is no evidence of any sexual violence or any recent sexual encounter." This was performed during Nicole Brown's autopsy by Dr. Golden.

• **Fuhrman's claim (pages 59–76):** Fuhrman devotes Chapter 5 of his book to criticizing us for the manner in which we conducted our June 13 "interrogation" with Simpson.

Our response (pages 65–67): This *interview* was not an "interrogation" for the reasons cited in our book. Yet, despite his criticism of the interview, Fuhrman writes on page 183 of his book: "Vince Bugliosi later said that with a legal pad and a hundred hours to prepare, he could have convicted Simpson on the transcript of that interview alone."

• **Fuhrman's claim (page 77):** "Regardless of what turns the investigation had taken up to Simpson's interrogation, Vannatter and Lange still had more than enough evidence to arrest him late on the afternoon of June 13. But they didn't."

Our response (pages 57–58): "Vannatter has no intention of arresting Simpson right now. The detective recognizes that he has a mandatory forty-eight hour filing deadline with the district attorney's office after an arrest is made. If he takes Simpson into custody and doesn't file his paperwork within that period of time, he must, under law, release him. With the whole world already watching this case, Vannatter knows that Deputy District Attorney Marcia Clark, as well as the LAPD, will want the blood-analysis work completed before the case is formally cleared and filed with the DA's office. Vannatter knows that they are several days away from receiving the critical blood reports from the LAPD/SID crime lab."

• **Fuhrman's claim (pages 78–79):** "The previous night [June 16], Simpson's new lawyer, Robert Shapiro, had convinced the detectives to allow Simpson to surrender instead of arresting him."

Our response (pages 148–153): This is not true. These pages in our book explain the previously untold story of the negotiations regarding Simpson's arrest. Neither of us had any conversation with Shapiro on the night of June 16 about this or any other matter. All of the conversations with Shapiro occurred on the morning of June 17, the day of Simpson's arrest.

• **Fuhrman's claim (pages 93–94):** "I was subpoenaed to appear before the grand jury and went to the criminal courts building at 210 W. Temple the week of June 20. I sat in the grand jury witness waiting room with Phillips, Vannatter, Lange, and others all day, talking, drinking coffee, and reading three-month-old magazines. But we were never called to testify."

Our response: This is not true. Both of us testified before the county grand jury investigating the Simpson case. Lange testified on Tuesday, June 21; Vannatter testified on Wednesday, June 22.

• **Fuhrman's claim (pages 94–95):** "I realized that the Rockingham glove proved one irrefutable fact if nothing else: Because it had the blood of all three people, it was the one piece of evidence that linked Simpson with the two victims."

Our response (pages 261–262): This is not true. Blood matching the DNA of Simpson and of the two victims was also found in Simpson's Bronco.

• **Fuhrman's claim (page 172):** "During the investigation, the Robbery/Homicide detectives did not pursue many potential leads because they were overwhelmed by the case and wedded to a certain chain of events."

Our response (pages 104–105 and 112, endnote 53): This is not true. We opened a "clue book," which consisted of 518 leads, all of which were investigated, including fifty that "pointed to a variety of motives and suspects having nothing to do with Simpson."

• **Fuhrman's claim (page 183):** Regarding the cup of Ben & Jerry's ice cream found at the crime scene, Fuhrman writes: "A great deal of testimony and countless hours of investigation were spent on this insignificant piece of evidence, including a drawn-out debate on what flavor the ice cream was (while early speculation had inaccurately identified it as Chunky Monkey, the ice cream in question was eventually determined to be Rainforest Crunch.)"

Our response (page 7): This is not true. "Countless hours" were not spent on the investigation of the ice cream. Also, the flavor was Chocolate Chip Cookie Dough.

• **Fuhrman's claim (page 184):** "I asked if we had a weather report for the night of the murders and the morning after. . . . This should have already been taken care of by Vannatter and Lange, as they were working an outdoor crime scene, and even if you note the weather conditions yourself—which I don't believe they did—you still have to get the weather report to corroborate your own findings."

Our response: This is not true. Although we did not note this in our book, we obtained all weather reports for the day of and the morning after the murders. This fact can be corroborated by our supervisors Captain William O. Gartland and Lieutenant John Rogers. Also, the documents about the weather are contained in the official "murder book" on the Simpson case.

• **Fuhrman's claim (pages 188–189):** Fuhrman alleges that he had a conversation with a "lady, who wishes to remain anonymous," who claimed to know of an affair between Nicole Brown and Ron Goldman. Fuhrman continues: "I took this conversation down as a statement over two years ago. The statement was typed on an LAPD statement sheet and given to Lange and Vannatter. I have not seen it since."

Our response: This is not true. We *never* received any such report from Fuhrman or anyone else. On page 116, we discussed the extent of our knowledge about the relationship between Brown and Goldman. Also, we are automatically suspicious of Fuhrman's claim of an "anonymous" source.

• **Fuhrman's claim (page 194):** Regarding the piece of wood found near the Bronco during the early morning hours of June

13 and its possible connection to a discarded murder weapon, Fuhrman writes, "We informed Lange and Vannatter, but they weren't interested. My suggestion to use police academy cadets to search the alleys and yards was politely ignored."

Our response (page 27, endnote 10): "Lange and Vannatter spent a considerable amount of time trying to match this splintered piece of wood to a broken fence or any other object on every conceivable route between South Bundy and North Rockingham. In the end, they could not determine where it came from or whether it had any connection to the murders."

Also see page 218, endnote 108: "In late June, Vannatter also directed a street search for the murder weapon, taking dozens of recruits from the LAPD Academy, organizing them in groups of ten with an RHD detective in charge of each. All of the groups walked the various possible two-mile routes from the South Bundy crime scene to the North Rockingham crime scene, checking everything from vacant lots to sewers. No weapon was ever found."

• **Fuhrman's claim (page 195):** "No one ever took tire impressions of the Bronco, or searched the alleys for tire marks."

Our response (page 247): "Lange determined that there were so many tracks superimposed over one another that isolating any of them for testing was an impossibility."

• **Fuhrman's claim (pages 200–206):** This section highlights a Connecticut limousine driver, John Upson, who had witnessed Simpson playing with a knife in the backseat of Upson's limousine. Fuhrman credits the plaintiff's attorneys in the wrongful-death civil case against Simpson for the discovery of this witness.

Our response (pages 211–212): We authorized the investigation of Upson's claim and sent Detective Vic Pietrantoni to Connecticut to interview the driver on June 24, 1994, just twelve days after the murders. (Upson also passed a polygraph test on this matter. We complained that the prosecution did not use his testimony in our "evidence dismissed" list on page 270 of our book.)

• **Fuhrman's claim (page 218):** "I saw Phillips give my notes to Vannatter when he arrived early in the morning of June 13, 1994, and watched Vannatter place them in his notebook without reading a word."

Our response (page 13): "Phillips asks Fuhrman for his general observation notes taken during his early walk-through. When Fuhrman complies, Phillips hands them to Vannatter, who immediately gives them to Lange. This is their standard operating procedure, since Lange will conduct the crime-scene search and ultimately prepare the final murder follow-up report for the district attorney's office—should an arrest be made."

• **Fuhrman's claim (page 218):** "I left [Marcia Clark's] office disgusted. The words, '[Lange and Vannatter] didn't read your notes,' echo in my mind every time I think about the Simpson case."

Our response (page 39): "[Lange] sees that the gate at the west end of the walkway is open and has two drops of blood on its inside lower rung. Phillips had earlier pointed this out to him, and Fuhrman had mentioned this blood evidence in his notes."

Also see page 49, endnote 17: "Fuhrman claimed in his notes that he had also observed a bloody fingerprint on the locking mechanism of the rear gate at the South Bundy crime scene. However, no such fingerprint was seen by anyone else. Also in his notes, Fuhrman speculated that the victims died from gunshot wounds, and that the killer had possibly been bitten by Brown's dog."

In short, we *did* read Fuhrman's notes and found that they provided erroneous and misleading information. (See our section in this appendix "Fuhrman's Crime-Scene Notes.")

• **Fuhrman's claim (page 221):** "By not calling Brad [Roberts] to corroborate my notes, Marcia Clark seemed to be protecting Vannatter and the entire prosecution from embarrassment."

Our response (page 226): This claim is ridiculous. A major theme in our book is the conflict between Marcia Clark and us. This tension culminated during a pretrial hearing when Clark failed to defend Vannatter's search warrant—which she had cleared before it was filed. Instead of "protecting Vannatter," as Fuhrman claims, Clark hung the detective out to dry. Also, Fuhrman's notes contained inaccurate suppositions that would have been impeached by Simpson's defense team.

• **Fuhrman's claim (pages 225–226):** "When Vannatter first called Marcia to the scene, she had not even heard of O.J. Simpson."

Our response (page 42): This is not true. Clark knew who Simpson was. She simply called him "a has-been football player."

APPENDIX

Fuhrman's Crime-Scene Notes

Regarding his crime-scene notes, Fuhrman writes on page 52 of his book: "Once my preliminary walk-through of the Bundy crime scene was complete, I carefully wrote my observations, including the print on the gate, in clear, neat notes. I had a meticulous system for taking notes at crime scenes." On page 16, Fuhrman added that he "was not about to jump to conclusions" during his early investigation.

However, a close examination of Fuhrman's three pages of numbered "meticulous" notes which appear on pages 19–21 of his book, demonstrates that he did, in fact, jump to conclusions, and that his careful observations were in error in several instances.

• **In note #3,** Fuhrman discussed the cause of death, writing, "unknown cause of death—poss GSW [gunshot wound]."

Our response: As is now common knowledge, the victims were slashed and stabbed. There is no evidence that any of the wounds were inflicted by a gun.

• **In note #5,** Fuhrman wrote, "Pizza menu by female victim's left leg."

Our response: The menu had come from the "Thai Flavor" restaurant. (See page 120: property report, Item #46.) This careless miscue by Fuhrman could have been impeached by Simpson's defense team if this menu had turned out to be crucial evidence.

• **In note #13,** Fuhrman speculated on the cause of the blood drops next to the bloody shoeprints leading away from the bodies. Fuhrman wrote, "Susp possibly biten [*sic*] by dog?"

Our response: There is absolutely no evidence that the killer was bitten by a dog. (See page 15, endnote 2.)

• **In note #15,** Fuhrman mentioned the "visible fingerprint."

Our response: No such fingerprint was reported by anyone else. (See page 49, endnote 17.)

• **In note #17,** Fuhrman described an item of headwear as a "ski mask."

Our response: The item found was a plain knit watchman's cap, not a "ski mask." (See page 119: property report, Item #38.) Fuhrman's erroneous observation led to a media leak regarding a bloody ski mask, which did not exist.

Fuhrman's three pages of notes were sloppy, jumped to conclusions, and provided erroneous information to the lead detectives.

In fact, other than the false and misleading statements Fuhrman made, *nothing* contained in his notes added *any* new information to the case beyond what had already been reported by the patrol officers who arrived at the scene before Fuhrman.

A final remark on Fuhrman's notes: Detectives conduct walk-throughs of a crime scene to familiarize themselves with the existing evidence found by police officers who arrive at the crime scene before them. Any and all evidence must be pointed out during these walk-throughs.

At no time during our walk-throughs on June 13, 1994, did anyone, including Fuhrman, ever mention "a bloody fingerprint" on the rear gate or anywhere else. When a detective finds a bloody fingerprint, bells and whistles should go off. A good detective doesn't just hide such crucial evidence in his notes. He tells someone; Fuhrman did not. We believe that this "bloody fingerprint" may have been nothing more than a blood smudge.

Miscellaneous Statements Contained in Fuhrman's Book

The following are quotes of a handful of statements Fuhrman makes about himself, which indicate, among other things, his inability to take responsibility for his actions (despite his claims to the contrary on page xxi in his Prologue):

• "I understand racism, and I understand the inequality that it produces" (page 114).

• "The defense needed to portray me as a racist in order to float their bizarre conspiracy theories. And the media was much more interested in the story of a rogue cop (which I wasn't) than a good detective (which I was)" (page 120).

• "Though the allegations against me were all either weak or untrue, the controversy continued" (page 133).

• "My application for a disability pension in 1982 has been scrutinized at length in the media. Conveniently excerpted portions of my file have been publicized, and I consider all discussion of the contents of that file to be a breach of confidentiality. While I refuse to discuss the specifics of that file, I will, however, speak candidly about my life at that time" (pages 106–107).

Note: In one file, prepared by psychiatrist Dr. Ronald R. Koegler, Fuhrman said that he began to dislike the military because "there were these Mexicans and niggers, volunteers, and they would tell me they weren't going to do something." (See Jeffrey Toobin, *The Run of His Life*, New York: Random House, page 148. *In fact, Fuhrman freely used the "N-word" long before the Simpson case.*)

Note: In another file, psychiatrist Dr. John Hochman filed a report, quoting Fuhrman as saying, "I have this urge to kill people that upset me." Hochman speculated that this and Fuhrman's similar statements were a "conscious attempt to look bad and an exaggeration of problems which could be a cry for help and/or overdramatization by a narcissistic, self-indulgent, emotionally unstable person who expects immediate attention and pity." (See Toobin, page 149. We ask readers to place Dr. Hochman's analysis in context with the contents of Fuhrman's book.)

• "[P]erjury must also be willful, and I can guarantee that at no point was I willfully lying to the court" (page 252).

• "My plea [of "no contest" to perjury] had nothing to do with what I have described here; it had to do with the ability to finance a defense and the realization that I could not receive a fair trial" (page 252).

• "Throughout the interviews [taped by Laura McKinny], I was creating fictional situations, sometimes based loosely on true incidents. Characters were developed from composites of many people, from police management down to the lowest criminals" (page 270).

Question: Was Fuhrman creating a fictional situation, using a composite character, when he specifically, by name, described his former boss and Judge Lance Ito's wife, Captain Margaret York, as a "fat slob" who "sucked her way to the top." (See *Evidence Dismissed*, page 274.)

Question: Was Fuhrman creating a fictional situation, using a composite character, when he said, "I am the key witness in the biggest case of the century. And if I go down, they lose the case. The glove is everything. Without the glove—bye-bye." (See *Evidence Dismissed*, page 275.)

• "When I testified in the Superior Court trial, I did not think about the tapes. Bailey asked me if I had ever used the 'N' word in addressing a person. I could truthfully answer that I had not. I never thought that screenplay notes and character dialogue could be misrepresented as my own words. I hadn't told Marcia about the tapes simply because I didn't remember them at first, and when I did, I didn't think they were at all relevant to the case" (page 273).

Question: Did Fuhrman really believe that his disgusting racist remarks, in which he used the "N-word" over forty times, had no relevance to the Simpson case—or is he lying here, too?

- "While the tapes were still in court action in North Carolina, I called Laura from my attorney's home, and pleaded with her to destroy the tapes" (page 273).

- "I took the Fifth because I had no choice. The prosecution had abandoned me, and I was left twisting in the wind" (page 289).

- "People wanted a sacrificial lamb so they wouldn't have to deal with the fact that a popular celebrity brutally murdered two people. The jury wanted an excuse to vote not guilty. The defense wanted to cast guilt on others. The prosecution and investigating detectives wanted someone to take the blame for their mistakes.

"So I was drawn and quartered in the forum of public opinion" (page 290).

- "Marcia and Chris wanted to think that they were all right and I was all wrong. But deep down they must have known that this was crap. They knew who screwed up this case. They knew who bungled the evidence. They knew who failed to collect evidence. They knew who lost evidence. They knew who ignored evidence. They knew who wrote bad search warrants. They knew who failed to follow up on clues. They knew who blew the interrogation. And it wasn't Mark Fuhrman" (pages 299–300).

Conclusion

Fuhrman's book shows that he has much in common with O.J. Simpson. Both men claim to take full responsibility for their lives and careers—but blame everyone else for their problems. Fuhrman, in particular, blames the prosecution, the defense team, the LAPD, and especially us. He seems to believe that Truth is like a balloon: It's no good unless you blow it up.

The only real mistake we made during the early hours of our investigation was not sending Fuhrman home on that morning after the murders of Nicole Brown and Ron Goldman.

Finally, we appreciate the nationwide support we are receiving in the wake of the publication of our book, which details the definitive story of the police investigation of the O.J. Simpson case. Yet, we feel somewhat frustrated by this latest demand by the media for us to defend ourselves, especially when the charges are being made by a proven racist and perjurer who took the Fifth Amendment rather than defend his work in our case.

Acknowledgments

Due to the sheer magnitude of this case no two detectives could have handled the tremendous amount of investigation and evidence, physical and testimonial, that was accumulated over the months. As a result, several other detectives and support personnel became involved at one stage or another. It is with a great deal of respect and admiration that we acknowledge others who were part of this investigation.

For his leadership and support, Captain William O. Gartland (WOG), Commanding Officer, Robbery/Homicide Division. Patti Jo Fairbanks, who can do it all. West L.A. homicide coordinator Det. Ron Phillips, Brad Roberts, Francine Mounger, and the officers of the LAPD West L.A. Division. Our "third" partner, Det. Vic Pietrantoni. Former Lt. John Rogers and Det. Bert Luper. Also from RHD, Dets. Ron Ito and Detective III Rich Crotsley, who handled literally hundreds of "clues." The computer gurus, Dennis Payne and Bill Parker.

To RHD detectives Richie Aldahl, Tom Appleby, Bud Arce, Ted Ball, Jim and Suzie Barry, Mike Berchem, Tom Brascia, Brian Carr, Lt. Pat Conmay, Denis Cremins, Lynn Cummings, Larry DeLosh, Lt. Don Foster, Bill Gailey, Frank Garcia, John Garcia, Jack Giroud, Jim Gollaz, Lt. Jim Grayson, Lt. Bill Hall, Rich Haro, Jimmy Harper, John Helvin, Buck Henry, Ray Hernandez, Norm Jackson, Rick Jackson, Steve Katz, Dennis Kilcoyne, J.R. Kwock, Lt. Ken Lady,

Danny Lang, Cliff LeFall, Ron Lewis, Otis Marlow, Dave Martin, John and Gloria Martin, Mike Mejia, Fred Miller, Lt. Al Moen, Wally Montgomery, Joe Najera, Leroy Orozco, Roseanne Perrino, Ed Ramirez, Jerry Stephens, Mike Thies, Paul Tippin, Mike Watson, Bud Watts, and all of the personnel at RHD. For the support staff, Paula Donahey, Chris Arce, Nancy Claiborne, and Rachel Valdez.

To the "brass," Deputy Chief John White, Chief Bernie Parks, Commander Jim McMurray, and retired Commander Keith Bushey; Chief of Police Willie L. Williams. Lts. Tony Alba, John Dunkin, and Bob Salkeld.

To our "real" lawyer, Bob Brewer of San Diego. Our "other" lawyers Woody Clarke, Rock Harmon, and Cheri Lewis.

To Chicago police detectives Ken Berris and Mike Fleming.

To Lt. Gary Schram and his entire unit at the DA's office.

To Ron Shipp for his courage.

To the FBI and Special Agents Bill Bodziak, Doug Deedrick, Kevin Kelly, Nick McKean, Bob Rattleman, and John Riggi.

To the U.S. Department of Defense Polygraph Institute's Scott Manners; and Captain Thomas Wright of the Anniston, Alabama, Police Department.

To former L.A. Chief of Police Daryl F. Gates.

To the entire L.A. Police Protective League Board of Directors.

To David Lloyd and Howard Chapman of New Scotland Yard, London.

For the support and advice of Paul Barron, Adam Dawson, Floyd Duncan, Rod Englert, Betty Fanning, Lois Gallina, Vicki Griffin, Jim and Ellie Kokotos, Enoch "Mac" McClain, Darryl Mounger, Dick Rudell, Ray Saffell, Mel Sandvig, Gail, Dawn, Cy, and Wally Smith, Bob Souza, Sherry and Bob Taylor, Randy Witkamp, and Russ Young.

For the support of Pastor Frank Witman and Asst. Pastor David Burgeson.

To Frank Weimann and Ron Goldfarb.

To Jeff Rutledge of Washington, D.C., for all of his assistance, advice, patience, research, and friendship.

To Mrs. Nancy Nolte in Boulder, Colorado.

To Roger Simmons and Ed Law of Frederick, Maryland.

To James Strothmann in Falls Church, Virginia.

To our friends at Pocket Books: Gina Centrello, Kara Welsh, Nancy Miller, Donna O'Neill, Donna Ruvituso, Nathaniel Bissort,

ACKNOWLEDGMENTS

Liz Hartman, Theresa Zoro, Elizabeth McNamara, Irene Yuss, Joann Foster, Stephen Llano, Craig Hillman, and, especially, Sue Carswell.

Also, our sincerest appreciation is extended to: Ed Becker, Barbara Bennet, Dick Billings, Chris Blatchford, Donna Brant, Ed Brown, Roi Brown, David Burnham, John Burns, Dave and Christina Convis, Henry Cupperman, Bob Davis, Judge Nancy Davis-Loomis, Tim Davis, Paul Dickson, Janet Donovan, Dick Dulgerian, George Farris, Lou Farris, Mike Gale, Jeff Goldberg, Joe Goulden, Jim Grady, Jon Greene, John Greenya, Art Harris, Bill Jordan, Bill Knoedelseder, Linda, Melissa, and Megan Lange, Larry Leamer, Capt. Bill Lewis, Bob Loomis, Steve Love, Scott Malone, Phil Manuel, Alice Martell, Joe and Jo Masson, Ron Matheson, Dennis McCarthy, Tom Mechling, Art Melendres, Ethelbert Miller, Karl Milligan, Terry Minton, "Mister In-Between," Jack Mitchell, Marsha Moldea, Mary Moldea, Lt. Larry Momchilov, Tony Morris, Lt. Rich Munsey, Don Murdoch, Gary Nesbitt, Jim Newton, Pete Noyes, Mark Olshaker, Tom O'Neill, Bob Pack, Mark Perry, Mike Pilgrim, Jack Platt, Jan Pottker, Peter Range, Barbara Raskin, Kristina Rebelo Anderson, Pete Reindel, Dave Robb, Serge Robleto, Shelly Saarela, Val Santiago, Carl Shoffler, John Sikorski, Kris Sofley, Rich Stavin, Mark Stewart, Joel Swerdlow, Jim Switzer, Bill Thomas, Donna Thomas, Rhys Thomas, Charlie Thompson, Jack Tobin, Steve Trattner, Jerry Trent, Dawn Trouard, Tom von Stein, Joe Vannatter, Matthew Vannatter, Rita Vannatter, Jim Warner, John Weisman, Courtney Wesley, Danny Wexler, Herb White, Peter Whitmore, Ben Wickham, Debbie Wise, Dick Wolford, Mimi Wolford, Ron Zito, and Fred Zuch.

And in memory of Joe Chandler.

Index